D0251069

DATE DUE

MURDER AND MYSTERY IN CHICAGO

MURDER and MYSTERY in CHICAGO

Edited by
Carol-Lynn Rössel Waugh,
Frank D. McSherry, Jr., and Martin H. Greenberg

DEMBNER BOOKS • New York

DEMBNER BOOKS
Published by Red Dembner Enterprises Corp.,
80 Eighth Avenue, New York, N.Y. 10011

Distributed by W. W. Norton & Company, Inc.,
500 Fifth Avenue, New York, N.Y. 10110

Library of Congress Cataloging in Publications Data

Murder and mystery in Chicago

   1. Detective and mystery stories, American—Illinois
—Chicago. 2. Chicago (Ill.)—Fiction. I. Waugh,
Carol-Lynn Rössel. II. Greenberg, Martin Harry.
III. McSherry, Frank D.
PS648.D4M8532 1988   813'.0872'083277311   87-30582
ISBN 0-934878-98-6

Design by Antler & Baldwin, Inc.

CONTENTS

Introduction		**vii**
At the Old Swimming Hole	Sara Paretsky	**1**
I'll Cut Your Throat Again, Kathleen	Fredric Brown	**21**
So Dark for April	Howard Browne	**39**
The Theft of the Overdue Library Book	Edward D. Hoch	**62**
The Play's the Thing	Robert Bloch	**84**
His Heart Could Break	Craig Rice	**92**
Dead Ringer	James M. Ullman	**113**
Malice at the Mike	Jon L. Breen	**130**
Before He Kills	Ray Russell	**141**
Brother Orchid	Richard Connell	**152**
The Spotted Pup	Dorothy B. Hughes	**169**
About the Authors		**252**

INTRODUCTION

Chicago?

Yes, I know the town.

My grandparents were scorched by the Great Chicago Fire of 1871, and my parents grew up in the city that rose from its ashes. I began my own life in Chicago with the advent of WWI and spent early childhood in Ravenswood, on the north side. Since many relatives lived on the south side of town, I came to know that area too. When my family bought a home in suburban Maywood, I discovered the west side.

It was there that my sister and I attended school during the peak years of the roaring twenties. But on weekends we were usually back in metropolitan Chicago. Saturdays started with downtown shopping and ended with a vaudeville show or a musical. Sundays found us at the Art Institute, the Field Museum, Lincoln Park on the north side or Jackson Park out south. I learned the geography of the city through the windows of streetcars, elevated trains, or double-decker buses. Sometimes my parents would even let me ride on the open-air upper level of a bus, if the wind on Michigan Avenue wasn't too strong.

Everything blew into the Windy City in the twenties—stench from its famous stockyards, smoke and steam from the daily discharge of a thousand trains. The odor of alcohol fermenting in tenement stills mingled with perfume rising from the crowded lobby of the new opera house that utilities-magnate Samuel Insull built to showcase his mistress. The smell of old money wafted from the stately mansions lining Lake Shore Drive. But throughout most of the city the predominant smell was perspiration as construction workers sweated through a building boom.

A giant stadium appeared in Grant Park, along with an aquarium; elsewhere new museums, new schools, and new picture palaces opened their doors. In residential areas the vacant lots began to vanish, and downtown Chicago soared upwards, reaching for the sky.

While some citizens worked all day, others played all night. Restaurants and cabarets and night-clubs proliferated and prospered. Chicago jazz set a tempo for the times.

It was indeed a toddling town during the heyday of Prohibition, the reign of Al Capone and other ganglords who ran Chicago with their machine-guns and the aid of Mayor "Big Bill" Thompson's political machine.

Chicagoans were thirsty people, and depended on gang-controlled bootleggers to bring them their booze. Gangland slayings were tolerated as a necessary evil, and the abrupt demise of a Dion O'Banion or a Hymie Weiss raised comparatively little concern. From time to time an innocent bystander was mowed down by mistake, but then nobody's perfect. Incidents like the massive but unsuccessful attack on Capone in his Cicero hotel headquarters meant little to us, although Cicero was a suburb not far from our own.

My family, like the vast majority of residents in and around Chicago, had no ties with bootlegging, gambling, prostitution, or other illegal activities. But that doesn't mean we didn't get our toes wet in Chicago's crime-wave. The bank where my father worked was robbed twice—first by hoodlums and then by its owners. I visited a speakeasy at the tender age of five, when Dad committed a criminal act by downing a glass of beer.

But as a general rule, my parents were more interested in literature than in lawbreaking. They encouraged me to read even before I attended school, and taught me that Chicago's newspapers contained more than comic-strips.

In those days, before the rise of radio or the advent of television, journalism's importance made a newspaper reporter seem glamorous. Wearing a felt hat pushed back on the forehead was a professional requirement, as was the constant consumption of alcohol. For many gentlemen of the Chicago press these attributes alone sufficed. But men like Ben Hecht and Charlie MacArthur were writing plays and books on the side; Carl Sandburg, Edgar Lee Masters and Maxwell Bodenheim produced poetry, Sherwood Anderson and Floyd Dell found a national audience with their fiction. Their success undoubtedly encouraged the ambitions of James T. Farrell and Nelson Algren in the following decade.

Chicago had plenty of writers, but not enough local publishers. As a result its talents inevitably ended up in New York. By the time I began writing for the pulps in the thirties, most of the local literary luminaries had wormed their way into the Big Apple.

The magazine I appeared in, *Weird Tales*, maintained an editorial office at 840 N. Michigan Avenue, but it wasn't owned by Chicagoans. And its one-cent-a-word-on-or-after-publication-or-at-gunpoint policy was hardly sufficient to support a writers' colony. Most of its contributors lived elsewhere. I myself had moved with the family to Milwaukee.

But I returned to Chicago when I could. On such occasions I usually paid a visit to the magazine offices where editor Farnsworth Wright and business manager William Sprenger fought the good fight against sagging sales, slow circulation, and other perils that plagued periodicals in the Great Depression. When they lost the battle and the magazine's owners sold it down the river to New York, my visits switched to another location in downtown Chicago.

The Ziff-Davis publishing empire, founded on the success of its hobby-magazines such as *Popular Photography*, acquired a moribund science fiction pulp, *Amazing Stories*. Under the editorship of another Milwaukeean, Raymond A. Palmer, it was quickly rejuvenated. And during the Forties a number of companion magazines—*Fantastic Adventures, Mammoth Detective, Mammoth Mystery,* and *Mammoth Western*—enjoyed a healthy existence. There was now enough of a potential market to attract local writers, including William P. McGivern, whom I met long before he rose to deserved fame as a novelist and screenwriter. Another eminence who went that route—and whose work is included here—is Howard Browne. In those days Browne served as an associate editor and wrote on the side, but when Palmer left to found his own magazine, Howard Browne took over as editor-in-chief. One of Browne's assistants, William Hamling, also left to start magazines of his own, so for a brief while during the fifties there were more pulps published in Chicago than ever before. And when Hugh Hefner brought out *Playboy* and Hamling published *Rogue*, the city could boast of its own slick-paper markets as well.

Among their contributors was a writer whose work can also be found in the following pages, Fredric Brown, plus that of the editor who piloted *Playboy* to fame, Ray Russell.

I met William B. Nolan in those heady days, and Fred Brown was for some years a fellow-resident of Milwaukee and a close friend. As for Ray Russell, my most memorable encounter with him took place on an afternoon thirty years ago, at the cocktail lounge of the Palmer House hotel. With us was the eminent Chicago critic and essayist, Vincent Starrett, and thanks to their eloquence, for a few hours the saloon became a salon.

But such occasions became infrequent. By the time Vincent Starrett passed on, most of the Chicago-based writers of mystery or suspense had already moved.

But the destination was no longer New York. Both Browne and Brown, Nolan and Russell, McGivern and I had made a rather remote western suburb of Chicago called Hollywood our new home.

Chicago itself had changed—its fast-thinking literary critics, fast-talking reporters and fast-typing pulp-writers were gone forever.

But as you will discover in the work that follows by expatriate Craig Rice, Rochester-based Ed Hoch, Santa Fe's Dorothy B. Hughes, New York City's Jon Breen and current Chicagoans Sara Paretsky and James Ullman, one constant remains.

Crime—past, present and future—continues to bring mayhem to the metropolis. Fortunately for the *aficionados* of detective, police-procedure, mystery and suspense fiction, it also continues to inspire writers and enthrall readers.

An extravagant claim, you say?

Not so. The proof is in your hands.

Read, and enjoy!

—Robert Bloch

AT THE OLD SWIMMING HOLE

SARA PARETSKY

I

The gym was dank—chlorine and sweat combined in a hot, sticky mass. Shouts from the trainers, from the swimmers, from the spectators, bounced from the high metal ceilings and back and forth from the benches lining the pool on two sides. The cacophony set up an unpleasant buzzing in my head.

I was not enjoying myself. My shirt was soaked through with sweat. Anyway, I was too old to sit cheering on a bleacher for two hours. But Alicia had been insistent—I had to be there in person for her to get points on her sponsor card.

Alicia Alonso Dauphine and I went to high school together. Her parents had bestowed a prima ballerina's name on her, but Alicia showed no aptitude for fine arts. From her earliest years, all she wanted was to muck around with engines. At eighteen, off she went to the University of Illinois to study aeronautics.

Despite her lack of interest in dance, Alicia was very athletic. Next to airplanes, the only thing she really cared about was competitive swimming. I used to cheer her when she was NCAA swimming champ, always with a bit of irritation about being locked in a dank, noisy gym for hours at a time—swimming is not a great spectator sport. But after all, what are friends for?

When Alicia joined Berman Aircraft as an associate engineer, we drifted our separate ways. We met occasionally at weddings, confirmations, bar mitzvahs (my, how our friends were aging! Childlessness seemed to suspend us in time, but each new ceremony in their lives marked a new milestone toward old age for the women we had played with in high school).

Then last week I'd gotten a call from Alicia. Berman was mounting a team for a citywide corporate competition—money would be raised through sponsors for the American Cancer Society. Both Alicia's mother and mine had died of cancer—would I sponsor her for so many meters? Doubling my contribution if she won? It was only after I'd made the pledge that I realized she expected me there in person. One of her sponsors had to show up to testify that she'd done it, and all the others were busy with their homes and children, and come on, V.I., what do you do all day long? I need you.

How can you know you're being manipulated and still let it happen? I hunched an impatient shoulder and turned back to the starting blocks.

From where I sat, Alicia was just another bathing-suited body with a cap. Her distinctive cheekbones were softened and flattened by the dim fluorescence. Not a wisp of her thick black hair trailed around her face. She was wearing a bright red tank suit—no extra straps or flounces to slow her down in the water.

The swimmers had been wandering around the side of the pool, swinging their arms to stretch out the muscles, not talking much while the timers argued some inaudible point with the referee. Now a police whistle shrilled faintly in the din and the competitors snapped to attention, moving toward the starting blocks at the far end of the pool.

We were about to watch the fifty-meter freestyle. I looked at the hand-scribbled card Alicia had given me before the meet. After the fifty-meter, she was in a 4x50 relay. Then I could leave.

The swimmers were mounting the blocks when someone began complaining again. The woman from the Ajax insurance team seemed to be having a problem with the lane marker on the inside of her lane. The referee reshuffled the swimmers, leaving the offending lane empty. The swimmers finally mounted the blocks again. Timers got into position.

Standing to see the start of the race, I was no longer certain which of the women was Alicia. Two of the other six contenders also wore red tank suits; with their features smoothed by caps and dimmed lighting, they all became anonymous. One red suit was in lane two, one in lane three, one in lane six.

The referee raised the starting gun. Swimmers got set. Arms swung back for the dive. Then the gun, and seven bodies flung themselves into the water. Perfect dive in lane six—had to be Alicia, surfacing, pulling away from all but one other swimmer, a fast little woman from the brokerage house of Feldstein, Holtz and Woods.

Problems for the red-suited woman in lane two. I hadn't seen her dive, but she was having trouble righting herself, couldn't seem to make headway in the lane. Now everyone was noticing her. Whistles were blowing; the man on the loudspeaker tried ineffectually to call for silence.

I pushed my way through the crowds on the benches and vaulted over the barrier dividing the spectators from the water. Useless over the din to order someone into the pool for her. Useless to point out the growing circle of red. I kicked off running shoes and dove from the side. Swimming underwater to the second lane. Not Alicia. Surely not. Seeing the water turn red around me. Find the woman. Surface. Drag her to the edge where, finally, a few galvanized hands pulled her out.

I scrambled from the pool and picked out someone in a striped referee's shirt. "Get a fire department ambulance as fast as you can." He stared at me with a stupid gape to his jaw. "Dial 911, damn it. Do it now!" I pushed him toward the door, hard, and he suddenly broke into a trot.

I knelt beside the woman. She was breathing, but shallowly. I felt her gently. Hard to find the source of bleeding with the wet suit, but I thought it came from the upper back. Demanding help from one of the bystanders, I carefully turned her to her side. Blood was oozing now, not pouring, from a wound below her left shoulder. Pack it with towels, elevate her feet, keep the crowd back. Wait. Wait. Watch the shallow breathing turn to choking. Mouth-to-mouth does no good. Who knows cardiopulmonary resuscitation? A muscular young man in skimpy bikini shorts comes forward and works at her chest. By the time the paramedics hustle in with stretcher and equipment, the shallow, choking breath has stopped. They take her to the hospital, but we all know it's no good.

As the stretcher-bearers trotted away, the rest of the room came back into focus. Alicia was standing at my side, black hair hanging damply to her shoulders, watching me with fierce concentration. Everyone else seemed to be shrieking in unison; the sound re-echoing from the rafters was more unbearable than ever.

I stood up, put my mouth close to Alicia's ear, and asked her to take me to whoever was in charge. She pointed to a man in an Izod T-shirt standing on the other side of the hole left by the dead swimmer's body.

I went to him immediately. "I'm V.I. Warshawski. I'm a private detective. That woman was murdered—shot through the back. Whoever shot her probably left during the confusion. But you'd better get the cops here now. And tell everyone over your megaphone that no one leaves until the police have seen them."

He looked contemptuously at my dripping jeans and shirt. "Do you have anything to back up this preposterous statement?"

I held out my hands. "Blood," I said briefly, then grabbed the microphone from him. "May I have your attention, please." My voice bounced around the hollow room. "My name is V.I. Warshawski; I am a detective. There has been a serious accident in the pool. Until the police have been here and talked to us, none of us must leave this area. I am asking the six timers who were at the far end of the pool to come here now."

There was silence for a minute, then renewed clamor. A handful of people picked their way along the edge of the pool toward me. The man in the Izod shirt was fulminating but lacked the guts to try to grab the mike.

When the timers came up to me, I said, "You six are the only ones who definitely could not have killed the woman. I want you to stand at the exits." I tapped each in turn and sent them to a post—two to the doors on the second floor at the top of the bleachers, two to the ground-floor exits, and one each to the doors leading to the men's and women's dressing rooms.

"Don't let anyone, regardless of *anything* he or she says, leave. If they have to use the bathroom, tough—hold it until the cops get here. Anyone tries to leave, keep them here. If they want to fight, let them go but get as complete a description as you can."

They trotted off to their stations. I gave Izod back his mike, made my way to a pay phone in the corner, and dialed the Eleventh Street homicide number.

II

Sergeant McGonnigal was not fighting sarcasm as hard as he might have. "You sent the guy to guard the upstairs exit and he waltzed away, probably taking the gun with him. He must be on his knees in some church right now thanking God for sending a pushy private investigator to this race."

I bit my lips. He couldn't be angrier with me than I was with myself. I sneezed and shivered in my damp, clammy clothes. "You're right, Sergeant. I wish you'd been at the meet instead of me. You'd probably have had ten uniformed officers with you who could've taken charge as soon as the starting gun was fired and avoided this mess. Do any of the timers know who the man was?"

We were in an office that the school athletic department had given the police for their investigation-scene headquarters. McGonnigal had been questioning all the timers, figuring their closeness to the pool gave them the best angle on what had happened. One was missing, the man I'd sent to the upper balcony exit.

The sergeant grudgingly told me he'd been over that ground with the other timers. None of them knew who the missing man was. Each of the companies in the meet had supplied volunteers to do the timing and other odd jobs. Everyone just assumed this man was from someone else's firm. No one had noticed him that closely; their attention was focused on the action in the pool. My brief glance at him gave the police their best description: medium height, light, short brown hair, wearing a pale green T-shirt and faded white denim shorts. Yes, baggy enough for a gun to fit in a pocket unnoticed.

"You know, Sergeant, I asked for the six timers at the far end of the pool because they were facing the swimmers, so none of them could have shot the dead woman in the back. This guy came forward. That means there's a timer missing—either the person actually down at the far end was in collusion, or you're missing a body."

McGonnigal made an angry gesture—not at me. Himself for not

having thought of it before. He detailed two uniformed cops to round up all the volunteers and find out who the errant timer was.

"Any more information on the dead woman?"

McGonnigal picked up a pad from the paper-littered desk in front of him. "Her name was Louise Carmody. You know that. She was twenty-four. She worked for the Ft. Dearborn Bank and Trust as a junior lending officer. You know that. Her boss is very shocked—you probably could guess that. And she has no enemies. No dead person ever does."

"Was she working on anything sensitive?"

He gave me a withering glance. "What twenty-four-year-old junior loan officer works on anything sensitive?"

"Lots," I said firmly. "No senior person ever does the grubby work. A junior officer crunches numbers or gathers basic data for crunching. Was she working on any project that someone might not want her to get data for?"

McGonnigal shrugged wearily but made a note on a second pad— the closest he would come to recognizing that I might have a good suggestion.

I sneezed again. "Do you need me for anything else? I'd like to get home and dry off."

"No, go. I'd just as soon you weren't around when Lieutenant Mallory arrives, anyway."

Bobby Mallory was McGonnigal's boss. He was also an old friend of my father, who had been a beat sergeant until his death fifteen years earlier. Bobby did not like women on the crime scene in any capacity— victim, perpetrator, or investigator—and he especially did not like his old friend Tony's daughter on the scene. I appreciated McGonnigal's unwillingness to witness any acrimony between his boss and me, and was getting up to leave when the uniformed cops came back.

The sixth timer had been found in a supply closet behind the men's lockers. He was concussed and groggy from a head wound and couldn't remember how he got to where he was. Couldn't remember anything past lunchtime. I waited long enough to hear that and slid from the room.

Alicia was waiting for me at the far end of the hall. She had changed from her suit into jeans and a pullover and was squatting on her heels, staring fiercely at nothing. When she saw me coming, she stood up and pushed her black hair out of her eyes.

"You look a mess, V.I."

"Thanks. I'm glad to get help and support from my friends after they've dragged me into a murder investigation."

"Oh, don't get angry—I didn't mean it that way. I'm sorry I dragged you into a murder investigation. No, I'm not, actually. I'm glad you were on hand. Can we talk?"

"After I put some dry clothes on and stop looking a mess."

She offered me her jacket. Since I'm five-eight to her five-four, it wasn't much of a cover, but I draped it gratefully over my shoulders to protect myself from the chilly October evening.

At my apartment Alicia followed me into the bathroom while I turned on the hot water. "Do you know who the dead woman was? The police wouldn't tell us."

"Yes," I responded irritably. "And if you'll give me twenty minutes to warm up, I'll tell you. Bathing is not a group sport in this apartment."

She trailed back out of the bathroom, her face set in tense lines. When I joined her in the living room some twenty minutes later, a towel around my damp hair, she was sitting in front of the television set changing channels.

"No news yet," she said briefly. "Who was the dead girl?"

"Louise Carmody. Junior loan officer at the Ft. Dearborn. You know her?"

Alicia shook her head. "Do the police know why she was shot?"

"They're just starting to investigate. What do you know about it?"

"Nothing. Are they going to put her name on the news?"

"Probably, if the family's been notified. Why is this important?"

"No reason. It just seems so ghoulish, reporters hovering around her dead body and everything."

"Could I have the truth, please?"

She sprang to her feet and glared at me. "It is the truth."

"Screw that. You don't know her name, you spin the TV dials to see the reports, and now you think it's ghoulish for the reporters to hover around? . . . Tell you what I think, Alicia. I think you know who did the shooting. They shuffled the swimmers, nobody knew who was in which lane. You started out in lane two, and you'd be dead if the woman from Ajax hadn't complained. Who wants to kill you?"

Her black eyes glittered in her white face. "No one. Why don't you have a little empathy, Vic? I might have been killed. There was a madman out there who shot a woman. Why don't you give me some sympathy?"

"I jumped into a pool to pull that woman out. I sat around in wet clothes for two hours talking to the cops. I'm beat. You want sympathy, go someplace else. The little I have is reserved for myself tonight.

"I'd really like to know why I had to be at the pool, if it wasn't to ward off a potential attacker. And if you'd told me the real reason, Louise Carmody might still be alive."

"Damn you, Vic, stop doubting every word I say. I told you why I needed you there—someone had to sign the card. Millie works during the day. So does Fredda. Katie has a new baby. Elene is becoming a grandmother for the first time. Get off my goddamn back."

"If you're not going to tell me the truth, and if you're going to scream at me about it, I'd just as soon you left."

She stood silent for a minute. "Sorry, Vic. I'll get a better grip on myself."

"Great. You do that. I'm fixing some supper—want any?"

She shook her head. When I returned with a plate of pasta and olives, Joan Druggen was just announcing the top local story. Alicia sat with her hands clenched as they stated the dead woman's name. After that, she didn't say much. Just asked if she could crash for the night—she lived in Warrenville, a good hour's drive from town, near Berman's aeronautic engineering labs.

I gave her pillows and a blanket for the couch and went to bed. I was pretty angry: I figured she wanted to sleep over because she was scared, and it infuriated me that she wouldn't talk about it.

When the phone woke me at 2:30, my throat was raw, the start of a cold brought on by sitting around in wet clothes for so long. A heavy voice asked for Alicia.

"I don't know who you're talking about," I said hoarsely.

"Be your age, Warshawski. She brought you to the gym. She isn't at her own place. She's gotta be with you. You don't want to wake her up, give her a message. She was lucky tonight. We want the money by noon, or she won't be so lucky a second time."

He hung up. I held the receiver a second longer and heard another click. The living room extension. I pulled on a dressing gown and padded down the hallway. The apartment door shut just as I got to the living room. I ran to the top of the stairs; Alicia's footsteps were echoing up and down the stairwell.

"Alicia! Alicia—you can't go out there alone. Come back here!"

The slamming of the entryway door was my only answer.

III

I didn't sleep well, my cold mixing with worry and anger over Alicia. At eight I hoisted my aching body out of bed and sat sneezing over some steaming fruit juice while I tried to focus my brain on possible action. Alicia owed somebody money. That somebody was pissed off enough to kill because he didn't have it. Bankers do not kill wayward loan customers. Loan sharks do, but what could Alicia have done to rack up so much indebtedness? Berman probably paid her seventy or eighty thousand a year for the special kinds of designs she did on aircraft wings. And she was the kind of client a bank usually values. So what did she need money for that only a shark would provide?

The clock was ticking. I called her office. She'd phoned in sick; the secretary didn't know where she was calling from but had assumed home. On a dim chance I tried her phone. No answer. Alicia had one brother, Tom, an insurance agent on the far south side. After a few tries I located his office in Flossmoor. He hadn't heard from Alicia for weeks. And no, he didn't know who she might owe money to.

Reluctantly Tom gave me their father's phone number in Florida. Mr. Dauphine hadn't heard from his daughter, either.

"If she calls you, or if she shows up, *please* let me know. She's in trouble up here, and the only way I can help her is by knowing where she is." I gave him the number without much expectation of hearing from him again.

I did know someone who might be able to give me a line on her debts. A year or so earlier, I'd done a major favor for Don Pasquale, a local mob leader. If she owed him money, he might listen to my intercession. If not, he might be able to tell me whom she had borrowed from.

Torfino's, an Elmwood Park restaurant where the don had a part-time office, put me through to his chief assistant, Ernesto. A well-remembered gravel voice told me I sounded awful.

"Thank you, Ernesto," I snuffled. "Did you hear about the death of Louise Carmody at the University of Illinois gym last night? She was probably shot by mistake, poor thing. The intended victim was a woman named Alicia Dauphine. We grew up together, so I feel a little solicitous on her behalf. She owes a lot of money to someone: I wondered if you know who."

"Name isn't familiar, Warshawski. I'll check around and call you back."

My cold made me feel as though I was at the bottom of a fish tank. I couldn't think fast enough or hard enough to imagine where Alicia might have gone to ground. Perhaps at her house, believing if she didn't answer the phone no one would think she was home? It wasn't a very clever idea, but it was the best I could do in my muffled, snuffled state.

The old farmhouse in Warrenville that Alicia had modernized lay behind the local high school. The boys were out practicing football. They were wearing light jerseys. I had on my winter coat—even though the day was warm, my cold made me shiver and want to be bundled up. Although we were close enough that I could see their mouthpieces, they didn't notice me as I walked around the house looking for signs of life.

Alicia's car was in the garage, but the house looked cold and unoccupied. As I made my way to the back, a black-and-white cat darted out from the bushes and began weaving itself around my ankles, mewing piteously. Alicia had three cats. This one wanted something to eat.

Alicia had installed a sophisticated burglar alarm system—she had an office in her home and often worked on preliminary designs there. An expert had gotten through the system into the pantry—some kind of epoxy had been sprayed on the wires to freeze them. Then, somehow disabling the phone link, the intruder had cut through the wires.

My stomach muscles tightened, and I wished futilely for the Smith & Wesson locked in my safe at home. My cold really had addled my brains for me not to take it on such an errand. Still, where burglars lead shall P.I.s hesitate? I opened the window, slid a leg over, and landed on the pantry floor. My feline friend followed more gracefully. She promptly abandoned me to start sniffing at the pantry walls.

Cautiously opening the door I slid into the kitchen. It was deserted, the refrigerator and clock motors humming gently, a dry dishcloth draped over the sink. In the living room another cat joined me and followed me into the electronic wonderland of Alicia's study. She had used built-in bookcases to house her computers and other gadgets. The printers were tucked along a side wall, and wires ran everywhere. Whoever had broken in was not interested in merchandise—the street value of her study contents would have brought in a nice return, but they stood unharmed.

By now I was dreading the trek upstairs. The second cat, a tabby, trotted briskly ahead of me, tail waving like a flag. Alicia's bedroom door was shut. I kicked it open with my right leg and pressed myself against the wall. Nothing. Dropping to my knees I looked in. The bed, tidily covered with an old-fashioned white spread, was empty. So was the bathroom. So was the guest room and an old sun porch glassed in and converted to a solarium.

The person who broke in had not come to steal—everything was preternaturally tidy. So he (she?) had come to attack Alicia. The hair stood up on the nape of my neck. Where was he? Not in the house. Hiding outside?

I started down the stairs again when I heard a noise, a heavy scraping. I froze, trying to locate the source. A movement caught my eye at the line of vision. The hatch to the crawl space had been shoved open; an arm swung down. For a split second only I stared at the arm and the gun in its grip, then leaped down the stairs two at a time.

A heavy thud—the man jumping onto the upper landing. The crack as the gun fired. A jolt in my left shoulder, and I gasped with shock and fell the last few steps to the bottom. Righted myself. Reached for the deadlock on the front door. Heard an outraged squawk, loud swearing, and a crash that sounded like a man falling downstairs. Then I had the door open and was staggering outside while an angry bundle of fur poured past me. One of the cats, a heroine, tripping my assailant and saving my life.

IV

I never really lost consciousness. The football players saw me stagger down the sidewalk and came trooping over. In their concern for me they failed to tackle the gunman, but they got me to a hospital, where a young intern eagerly set about removing the slug from my shoulder; the winter coat had protected me from major damage.

Between my cold and the gunshot, I was just as happy to let him incarcerate me for a few days.

They tucked me into bed, and I fell into a heavy, uneasy sleep. I had jumped into the black waters of Lake Michigan in search of Alicia, trying to reach her ahead of a shark. She was lurking just out of reach. She didn't know that her oxygen tank ran out at noon.

When I woke finally, soaked with sweat, it was dark outside. The room was lit faintly by a fluorescent light over the sink. A lean man in a brown wool business suit was sitting next to the bed. When he saw me looking at him, he reached into his coat.

If he was going to shoot me, there wasn't a thing I could do about it—I was too limp from my heavy sleep to move. Instead of a gun, though, he pulled out an ID case.

"Miss Warshawski? Peter Carlton, Federal Bureau of Investigation. I know you're not feeling well, but I need to talk to you about Alice Dauphine."

"So the shark ate her," I said.

"What?" he demanded sharply. "What does that mean?"

"Nothing. Where is she?"

"We don't know. That's what we want to talk to you about. She went home with you after the swimming meet yesterday. Correct?"

"Gosh, Mr. Carlton. I love watching my tax dollars at work. If you've been following her, you must have a better fix on her whereabouts than I do. I last saw her around 2:30 this morning. If it's still today, that is."

"What did she talk to you about?"

My mind was starting to unfog. "Why is the Bureau interested in Miss Dauphine?"

He didn't want to tell me. All he wanted was every word Alicia had said to me. When I wouldn't budge, he started in on why I was in her house and what I had noticed there.

Finally I said, "Mr. Carlton, if you can't tell me why you're interested in Miss Dauphine, there's no way I can respond to your questions. I don't believe the Bureau—or the police—or anyone, come to that—has any right to pry into the affairs of citizens in the hopes of turning up some scandal. You tell me why you're interested, and I'll tell you if I know anything relevant to that interest."

With an ill grace he said, "We believe she has been selling Defense Department secrets to the Russians."

"No," I said flatly. "She wouldn't."

"Some wing designs she was working on have disappeared. She's disappeared. And a Soviet functionary in St. Charles has disappeared."

"Sounds pretty circumstantial to me. The wing designs might be in her home. They could easily be on a disk someplace—she did all her drafting on computer."

They'd been through her computer files at home and at work and found nothing. Her boss did not have copies of the latest design, only of the early stuff. I thought about the heavy voice on the phone demanding money, but loyalty to Alicia made me keep it to myself—give her a chance to tell her story first.

I did give him everything Alicia had said, her nervousness and her sudden departure. That I was worried about her and went to see if she was in her house. And was shot by an intruder hiding in the crawl space. Who might have taken her designs. Although nothing looked pilfered.

He didn't believe me. I don't know if he thought I knew something I wasn't telling, or if he thought I had joined Alicia in selling secrets to the Russians. But he kept at me for so long that I finally pushed my call button. When the nurse arrived, I explained that I was worn out and could she please show my visitor out? He left but promised me that he would return.

Cursing my weakness, I fell asleep again. When I next woke it was morning, and both my cold and my shoulder were much improved. When the doctors came by on their morning visit, I got their agreement to a discharge. Before I bathed and left, the Warrenville police sent out a man who took a detailed statement.

I called my answering service from a phone in the lobby. Ernesto had been in touch. I reached him at Torfino's.

"Saw about your accident in the papers, Warshawski. How you feeling? . . . About Dauphine. Apparently she's signed a note for $750,000 to Art Smollensk. Can't do anything to help you out. The don sends his best wishes for your recovery."

Art Smollensk, gambling king. When I worked for the public defender, I'd had to defend some of his small-time employees—people at the level of smashing someone's fingers in his car door. The ones who did hits and arson usually could afford their own attorneys.

Alicia as a gambler made no sense to me—but we hadn't been close for over a decade. There were lots of things I didn't know about her.

At home for a change of clothes I stopped in the basement, where I store useless mementos in a locked stall. After fifteen minutes of shifting boxes around, I was sweating and my left shoulder was throbbing and oozing stickily, but I'd located my high school yearbook. I took it upstairs with me and thumbed through it, trying to gain inspiration on where Alicia might have gone to earth.

None came. I was about to leave again when the phone rang. It was Alicia, talking against a background of noise. "Thank God you're safe, Vic. I saw about the shooting in the paper. Please don't worry about me. I'm okay. Stay away and don't worry."

She hung up before I could ask her anything. I concentrated, not on what she'd said, but what had been in the background. Metal doors banging open and shut. Lots of loud, wild talking. Not an airport—the talking was too loud for that, and there weren't any intercom announcements in the background. I knew what it was. If I'd just let my mind relax, it would come to me.

Idly flipping through the yearbook, I looked for faces Alicia might trust. I found my own staring from a group photo of the girls' basketball team. I'd been a guard—Victoria the protectress from way back. On the next page, Alicia smiled fiercely, holding a swimming trophy. Her coach, who also taught Latin, had desperately wanted Alicia to train for the Olympics, but Alicia had had her heart set on the U of I and engineering.

Suddenly I knew what the clanking was, where Alicia was. No other sound like that exists anywhere on earth.

V

Alicia and I grew up under the shadow of the steel mills in South Chicago. Nowhere else has the deterioration of American industry shown up more clearly. Wisconsin Steel is padlocked shut. The South Works are a fragment of their former monstrous grandeur. Unemployment is over thirty percent, and the number of jobless youths lounging in the bars and on the streets had grown from the days when I hurried past them to the safety of my mother's house.

The high school was more derelict than I remembered. Many windows were boarded over. The asphalt playground was cracked and covered with litter, and the bleachers around the football field were badly weathered.

The guard at the doorway demanded my business. I showed her my P.I. license and said I needed to talk to the women's gym teacher on confidential business. After some dickering—hostile on her side, snuffly on mine—she gave me a pass. I didn't need directions down the scuffed corridors, past the battered lockers, past the smell of rancid oil coming from the cafeteria, to the noise and life of the gym.

Teenage girls in blue shirts and white shorts—the school colors— were shrieking, jumping, wailing in pursuit of volleyballs. I watched the pandemonium until the buzzer ended the period, then walked up to the instructor.

She was panting and sweating and gave me an incurious glance, looking only briefly at the pass I held out for her. "Yes?"

"You have a new swimming coach, don't you?"

"Just a volunteer. Are you from the union? She isn't drawing a paycheck. But Miss Finley, the coach, is desperately shorthanded—she teaches Latin, you know—and this woman is a big help."

"I'm not from the union. I'm her trainer. I need to talk to her—find out why she's dropped out and whether she plans to compete in any of her meets this fall."

The teacher gave me the hard look of someone used to sizing up fabricated excuses. I didn't think she believed me, but she told me I could go into the pool area and talk to the swim coach.

The pool dated to the time when this high school served an affluent neighborhood. It was twenty-five yards long, built with skylights along the outer wall. You reached it through the changing rooms, separate ones with showers for girls and boys. It didn't have an outside hallway entrance.

Alicia was perched alone on the high dive. A few students, boys and girls, were splashing about in the pool, but no organized training was in progress. Alicia was staring at nothing.

I cupped my hands and called up to her, "Do you want me to climb up, or are you going to come down?"

She shot off the board in a perfect arc, barely rippling the surface of the water. The kids watched with envy. I was pretty jealous, myself—nothing I do is done with that much grace.

She surfaced near me but looked at the students. "I want you guys swimming laps," she said sharply. "What do you think this is—summer camp?"

They left us reluctantly and began swimming.

"How did you find me?"

"It was easy. I was looking through the yearbook, trying to think of someone you would trust. Miss Finley was the simple answer—I remembered how you practically lived in her house for two years. You liked to read *Jane Eyre* together, and she adored you."

"You are in deep trouble. Smollensk is after you, and so is the FBI. You can't hide here forever. You'd better talk to the Bureau guys. They won't love you, but at least they're not going to shoot you."

"The FBI? Whatever for?"

"Your designs, sweetie pie. Your designs and the Russians. The FBI are the people who look into that kind of thing."

"Vic. I don't know what you're talking about." The words were said with such slow deliberateness that I was almost persuaded.

"The $750,000 you owe Art Smollensk."

She shook her head, then said, "Oh. Yes. That."

"Yes, that. I guess it seems like more money to me than it does to you. Or had you forgotten Louise Carmody getting shot? . . . Anyway, a known Russian spy left Fermilab yesterday or the day before, and you're gone, and some of your wing designs are gone, and the FBI thinks you've sold them overseas and maybe gone East yourself. I didn't tell them about Art, but they'll probably get there before too long."

"How sure are they that the designs are gone?"

"Your boss can't find them. Maybe you have a duplicate set at home nobody knows about."

She shook her head again. "I don't leave that kind of thing at home. I had them last Saturday, working, but I took the diskettes back . . ." Her voice trailed off as a look of horror washed across her face. "Oh, no. This is worse than I thought." She hoisted herself out of the pool. "I've got to go. Got to get away before someone else figures out I'm here."

"Alicia, for Christ's sake. What has happened?"

She stopped and looked at me, tears swimming in her black eyes. "If I could tell anyone, it would be you, Vic." Then she was jogging into the girls' changing room, leaving the students in the pool swimming laps.

I stuck with her. "Where are you going? The Feds have a hook on any place you have friends or relations. Smollensk does, too."

That stopped her. "Tom, too?"

"Tom first, last, and foremost. He's the only relative you have in Chicago." She was starting to shiver in the bare corridor. I grabbed her and shook her. "Tell me the truth, Alicia. I can't fly blind. I already took a bullet in the shoulder."

Suddenly she was sobbing on my chest. "Oh, Vic. It's been so awful. You can't know . . . you can't understand . . . you won't believe . . ." She was hiccuping.

I led her into the shower room and found a towel. Rubbing her down, I got the story in choking bits and pieces.

Tom was the gambler. He'd gotten into it in a small way in high school and college. After he went into business for himself, the habit grew. He'd mortgaged his insurance agency assets, taken out a second mortgage on the house, but couldn't stop.

"He came to me two weeks ago. Told me he was going to start filing claims with his companies, collect the money." She gave a twisted smile. "He didn't have to put that kind of pressure on—I can't help helping him."

"But, Alicia, why? And how does Art Smollensk have your name?"

"Is that the man Tom owes money to? I think he uses my name— Alonso, my middle name—I know he does; I just don't like to think about it. Someone came around threatening me three years ago. I told Tom never to use my name again, and he didn't for a long time, but now I guess he was desperate—$750,000, you know. . . .

"As to why I help him . . . You never had any brothers or sisters, so maybe you can't understand. When Mom died, I was thirteen, he was six. I looked after him. Got him out of trouble. All kinds of stuff. It gets to be a habit, I guess. Or an obligation. That's why I've never married, you know, never had any children of my own. I don't want any more responsibilities like this one."

"And the designs?"

She looked horrified again. "He came over for dinner on Saturday. I'd been working all day on the things, and he came into the study when I was logging off. I didn't tell him it was Defense Department work, but it's not too hard to figure out what I do is defense-related—after all, that's all Berman does; we don't make commercial aircraft. I haven't had a chance to look at the designs since—I worked out all day Sunday getting ready for that damned meet Monday. Tom must have taken my diskettes and swapped the labels with some others—I've got tons of them lying around."

She gave a twisted smile. "It was a gamble: a gamble that there'd be something valuable on them and a gamble I wouldn't discover the switch before he got rid of them. But he's a gambler."

"I see. . . . Look, Alicia. You can only be responsible for Tom so far. Even if you could bail him out this time—and I don't see how you possibly can—there'll be a next time. And you may not survive this one to help him again. Let's call the FBI."

She squeezed her eyes shut. "You don't understand, Vic. You can't possibly understand."

While I was trying to reason her into phoning the Bureau, Miss Finley, swim coach-cum-romantic-Latin-teacher, came briskly into the locker room. "Allie! One of the girls came to get me. Are you all—" She did a double-take. "Victoria! Good to see you. Have you come to help Allie? I told her she could count on you."

"Have you told her what's going on?" I demanded of Alicia.

Yes, Miss Finley knew most of the story. Agreed that it was very worrying but said Allie could not possibly turn in her own brother. She had given Allie a gym mat and some bedding to sleep on—she could just stay at the gym until the furor died down and they could think of something else to do.

I sat helplessly as Miss Finley led Alicia off to get some dry clothes. At last, when they didn't rejoin me, I sought them out, poking through half-remembered halls and doors until I found the staff coaching office. Alicia was alone, looking about fifteen in an old cheerleader's uniform Miss Finley had dug up for her.

"Miss Finley teaching?" I asked sharply.

Alicia looked guilty but defiant. "Yes. Two-thirty class. Look. The critical thing is to get those diskettes back. I called Tom, explained it to him. Told him I'd try to help him raise the money but that we couldn't let the Russians have those things. He agreed, so he's bringing them out here."

The room rocked slightly around us. "No. I know you don't have much of a sense of humor, but this is a joke, isn't it?"

She didn't understand. Wouldn't understand that if the Russian had already left the country, Tom no longer had the material. That if Tom was coming here, she was the scapegoat. At last, despairing, I said, "Where is he meeting you? Here?"

"I told him I'd be at the pool."

"Will you do one thing my way? Will you go to Miss Finley's class and conjugate verbs for forty-five minutes and let me meet him at the pool? Please?"

At last, her jaw set stubbornly, she agreed. She still wouldn't let me call the Bureau, though. "Not until I've talked to Tom myself. It may all be a mistake, you know."

We both knew it wasn't, but I saw her into the Latin class without making the phone call I knew it was my duty to make and returned to the pool. Driving out the two students still splashing around in the water, I put signs on the locker room doors saying the water was contaminated and there would be no swimming until further notice.

I turned out the lights and settled in a corner of the room remote from the outside windows to wait. And go over and over in my mind the story. I believed it. Was I fooling myself? Was that why she wouldn't call the Feds?

At last Tom came in through the men's locker room entrance. "Allie? Allie?" His voice bounced off the high rafters and echoed around me. I was well back in the back shadows, my Smith & Wesson in hand; he didn't see me.

After half a minute or so another man joined him. I didn't recognize the stranger, but his baggy clothes marked him as part of Smollensk's group, not the Bureau. He talked softly to Tom for a minute. Then they went into the girl's locker room together.

When they returned, I had moved part way up the side of the pool, ready to follow them if they went back into the main part of the high school looking for Alicia.

"Tom!" I called. "It's V.I. Warshawski. I know the whole story. Give me the diskettes."

"Warshawski!" he yelled. "What the hell are you doing here?"

I sensed rather than saw the movement his friend made. I shot at him and dived into the water. His bullet zipped as it hit the tiles where I'd been standing. My wet clothes and my sore shoulder made it hard to move. Another bullet hit the water by my head, and I went under again, fumbling with my heavy jacket, getting it free, surfacing, hearing Alicia's sharp, "Tom, why are you shooting at Vic? Stop it now. Stop it and give me back the diskettes."

Another flurry of shots, this time away from me, giving me a chance to get to the side of the pool, to climb out. Alicia lay on the floor near the door to the girls' locker room. Tom stood silently by. The gunman was jamming more bullets into his gun.

As fast as I could in my sodden clothes I lumbered to the hitman, grabbing his arm, squeezing, feeling blood start to seep from my shoulder, stepping on his instep, putting all the force of my body into my leg. Tom, though, Tom was taking the gun from him. Tom was going to shoot me.

"Drop that gun, Tom Dauphine." It was Miss Finley. Years of teaching in a tough school gave creditable authority to her; Tom dropped the gun.

VI

Alicia lived long enough to tell the truth to the FBI. It was small comfort to me. Small consolation to see Tom's statement. He hoped he could get Smollensk to kill his sister before she said anything. If that happened, he had a good gamble on her dying a traitor in their eyes— after all, her designs were gone, and her name was in Smollensk's files. Maybe the truth never would have come out. Worth a gamble to a betting man.

The Feds arrived about five minutes after the shooting stopped. They'd been watching Tom, just not closely enough. They were sore that they'd let Alicia get shot. So they dumped some charges on me— obstructing federal authorities, not telling them where Alicia was, not calling as soon as I had the truth from her, God knows what else. I spent several days in jail. It seemed like a suitable penance, just not enough of one.

I'LL CUT YOUR THROAT AGAIN, KATHLEEN

FREDRIC BROWN

I heard the footsteps coming down the hall and I was watching the door—the door that had no knob on my side of it—when it opened.

I thought I'd recognized the step, and I'd been right. It was the young, nice one, the one whose bright hair made so brilliant a contrast with his white uniform coat.

I said, "Hello, Red," and he said, "Hello, Mr. Marlin. I—I'll take you down to the office. The doctors are there now." He sounded more nervous than I felt.

"How much time have I got, Red?"

"How much— Oh, I see what you mean. They're examining a couple of others ahead of you. You've got time."

So I didn't get up off the edge of the bed. I held my hands out in front of me, backs up and the fingers rigid. They didn't tremble any more. My fingers were as steady as those of a statue, and about as useful. Oh, I could move them. I could even clench them into fists slowly. But for playing sax and clarinet they were about as good as hands of bananas. I turned them over—and there on my wrists were the two ugly scars where, a little less than a year ago, I'd slashed them with a straight razor. Deeply enough to have cut some of the tendons that moved the fingers.

I moved my fingers now, curling them inward toward the palm, slowly. The intern was watching.

"They'll come back, Mr. Marlin," he said. "Exercise—that's all they need." It wasn't true. He knew that I knew he knew it, for when I didn't bother to answer, he went on, almost defensively, "Anyway, you can still arrange and conduct. You can hold a baton all right. And—I got an idea for you, Mr. Marlin."

"Yes, Red?"

"Trombone. Why don't you take up trombone? You could learn it fast, and you don't need finger action to play trombone."

Slowly, I shook my head. I didn't try to explain. It was something you couldn't explain, anyway. It wasn't only the physical ability to play an instrument that was gone. It was more than that.

I looked at my hands again and then I put them carefully away in my pockets, where I wouldn't have to look at them.

I looked up at the intern's face again. There was a look on it that I recognized and remembered—the look I'd seen on thousands of young faces across footlights—hero worship. Out of the past it came to me, that look.

He could still look at me that way, even after—

"Red," I asked him, "don't you think I'm insane?"

"Of course not, Mr. Marlin. I don't think you were ever—" He bogged down on that.

I needed him. Maybe it was cruel, but it was crueler to me. I said, "You don't think I was ever crazy? You think I was sane when I tried to kill my wife?"

"Well—it was just temporary. You had a breakdown. You'd been working too hard—twenty hours a day, about. You were near the top with your band. Me, Mr. Marlin, *I* think you were *at* the top. You had it on all of them, only most of the public hadn't found out yet. They would have, if—"

"If I hadn't slipped a cog," I said. I thought, what a way to express going crazy, trying to kill your wife, trying to kill yourself, and losing your memory.

Red looked at his wrist watch, then pulled up a chair and sat down facing me. He talked fast.

"We haven't got too long, Mr. Marlin," he said. "And I want you to pass those doctors and get out of here. You'll be all right once you get out of this joint. Your memory will come back, a little at a time—when you're in the right surroundings."

I shrugged. It didn't seem to matter much. I said, "Okay, brief me. It didn't work last time, but—I'll try."

"You're Johnny Marlin," he said. *"The* Johnny Marlin. You play a mean clarinet, but that's sideline. You're the best alto sax in the business, *I* think. You were fourth in the Down Beat poll a year ago, but—"

I interrupted him. "You mean I *did* play clarinet and sax. Not any more, Red. Can't you get that through your head?" I hadn't meant to sound so rough about it, but my voice got out of control.

Red didn't seem to hear me. His eyes went to his wrist watch again and then came back to me. He started talking again.

"We got ten minutes, maybe. I wish I knew what you remember and what you don't about all I've been telling you the last month. What's your right name—I mean, before you took a professional name?"

"John Dettmann," I said. "Born June first, nineteen-twenty, on the wrong side of the tracks. Orphaned at five. Released from orphanage at sixteen. Worked as bus boy in Cleveland and saved up enough money to buy a clarinet, and took lessons. Bought a sax a year later, and got my first job with a band at eighteen."

"What band?"

"Heinie Wills'—local band in Cleveland, playing at Danceland there. Played third alto a while, then first alto. Next worked for a six-man combo called—What was it, Red? I don't remember."

"The Basin Streeters, Mr. Marlin. Look, do you really remember any of this, or is it just from what I've told you?"

"Mostly from what you've told me, Red. Sometimes, I get kind of vague pictures, but it's pretty foggy. Let's get on with it. So the Basin Streeters did a lot of traveling for a while and I left them in Chi for my first stretch with a name band— Look, I think I've got that list of bands pretty well memorized. There isn't much time. Let's skip it.

"I joined the army in forty-two—I'd have been twenty-two then. A year at Fort Billings, and then England. Kayoed by a bomb in London before I ever got to pull a trigger except on rifle range. A month in a hospital there, shipped back, six months in a mental hospital here, and let out on a P.N." He knew as well as I did what P.N. meant, but I translated it for us. "Psycho-neurotic. Nuts. Crazy."

He opened his mouth to argue the point, and then decided there wasn't time.

"So I saved my money," I said, "before and during the army, and I started my own band. That would have been—late forty-four?"

Red nodded. "Remember the list of places you've played, the names of your sidemen, what I told you about them?"

"Pretty well," I said. There wouldn't be time to go into that, anyway. I said, "And early in forty-five, while I was still getting started, I got married. To Kathy Courteen. *The* Kathy Courteen, who owns a slice of Chicago, who's got more money than sense. She must have, if she married me. We were married June tenth, nineteen forty-five. Why *did* she marry me, Red?"

"Why shouldn't she," he said. "You're *Johnny Marlin!*"

The funny part of it is, he wasn't kidding. I could tell by his voice he meant it. He thought being Johnny Marlin had really been something. I looked down at my hands. They'd got loose out of my pockets again.

I think I knew, suddenly, why I wanted to get out of this gilt-lined nuthouse that was costing Kathy Courteen—Kathy Marlin, I mean—the price of a fur coat every week to keep me in. It wasn't because I wanted *out*, really. It was because I wanted to get away from the hero worship of this red-headed kid who'd gone nuts about Johnny Marlin's band, and Johnny Marlin's saxophone.

"Have you ever seen Kathy, Red?" I asked.

He shook his head, "I've seen pictures of her, newspaper pictures of her. She's beautiful."

"Even with a scar across her throat?" I asked.

His eyes avoided mine. They went to his watch again, and he stood up quickly. "We'd better get down there," he said.

He went to the knobless door, opened it with a key, and politely held it open for me to precede him out into the hallway.

That look in his eyes made me feel foolish, as always. I don't know how he did it, but Red always managed to look *up* at me, from a height a good six inches taller than mine.

Then, side by side, we went down the great stairway of that plush-lined madhouse that had once been a million dollar mansion and was now a million dollar sanitarium with more employees than inmates.

We went into the office and the gray-haired nurse behind the desk nodded and said, "They're ready for you."

"Luck, Mr. Marlin," Red said. "I'm pulling for you."

So I went through the door. There were three of them, as last time.

"Sit down, please, Mr. Marlin," Dr. Glasspiegel, the head one, said.

They sat each upon one side of the square table, leaving the fourth side and the fourth chair for me. I slid into it. I put my hands in my pockets again. I knew if I looked at them or thought about them, I might say something foolish, and then I'd be here a while again.

Then they were asking me questions, taking turns at it. Some about my past—and Red's coaching had been good. Once or twice, but not often, I had to stall and admit my memory was hazy on a point or two. And some of the questions were about the present, and they were easy. I mean, it was easy to see what answers they wanted to those questions, and to give them.

But it had been like this the last time, I remembered, over a month ago. And I'd missed somewhere. They hadn't let me go. Maybe, I thought, because they got too much money out of keeping me here. I didn't really think that. These men were the best in their profession.

There was a lull in the questioning. They seemed to be waiting for something. For what? I wondered, and it came to me that the last interview had been like this, too.

The door behind me opened, quietly, but I heard it. And I remembered—that had happened last time, too. Just as they told me I could leave and they'd talk it over, someone else had come in. I'd passed him as I'd left the room.

And, suddenly, I knew what I'd missed up on. It had been someone I'd been supposed to recognize, and I hadn't. And here was the same test again. Before I turned, I tried to remember what Red had told me about people I'd known—but there was so little physical description to it. It seemed hopeless.

"You may return to your room now, Mr. Marlin," Dr. Glasspiegel was saying. "We—ah—wish to discuss your case."

"Thanks," I said, and stood up.

I saw that he'd taken off his shell rimmed glasses and was tapping them nervously on the back of his hand, which lay on the table before him. I thought, okay, so now I know the catch and next time I'll make the grade. I'll have Red get me pictures of my band and other bands I've played with and as many newspaper pictures as he can find of people I knew.

I turned. The man in the doorway, standing there as though waiting for me to leave, was short and fat. There was a tense look in his face, even though his eyes were avoiding mine. He was looking past me, at the doctors. I tried to think fast. Who did I know that was short and—

I took a chance. I'd had a trumpet player named Tubby Hayes. "Tubby!" I said.

And hit the jackpot. His face lighted up like a neon sign and he grinned a yard wide and stuck out his hand.

"Johnny! Johnny, it's good to see you." He was making like a pump handle with my arm.

"Tubby Hayes!" I said, to let them know I knew his last name, too. "Don't tell me you're nuts, too. That why you're here?"

He laughed, nervously. "I came to get you, Johnny. That is, uh, if—" He looked past me.

Dr. Glasspiegel was clearing his throat. He and the other doctors were standing now.

"Yes," he said, "I believe it will be all right for Mr. Marlin to leave."

He put his hand on my shoulder. They were all standing about me now.

"Your reactions are normal, Mr. Marlin," he said. "Your memory is still a bit impaired but—ah—it will improve gradually. More rapidly, I believe, amid familiar surroundings than here. You—ah—have plans?"

"No," I said, frankly.

"Don't overwork again. Take things easy for a while. And . . ."

There was a lot more advice. And then signing things, and getting ready. It was almost an hour before we got into a cab, Tubby and I.

He gave the address, and I recognized it. The Carleton. That was where I'd lived, that last year. Where Kathy still lived.

"How's Kathy?" I asked.

"Fine, Johnny. I guess she is. I mean—"

"You mean what?"

He looked a bit embarrassed. "Well—I mean I haven't seen her. She never liked us boys, Johnny. You know that. But she was square with us. You know we decided we couldn't hold together without you, Johnny, and might as well break up. Well, she paid us what we had coming—the three weeks you were on the cuff, I mean—and doubled it, a three-weeks bonus to tide us over."

"The boys doing okay, Tubby?"

"Yep, Johnny. All of them. Well—except Harry. He kind of got lost in the snow if you know what I mean."

"That's tough," I said, and didn't elaborate. I didn't know whether I was supposed to know that Harry had been taking cocaine or not. And there had been two Harrys with the band, at that.

So the band was busted up. In a way I was glad. If someone had taken over and held it together, maybe there'd have been an argument about trying to get me to come back.

"A month ago, Tubby," I said, "they examined me at the sanitarium and I flunked. I think it was because I didn't recognize somebody. Was it you? Were you there then?"

"You walked right by me, through the door, Johnny. You never saw me."

"You there—for that purpose? Both times?"

"Yes, Johnny. That Doc Glasspiegel suggested it. He got to know me, and to think of me, I guess, because I dropped around so often to ask about you. Why wouldn't they let me see you?"

"Rules," I said. "That's Glasspiegel's system, part of it. Complete isolation during the period of cure. I haven't even seen Kathy."

"No!" said Tubby. "They told me you couldn't have visitors, but I didn't know it went that far." He sighed. "She sure must be head over heels for you, Johnny. What I hear, she's carried the torch."

"God knows why," I said. "After I cut—"

"Shut up," Tubby said sharply. "You aren't to think or talk about that. Glasspiegel told me that, while you were getting ready."

"Okay," I said. It didn't matter. "Does Kathy know we're coming?"

"We? I'm not going in, Johnny. I'm just riding to the door with you. No, she doesn't know. You asked the doc not to tell her, didn't you?''

"I didn't want a reception. I just want to walk in quietly. Sure, I asked the doctor, but I thought maybe he'd warn her anyway. So she could hide the knives."

"Now, Johnny—"

"Okay," I said.

I looked out the window of the cab. I knew where we were and just how far from the Carleton. Funny my topography hadn't gone the way the rest of my memory had. But I still knew the streets and their names, even though I couldn't recognize my best friend or my wife. The mind is a funny thing, I thought.

"One worry you won't have," Tubby Hayes said. "That lush brother of hers, Myron Courteen, the one that was always in your hair."

The red-headed intern had mentioned that Kathy had a brother. Apparently, I wasn't supposed to like him.

So I said, "Did someone drop him down a well?"

"Headed west. He's a Los Angeles playboy now. Guess he finally quarrelled with Kathy and she settled an allowance on him and let him go."

We were getting close to the Carleton—only a half dozen blocks to go—and suddenly I realized there was a lot that I didn't know, and should know.

"Let's have a drink, Tubby," I said. "I—I'm not quite ready to go home yet."

"Sure, Johnny," he said, and then spoke to the cab driver.

We swung in to the curb in front of a swanky neon-plated tavern. It didn't look familiar, like the rest of the street did. Tubby saw me looking.

"Yeah, it's new," he said. "Been here only a few months."

We went in and sat at a dimly lighted bar. Tubby ordered two scotch-and-sodas without asking me, so I guess that's what I used to drink. I didn't remember. Anyway, it tasted all right, and I hadn't had a drink for eleven months, so even the first sip of it hit me a little.

And when I'd drunk it all, it tasted better than all right. I looked at myself in the blue mirror back of the bar. I thought, there's always this. I can always drink myself to death—on Kathy's money. I knew I didn't have any myself because Tubby had said I was three weeks on the cuff with the band.

We ordered a second round and I asked Tubby, "How come this Myron hasn't money of his own, if he's Kathy's brother?" He looked at me strangely. I'd been doing all right up to now. I said, "Yeah, there are things I'm still hazy about."

"Oh," he said. "Well, that one's easy. Myron is worse than a black sheep for the Courteens. He's a no-good louse and an all-around stinker. He was disinherited, and Kathy got it all. But she takes care of him."

He took a sip of his drink and put it down again. "You know, Johnny," he said, "None of us liked Kathy much because she was against you having the band and wanted you to herself. But we were wrong about her. She's swell. The way she sticks to her menfolk no matter what they do. Even Myron."

"Even me," I said.

"Well—she saved your life, Johnny. With blood—" He stopped abruptly. "Forget it, Johnny."

I finished my second drink. I said, "I'll tell you the truth, Tubby. I can't forget it—because I don't remember it. But I've got to know, before I face her. What did happen that night?"

"Johnny, I—"

"Tell me," I said. "Straight."

He sighed. "Okay, Johnny. You'd been working close to twenty-four hours a day trying to put us over, and we'd tried to get you to slow down and so did Kathy."

"Skip the build-up."

"That night, after we played at the hotel, we rehearsed some new stuff. You acted funny, then, Johnny. You forgot stuff, and you had a headache. We made you go home early, in spite of yourself. And when you got home—well, you slipped a cog, Johnny. You picked a quarrel with your wife—I don't know what you accused her of. And you went nuts. You got your razor—you always used to shave with a straight-edge—and, well, you tried to kill her. And then yourself."

"You're skipping the details," I said. "How did she save my life?"

"Well, Johnny, you hadn't killed her like you thought. The cut went deep on one side of her throat but—she must have been pulling away—it went light across the center and didn't get the jugular or anything. But there was a lot of blood and she fainted, and you thought she was dead, I guess, and slashed your own wrists. But she came to, and found you bleeding to death fast. Bleeding like she was, she got tourniquets on both your arms and held 'em, and kept yelling until one of the servants woke up and got the Carleton house-doctor. That's all, Johnny."

"It's enough, isn't it?" I thought a while and then I added, "Thanks, Tubby. Look, you run along and leave me. I want to think it out and sweat it out alone, and then I'll walk the rest of the way. Okay?"

"Okay, Johnny," he said. "You'll call me up soon?"

"Sure," I said. "Thanks for everything."

"You'll be all right, Johnny?"

"Sure. I'm all right."

After he left, I ordered another drink. My third, and it would have to be my last, because I was really feeling them. I didn't want to go home drunk, to face Kathy.

I sat there, sipping it slowly, looking at myself in that blue mirror back of the bar. I wasn't a bad looking guy, in a blue mirror. Only I should be dead instead of sitting there. I should have died that night eleven months ago. I'd tried to die.

I was almost alone at the bar. There was one couple drinking martinis at the far end of it. The girl was a blonde who looked like a chorus girl. I wondered idly if Kathy was a blonde. I hadn't thought to ask anyone. If Kathy walked in here now, I thought, I wouldn't know her.

The blonde down there picked up some change off the bar and walked over to the juke box. She put in a coin and punched some buttons, and then swayed her hips back to the bar. The juke box started playing and it was an old record and a good one—the Harry James version of the *Memphis Blues*. Blue and brassy stuff from the days back before Harry went commercial.

I sat there listening, and feeling like the devil. I thought, I've got to get over it. Every time I hear stuff like that I can't go on wanting to kill myself just because I can't play any more myself. I'm not the only guy in the world who can't play music. And the others get by.

*   *   *

My hands were lying on the bar in front of me and I tried them again, while I listened, and they wouldn't work. They wouldn't ever work again. My thumbs were okay, but the four fingers on each hand opened and closed together and not separately, as though they were webbed together.

Maybe the scotch was making me feel better, but—maybe, I decided—maybe it wouldn't be too bad—

Then the Harry James ended and another record slid onto the turntable and started, and it was going to be blue, too. *Mood Indigo*. I recognized the opening bar of the introduction. I wondered idly if all the records were blues, chosen to match the blue back-bar mirrors.

Deep blue stuff, anyway, and well handled and arranged, whoever was doing it. A few scotches and a blue mood, and that *Mood Indigo* can take hold of your insides and wring them. And this waxing of it was solid, pretty solid. The brasses tossed it to the reeds and then the piano took it for a moment, backed by wire-brush stuff on the skins, and modulated it into a higher key and built it up and you knew something was coming.

And then something came, and it was an alto sax, a sax with a tone like blue velvet, swinging high, wide and off the beat, and tossing in little arabesques of counterpoint so casually that it never seemed to leave the melody to do it. An alto sax riding high and riding hot, and with a tone like molten gold.

I unwound my fingers from around the scotch-and-soda glass and got up and walked across the room to the juke box. I knew already, but I looked. The record playing was Number 9, and Number 9 was *Mood Indigo*—Johnny Marlin.

For a black second I felt that I had to stop it, that I had to smash my fist through the glass and jerk the tone-arm off the record. I had to because it was doing things to me. That sound out of the past was making me remember, and I knew suddenly that the only way I could keep on wanting to live at all was *not* to remember.

Maybe I would have smashed the glass. I don't know. But instead I saw the cord and plug where the juke box plugged into the wall outlet beside it. I jerked on the cord and the box went dark and silent. Then I walked out into the dusk, with the three of them staring at me—the blonde and her escort and the bartender.

The bartender called out "Hey!" but didn't go on with it when I went on out without turning. I saw them in the mirror on the inside of the door as I opened it, a frozen tableau that slid sidewise off the mirror as the door opened.

I must have walked the six blocks to the Carleton, through the gathering twilight. I crossed the wide mahogany-paneled lobby to the elevator. The uniformed operator looked familiar to me—more familiar than Tubby. At least there was an impression that I'd seen him before.

"Good evening, Mr. Marlin," he said, and didn't ask me what floor I wanted.

But his voice sounded strange, tense, and he waited a moment, stuck his head out of the elevator and looked around, before he closed the door. I got the impression that he was hoping for another passenger, that he hated to shut himself and me in that tiny closed room.

But no one else came into the lobby and he slid the door shut and moved the handle. The building slid downward past us and came to rest at the eleventh floor. I stepped out into another mahogany-paneled hall and the elevator door slid shut behind me.

It was a short hallway, on this floor, with only four doors leading to what must be quite large suites. I knew which door was mine—or should I say Kathy's. My money never paid for a suite like that.

There was a leather case of keys in my pocket. One of them, I felt sure, would have fitted that door. But I didn't want just to walk in somehow. I rang the bell instead.

It wasn't Kathy who opened the door. I knew that because she was wearing a maid's uniform. And she must, I thought, be new. She looked at me blankly.

"Mrs. Marlin in?" I asked.

"No sir. She'll be back soon, sir."

I went on in. "I'll wait," I said. I followed her until she opened the door of a room that looked like a library.

"In here, please," she said. "And may I have your name?"

"Marlin," I said, as I walked past her. "Johnny Marlin."

She caught her breath a little, audibly. Then she said, "Yes, sir," and hurried away.

Her heels didn't click on the thick carpeting of the hall, but I could tell she was hurrying. Hurrying away from a homicidal maniac, back to the farthest reaches of the apartment, probably to the protective company of a cook who would keep a cleaver handy, once she heard the news that the mad master of the manse was back. And likely there'd be new servants, if any, tomorrow.

I walked up and down a while, and then decided I wanted to go to my room. I thought, if I don't think about it I can go there. My subconscious will know the way. And it worked; I went to my room.

I sat on the edge of the bed a while, with my head in my hands, wondering why I'd come here. Then I looked around. It was a big room, paneled like the rest of the joint, beautifully and tastefully furnished. Little Johnny Dettmann of the Cleveland slums had come a long way to have a room like that, all to himself. There was a Capehart radio-phonograph across the room from me, and a big cabinet of albums. Most of the pictures on the walls were framed photographs of bands. In a silver frame on the dresser was the picture of a woman.

That would be Kathy, of course. I crossed over and looked at it. She was beautiful, all right, a big-eyed brunette with pouting, kissable lips. And the fog was getting thinner. I almost knew and remembered her.

I looked a long time at that photograph, and then I put it down and went to the closet door. I opened it and there were a lot of suits in that closet, and a lot of pairs of shoes and a choice of hats. I remembered; John Dettmann had worn a sweater to high school one year because he didn't have a suit coat.

But there was something missing in that closet. The instrument cases. On the floor, there at the right, should have been two combination cases for sax and clarinet. Inside them should have been two gold-plated alto saxes and two sleek black Selmer clarinets. At the back of the closet should have been a bigger case that held a baritone sax I sometimes fooled around with at home.

They were all gone, and I was grateful to Kathy for that. She must have understood how it would make me feel to have them around.

I closed the closet door gently, and opened the door next to it, the bathroom. I went in and stood looking at myself in the mirror over the wash bowl. It wasn't a blue mirror. I studied my face, and it was an ordinary face. There wasn't any reason in that mirror why anyone should love me the way my wife must. I wasn't tall and I wasn't handsome. I was just a mug who had played a lot of sax—once.

The mirror was the door of a built-in medicine cabinet sunk into the tile wall and I opened it. Yes, all my toilet stuff was neatly laid out on the shelves of the cabinet, as though I'd never been away, or as though I'd been expected back daily. Even—and I almost took a step backwards—both of my straight-edge razors—the kind of razor a barber uses—lay there on the bottom shelf besides the shaving mug and brush.

Was Kathy crazy to leave them there, after what I'd used such a thing for? Had it even been one of these very razors? I could, of course, have had three of them, but— No, I remembered, there were only two, a matched pair.

In the sanitarium, I'd used an electric razor, naturally. All of them there did, even ones there for less deadly reasons than mine. And I was going to keep on using one. I'd take these and drop them down the incinerator, right now. If my wife was foolhardy enough to leave those things in a madman's room, *I* wasn't. How could I be sure I'd never go off the beam again?

My hand shook a little as I picked them up and closed the mirrored door. I'd take them right now and get rid of them. I went out of the bathroom and was crossing my own room, out in the middle of it, when there was a soft tap on the door—the connecting door from Kathy's room. "Johnny—" her voice said.

I thrust the razors out of sight into my coat pocket, and answered— I don't remember exactly what. My heart seemed to be in my throat, blocking my voice. And the door opened and Kathy came in—came in like the wind in a headlong rush that brought her into my arms. And with her face buried in my shoulder.

"Johnny, Johnny," she was saying, "I'm so glad you're back."

Then we kissed, and it lasted a long time, that kiss. But it didn't do anything to me. If I'd been in love with Kathy once, I'd have to start all over again, now. Oh, it was nice kissing her, as it would be nice kissing any beautiful woman. It wouldn't be hard to fall again. But so much easier and better, I thought, if I could push away all of the fog, if I could remember.

"I'm glad to be back, Kathy," I said.

Her arms tightened about me, almost convulsively. There was a big lounge chair next to the Capehart. I picked her up bodily, since she didn't want to let go of me, and crossed to the chair. I sat in it with her on my lap. After a minute, she straightened up and her eyes met mine, questioningly.

The question was, "Do you love me, Johnny?"

But I couldn't meet it just then. I'd pretend, of course, when I got my bearings, and after a while my memory would come the rest of the way back—or I'd manage to love her again, instead. But just then, I ducked the question and her eyes.

Instead, I looked at her throat and saw the scar. It wasn't as bad as I'd feared. It was a thin, long line that wouldn't have been noticeable over a yard away.

"Plastic surgery, Johnny," she said. "It can do wonders. Another year and it won't show at all. It—it doesn't matter." Then, as though to forestall my saying anything more about it, she said quickly, "I gave away your saxophones, Johnny. I—I figured you wouldn't want them around. The doctors say you'll never be able to—to play again."

I nodded. I said, "I guess it's best not to have them around."

"It's going to be so wonderful, Johnny. Maybe you'll hate me for saying it, but I'm—almost—glad. You know that was what came between us, your band and your playing. And it won't now, will it? You won't want to try another band—just directing and not playing—or anything foolish like that, will you, Johnny?"

"No, Kathy," I said.

Nothing, I thought, would mean anything without playing. I'd been trying to forget that. I closed my eyes and tried, for a moment, not to think.

"It'll be so wonderful, Johnny. You can do all the things I wanted you to do, and that you wouldn't. We can travel, spend our winters in Florida, and entertain. When France is normal again, we can live on the Riviera part of the time, and we can ski in the Tyrol and play the wheels at Monte Carlo and—and everything I've wanted to do, Johnny."

"It's nice to have a few million," I said.

She pulled back a little and looked at me. "Johnny, you're not going to start *that* again, are you? Oh, Johnny, you can't—now."

No, I thought, I can't. Heaven knows why she wants him to be one, but little Johnny Dettmann is a kept man, now, a rich girl's darling. He can't make money the only way he knows how now. He couldn't even hold a job as a bus boy or dig ditches. But he'll learn to balance teacups on his knee and smile at dowagers. He'll have to. It was coming back to me now, that endless argument.

But the argument was over now. There wasn't any longer anything to argue about.

"Kiss me, Johnny," Kathy said, and when I had, she said, "Let's have some music, huh? And maybe a dance—you haven't forgotten how to dance, have you, Johnny?"

She jumped up from my lap and went to the record album cabinet.

"Some of mine, will you, Kathy?" I asked. I thought, I might as well get used to it now, all at once. So I won't feel again, ever, as I had when I'd almost put my fist through that juke box window.

"Of course, Johnny."

She took them from one of the albums, half a dozen of them, and put them on the Capehart. The first one started, and it was a silly gay tune we'd once waxed—*"Chickery chick, cha la, cha la. . . ."* And she came back, holding out her hands to me to get up and dance, and I did, and I still knew how to dance.

And we danced over to the French doors that led to the balcony and opened them, and out onto the marble floor of the little railed balcony, into the cool darkness of the evening, with a full moon riding high in the sky overhead.

Chickery chick—a nice tune, if a silly tune. No vocal, of course. We'd never gone for them. Not gut-bucket stuff, either, but smooth rhythm, with a beat. And a high-riding alto sax, smooth as silk.

And I was remembering the argument. It had been one, a vicious one. Musician versus playboy as my career. I was remembering *Kathy* now, and suddenly tried not to. Maybe it would be better to forget all that bitterness, the quarreling and the overwork and everything that led up to the blankness of the breakdown.

But our feet moved smoothly on the marble. Kathy danced well. And the record ended.

"It's going to be wonderful, Johnny," she whispered, "having you all to myself . . . You're *mine* now, Johnny."

"Yes," I said. I thought, I've *got* to be.

The second record started, and it was a contrast. A number as blue as *Mood Indigo,* and dirtier. *St. James Infirmary*, as waxed by Johnny Marlin and his orchestra. And I remembered the hot day in the studio when we'd waxed it. Again no vocal, but as we started dancing again, the words ran through my mind with the liquid gold of the alto sax I'd once played.

"I went down to St. James Infirmary . . . Saw my *ba*by there . . . Stretched on a long white table . . . So sweet, so cold, so—"

I jerked away from her, ran inside and shut off the phonograph. I caught sight of my face in the mirror over the dresser as I passed. It was white as a corpse's face. I went back to the balcony. Kathy still stood there—she hadn't moved.

"Johnny, what—?"

"That tune," I said. "Those words. I *remember*, Kathy. I remember that night. *I didn't do it.*"

I felt weak. I leaned back against the wall behind me. Kathy came closer.

"Johnny—what do you mean?"

"I remember," I said. "I walked in, and you were lying there—with blood all over your throat and your dress—*when I came in the room.* I *don't* remember after that—but that's what must have knocked me off my base, after everything else. That's when I went crazy, not before."

"Johnny—you're wrong—"

The weakness was gone now. I stood straighter.

"Your brother," I said. "He hated you because you ran his life, like you wanted to run mine, because you had the money he thought should be his, and you doled it out to him and *ran* him. Sure, he hated you. I remember him now. Kathy, I remember. That was about the time he got past liquor and was playing with dope. Cocaine, wasn't it? And that night he came in, skyhigh and murderous, before I did. And tried to kill you, and probably thought he did. And ran. It must have been just before I came in."

"Johnny, please—you're wrong—"

"You came to, after I keeled over," I said. "It—it sounds incredible, Kathy, but it had to be that way. And, Kathy, that cold mind of yours saw a way to get everything it wanted. To protect your brother, and to get me, the way you wanted me. It was perfect, Kathy. Fix me so I'd never play again, and at the same time put me in a spot where I'd be tied to you forever because I'd think I tried to kill you."

I said, "You get your way, don't you, Kathy? At any cost. But you didn't want me to die. I'll bet you had those tourniquets ready *before you slashed my wrists.*"

She was beautiful, standing there in the moonlight. She stood there tall and straight, and she came the step between us and put her soft arms around me.

"But Johnny, don't I win?" she said.

She was beautiful, leaning back to look up into my face. Yes, she'd won. *So sweet, so cold, so bare.* So bare her throat that even in the moonlight I could see the faint scar, the dotted line. And one of my crippled hands, in my pocket, fumbled open one of the razors, and brought it out of my pocket, and up, and across.

SO DARK FOR APRIL

HOWARD BROWNE

I

When I got through telling the sergeant at Central Homicide about it, he said to sit tight and not touch anything, that somebody would be right over. I told him I wouldn't even breathe any more than was absolutely necessary and put back the receiver and went into the reception room to take another look at the body.

He was at the far end of the couch, slumped in a sitting position, with his chin on his chest and an arm hanging down. A wick of iron-gray hair made a curve against the waxen skin of a high forehead, his half-open eyes showed far too much white, and a trickle of dark blood had traced a crooked line below one corner of a slack-lipped mouth. His coat hung open, letting me see a circular red stain under the pocket of a soiled white shirt. From the center of the stain protruded the brown bone handle of a switchblade knife.

I moved over to lean against the window frame and light a cigarette. It was one of those foggy wet mornings we get early in April, with a chill wind off the lake and the sky as dull as a deodorant commercial. Umbrellas blossomed along the walks eight floors below and long lines of cars slithered past with a hooded look.

I stood there breathing smoke and staring at the dead man. He was nobody I had ever seen before. He wore a handsomely tailored suit coat of gray flannel, dirty brown gabardine slacks spattered with green paint and an oil stain across one knee, and brown bench-made shoes. His shirt

39

was open at the throat, showing a fringe of dark hair, and he wasn't wearing a tie.

The rummage-sale air of those slacks bothered me. This was no Skid Row fugitive. His nails had that cared-for look, his face, even in death, held a vague air of respectability, and they didn't trim hair that way at barber college.

I bent down and turned back the left side of his coat. The edge of a black wallet showed in the inner pocket. That was where I stopped. This was cop business. Let the boys who were paid for it paw the corpse.

A black satin label winked up at me. I put my eyes close enough to read the stitched letters in it. A C G—in a kind of Old English script. The letters seemed too big to be simply a personal monogram, but then there's no accounting for tastes.

I let the lapel drop back to the way I had found it. The dead man didn't seem to care either way. Something glistened palely between the frayed cuffs and the tops of the custom-made shoes. I said, "Huh?" out loud and bent down to make sure.

No mistake. It made no sense but there it was. The pale white shine was naked flesh.

The dead man wasn't wearing socks.

II

Detective Sergeant Lund said, "Right smack-dab through the old ticker. He never even had time to clear his throat. Not this guy."

His curiously soft voice held a kind of grim respect. He straightened up and backed away a couple of steps and took off his hat and shook rain water from it onto the carpet and stared thoughtfully at me out of gun-metal eyes.

I moved a shoulder and said nothing. At the wicker table across the room the two plainclothes men were unshipping tape measures and flashbulbs and fingerprint kits. Rain tapped the glass behind me with icy fingers.

"Your turn, Pine," Lund said in the same soft voice.

"He was like that when I came in," I said promptly. I looked at my strapwatch. "Exactly thirty-two minutes ago."

"How'd he get in here?"

"I usually leave the reception room unlocked, in case I have a client and the client cares to wait."

One corner of his mouth moved up faintly. "Somebody sure wanted this guy to wait, hey?"

I shrugged. He took a turn along the room and back again, hands deep in the pockets of his topcoat. Abruptly he said, "It says on your door you're a private dick. This a client?"

"No. I never saw him before."

"What's his name?"

"I don't know."

"No identification on him?"

"I didn't look. The sergeant at Central said not to."

He seemed mildly astonished. "A man dies in your office and you don't even show a little healthy curiosity? Don't be afraid of me, Pine. I haven't chewed off anybody's arm in over a week."

"I obey the law," I said mildly.

"Well, well," he said. He grinned suddenly, and after a moment I grinned back. Mine was no phonier than his. He snapped a thumb lightly against the point of his narrow chin a time or two while thinking a secret thought, then turned back to the body.

He went through the pockets with the deft delicacy of a professional dip. The blood, the knife handle, the sightless eyes meant about half as much to him as last week's laundry. When he straightened again there was a small neat pile of personal effects on one of the couch pillows and the dead man's pockets were as empty as his eyes.

The wallet was on top. Lund speared it, flipped it open. The transparent identification panels were empty, as was the bill compartment. Shoved into the latter, however, were three or four cards. Lund looked them over slowly and carefully, his thick brows drawn into a lazy V above his long, pointed nose.

"Credit cards on a couple Loop hotels," he said, almost to himself. "Plus one of these indentification cards you get with a wallet. According to what it says here, this guy is Franklin Andrus, 5861 Winthrop Avenue. One business card. It calls him a sales representative for the Reliable Amusement Machine Corporation, Dayton, Ohio. No telephone shown and nobody listed to notify. Any of this mean anything to you, Mr. Pine?"

"Sorry."

"Uh-huh. You ain't playing this too close, are you?"

"I'm not even in the game," I said.

"Initials in his coat don't agree with the name on these here cards. That must mean something, hey?"

I stared at the bridge of his nose. "His coat and somebody else's cards. Or his cards and somebody else's coat. Or neither. Or both."

His mouth hardened. "You trying to kid me, mister?"

"I guess that would be pretty hard to do, Sergeant."

He turned on his heel and went through the communicating door to my inner office, still carrying the wallet. He didn't bother to shut it, and through the opening I could see him reach for the phone without sitting down and dial a number with quick hard stabs of a forefinger. What he said when he got his party was too low-voiced for me to catch.

Two minutes later, he was back. He scooped up the stuff from the couch and said, "Let's talk, hey? Let's us try out that nice private office of yours."

I followed him in and drew up the Venetian blind and opened the window a crack to let out the smell of yesterday's cigarettes. On the outer ledge four pigeons were organizing a bombing raid. Lund shoved the phone and ashtray aside, dumped his collection on the desk pad and snapped on the lamp. I sat down behind the desk and watched him pull up the customer's chair across from me.

I got out my cigarettes. He took one, sniffed at it for no reason I knew of and struck a match for us both. He leaned back and hooked an arm over the chair back and put his dull gray eyes on me.

"Nice and cozy," he said. "All the comforts. Too bad they're not all like this."

"I could turn on the radio," I said. "Maybe get a little dance music."

He grunted with mild amusement. All the narrow-eyed suspicion had been tucked out of sight. He drew on his cigarette and blew a long blue plume of smoke at the ceiling. Another minute and he'd have his shoes off.

He let his gaze drift about the dingy office, taking in the Varga calendar, the filing cases, the worn tan linoleum. He said, "The place could stand a little paint, hey?"

"You drumming up business for your day off?" I asked.

That got another grunt out of him. "You sound kind of on the excited side, Pine. Don't be like that. You wouldn't be the first private boy got a customer shot out from under him, so to speak."

I felt my face burn. "He's not a customer. I told you that."

"I guess you did, at that," he said calmly. "It don't mean I have to believe it. Client getting pushed right in your own office don't look so good, hey? What the newshounds call a bad press."

I bit down on my teeth. "You just having fun, Sergeant, or does all this lead somewhere?"

"Why, we're just talking," he said mildly. "Just killing time, you might say, until the coroner shows up. That and looking over the rest of what the guy had on him."

He stuck out an untidy finger and poked at the pile. Besides the wallet, there were several small square transparent envelopes, some loose change, a pocket comb, and a small pair of gold tweezers.

He brought his eyes up to stare coldly at me, his mellow mood gone as quickly as it had arrived. He said harshly, "Let's lay off the clowning around, mister. You were working for him. I want to know doing what."

"I wouldn't bother to lie to you," I said. "I never saw the guy before in my life, I never talked to him on the phone, or got a letter from him. Period."

His sneer was a foot wide. "You must think I'm green!"

"I'm not doing any thinking," I said.

"I hope to tell you, you aren't. Listen, I can book you, brother!"

"For what?"

"Obstructing justice, resisting an officer. What do you care? I'm saying I can book you!"

I didn't say anything. Some of the angry color faded slowly from his high cheeks. Finally he sighed heavily and picked up the necktie and gave it a savage jerk between his square hands and threw it down again.

"Nuts," he said pettishly. "I don't want to fight with you. I'm trying to do a job. All I want is a little cooperation. This guy just don't walk in here blind. You're a private dick, or so your door says. Your job is people in trouble. I say it's too big a coincidence him picking your office to get knocked off in. Go on, tell me I'm wrong."

"I'm not saying you're wrong," I said. "I'm saying what I've already said. He's a stranger to me. He could have come in here to get out of the wet or to sell me a slot machine or to just sit down and rest his arches. I admit he might have come here to hire me. It has happened, although not often enough. Maybe somebody didn't want him spilling any touchy secrets to me, and fixed him so he couldn't."

"But you never saw him before?"

"You're beginning to get the idea," I said.

"Go ahead," he said bitterly. "Crack wise."

The sound of the reception room door opening and closing cut off what Lund was about to say. A short plump man went past the half-open door of the inner office, carrying a black bag. Lund got up without a word and went out there, leaving me where I sat.

Some time passed. Quite a lot of time. The murmur of voices from the next room went on and on. Flash bulbs made soundless explosions of light and a small vacuum cleaner whirred. I stayed where I was and burned a lot of tobacco and crossed my legs and dangled my foot and listened to the April rain and thought my thoughts.

Thoughts about a man who might still be alive if I hadn't slept an hour later than usual. A man with mismatched clothing and no socks and an empty wallet. A man who would want to go on living, even in an age when living was complicated and not very rewarding. A man who had managed for fifty-odd years to hang on to the only life he'd ever be given to live before a switch-blade knife and a strong hand combined to pinch it off.

I went on sitting. The rain went on falling. It was so dark for April.

After a while the corridor door opened to let in two men in white coats. They carried a long wicker basket between them. They passed my door without looking in. There was more indistinct murmuring, then a young voice said, "Easy with them legs, Eddie," and the basket was taken out again. It was harder to carry the second time.

Sergeant Lund walked in, his face expressionless. He sat down heavily and lighted a cigarette and waved out the match and continued to hold it. He said, "Andrus died between eight-thirty and ten. The elevator man don't recall bringing him up. What time did you get here?"

"Ten-thirty, about. Few minutes either way."

"You wouldn't happen to own a switch-blade knife, hey?"

"With a brown bone handle?" I said.

He bent the used match and dropped it in the general vicinity of the ashtray. "Seven-inch blade," he muttered. "Like a bayonet." He put the cigarette in a corner of his mouth and left it there. "This is a real cute killing, Pine. You notice how Andrus was dressed?"

"No socks," I said.

"That isn't the half of it, brother. New coat, old pants, fancy shoes. No hat and no topcoat. In weather like this? What's the sense?"

I spread my hands. "By me, Sergeant."

"You sure you wasn't work—"

"Don't say it!" I shouted.

The phone rang. A voice like a buzz-saw asked for Lund. He grunted into the mouthpiece, listened stolidly for nearly a full minute, then said, "Yeah," twice and passed back the receiver. I replaced it and watched him drag himself out of the chair, his expression a study in angry frustration.

"I had Rogers Park send a squad over to that Winthrop Avenue address," he growled. "Not only they don't find no trace of a Franklin Andrus; they don't even find the address! An empty lot! All right. The lab boys will turn up something. Laundry marks, cuff dust, clothing labels. It'll take 'em a day or two, but I can wait. The old routine takes time but it always works."

"Almost always," I said absently.

He glowered across the desk at me. "One thing I hope, mister. I hope you been holding out on me and I find it out. That's going to be jake with me."

He gathered up the dead man's possessions and stalked out. A little later one of the plainclothes men slipped in with his kit and took my fingerprints. He was nice about it, explaining they were only for elimination purposes.

III

By one o'clock I was back from having a sandwich and coffee at the corner drugstore. The reception room was empty, with only a couple of used flash bulbs, some smudges of fingerprint powder here and there and the smell of cheap cigars and damp cloth to remind me of my morning visitors. Without the dead man on it, the couch seemed larger than usual. There were no bloodstains. I looked to make sure.

I walked slowly into the other room and shucked off my trench coat. From the adjoining office came the faint whine of a dentist's drill.

A damp breeze crawled in at the window and rattled the cords on the blind. Cars hooted in the street below. Sounds that made the silence around me even more silent. And the rain went on and on.

I sat down behind the desk and emptied the ashtray into the wastebasket and wiped off the glass top. I put away the cloth and got out a cigarette and sat there turning it, unlighted, between a thumb and forefinger.

He had been a nice-looking man. Fifty-five at the most. A man with a problem on his mind. Let's say he wakes up this morning and decides to take his problem to a private detective. So he gets out the classified book and looks under the right heading. There aren't many, not even for a town the size of Chicago. The big agencies he passes up, maybe because he figures he'll have to go through a handful of henna-haired secretaries before reaching the right guy. Then, not too far down the column, he comes across the name Paul Pine. A nice short name. Anybody can pronounce. it.

So he takes a cab or a bus and comes on down. He hasn't driven a car; no car keys and no license on him. The waiting room is unlocked but no alert gimlet-eyed private detective around. So this nice-looking man with a problem sits down to wait . . . and somebody walks in and sticks a quarterpound of steel in him.

That was it. That explained everything. Everything but what his problem was and why he wasn't wearing socks and why his wallet was empty and why his identification showed an address that didn't exist.

I got up and took a couple of turns around the room. This was no skin off my shins. The boys from Homicide would have it all wrapped up in a day or so. The old routine Lund had called it. I didn't owe that nice old man a thing. He hadn't paid me a dime. No connection between us at all.

Except that he had come to me for help and got a mouthful of blood instead.

I sat down again and tried the phone book. No Franklin Andrus listed. No local branch of the Reliable Amusement Machine Corp. I shoved the book away and began to think about the articles that had come out of the dead man's pockets. Gold tweezers, a pocket comb, five small transparent envelopes, seventy-three cents in change, a dark blue necktie. There had been a department store label on the tie—Marshall

Field. I knew that because I had looked while Lund was out of the room. But Field's has hundreds of neckties. No help there.

Is that all, Pine, I thought to myself. End of the line? You mean you're licked? A nice, clean-necked, broad-shouldered, late-sleeping detective like you?

I walked the floor some more. I went over to the window and leaned my forehead against its coolness. My breath misted the glass and I wrote my name in the mist with the end of my finger. That didn't seem to help any. I went on thinking.

Maybe what *hadn't* come out of his pockets was important. No keys, for instance. Not even to his apartment. Maybe he lived in a hotel. Not even cigarettes or a book of matches. Maybe he didn't smoke. Not even a handkerchief. Maybe he didn't have a cold.

I sat down again. There had been initials in his coat. A C G. No periods and stitched professionally in fancy letters against a square of black satin. Rather large, as I recalled. Too bad I hadn't looked inside the pocket for the tailor's label. Unless . . .

This time I used the classified book. T—for Tailors—Men's. I ran through the columns to the G's. There it was, bright and shining and filled with promise. A. Cullinham Grandfils, Custom Tailor. On Michigan Avenue, in the 600 block. Right in the center of the town's swankiest shopping district.

I closed the window, climbed into my trench coat and hat and locked up. The smell of dime cigars still hung heavy in the outer office. Even the hall seemed full of it.

IV

It was made to look like a Greek temple, if you didn't look too close. It had a white limestone front and a narrow doorway with a circular hunk of stained glass above that. Off to one side was a single display window about the size of a visiting card. Behind the glass was a slanting pedestal covered with black velvet and on the velvet a small square of gray cloth that looked as though it might be of cheviot. Nothing else. No price tags, no suits, no firm name spelled out in severely stylized letters.

And probably no bargain basement.

I heaved back the heavy glass door and walked into a large room with soft dusty rose walls, a vaulted ceiling, moss green carpeting, and indirect lighting like a benediction. Scattered tastefully about were upholstered chairs and couches, blond in the wood and square in the lines. A few chrome ashstands, an end table or two, and at the far end a blond desk and a man sitting behind it.

The man stood up as I came in. He floated down the room toward me, a tall slender number in a cutaway coat, striped trousers and a gates-ajar collar. He looked like a high-class undertaker. He had a high reedy voice that said:

"Good afternoon, sir. May I be of service?"

"Are you the high priest?" I said.

His mouth fell open. "I beg your pardon?"

"Maybe I'm in the wrong place," I said. "I'm looking for the tailor shop. No name outside but the number checks."

His backbone got even stiffer, although I hadn't thought that possible. "This," he said in a strangled voice, "is A. Cullinham Grandfils. Are you interested in a garment?"

"A what?"

"A garment."

"You mean a suit?"

"Ah—yes, sir."

"I've got a suit," I said. I unbuttoned my coat and showed it to him. All he did was look pained.

"What I came by for," I said, "was to get the address of a customer of yours. I'm not sure but I think his name's Andrus— Franklin Andrus."

He folded his arms and brought up a hand and turned his wrist delicately and rested his chin between his thumb and forefinger. "I'm afraid not. No. Sorry."

"You don't know the name?"

"I'm not referring to the name. What I am attempting to convey to you is that we do not give out information on our people."

I said, "Oh," and went on staring at him. He looked like the type you can bend easy. I dug out the old deputy sheriff's star I carried for emergencies like this and showed it to him, keeping the lettering covered with the ball of my thumb. He jerked down his arms and backed away as though I'd pulled a gun on him.

"This is official," I said in a tough-cop voice. "I'm not here to horse around. Do you cooperate or do we slap you with a subpoena?"

"You'll have to discuss the matter with Mr. Grandfils," he squeaked. "I simply am no—I have no authority to—You'll just have to—"

"Then trot him out, Curly. I don't have all day."

"Mr. Grandfils is in his office. Come this way, please,"

We went along the room and through a glass door at the far end and along a short hall to another door: a solid panel of limed oak with the words A. Cullinham Grandfils, Private, on it in raised silver letters. The door was knocked on and a muffled voice came through and I was inside.

A little round man was perched in an enormous leather chair behind an acre of teakwood and glass. His head was as bald as a collection plate on Monday morning. A pair of heavy horn-rimmed glasses straddled a button nose above a tiny mouth and a chin like a ping-pong ball. He blinked owlishly at me and said, "What is it, Marvin?" in a voice so deep I jumped.

"This—ah—gentleman is the police, Mr. Grandfils. He has demanded information I simply haven't the right to—"

"That will be all, Marvin."

I didn't even hear him leave.

"I can't stand that two-bit diplomat," the little man said. "He makes the bottom of my foot itch."

I didn't say anything.

"Unfortunately he happens to be useful," he went on. "The women gush at him and he gushes back. Good for business."

"I thought you only sold men's suits," I said.

"Who do you think picks them out? Take off that coat and sit down. I don't know your name."

I told him my name and got rid of the trench coat and hat and drew up a teakwood chair trimmed in silver and sat on it. He made a quarter-turn in the big chair and his glasses flashed at me in the soft light.

"Police, eh?" he said suddenly. "Well, you've got the build for it. Where did you get that ridiculous suit?"

"This ridiculous suit set me back sixty-five bucks," I said.

"It looks it. What are you after, sir?"

"The address of one of your customers."

"I see. Why should I give it to you?"

"He was murdered. The address on his identification was incorrect."

"Murdered!" His mouth dropped open, causing the glasses to slip down on his nose. "Good heavens! One of my people?"

"He was wearing one of your coats," I said.

He passed a tremulous hand across the top of his head. All it smoothed down was scalp. "What was his name?"

"Andrus. Franklin Andrus."

He shook his head immediately. "No, Mr. Pine. None of my people has that name. You have made a mistake."

"The coat fitted him," I said doggedly. "He belonged in it. I might have the name wrong but not the coat. It was his coat."

He picked a silver paper-knife from the silver trimmed tan desk blotter and rapped it lightly over and over against the knuckles of his left hand. "Perhaps you're right," he said. "My coats are made to fit. Describe this man to me."

I gave the description, right down to the kidney-shaped freckle on the lobe of the left ear. Grandfils heard me out, thought over at length what I'd said, then shook his head slowly.

"In a general way," he said, "I know of a dozen men like that who come to me. The minor touches you've given me are things I never noticed about any of them. I'm not a trained observer and you are. Isn't there something else you can tell me about him? Something you've perhaps inadvertently overlooked?"

It hardly seemed likely but I thought back anyway. I said, "The rest of his clothing was a little unusual. That might mean something to you."

"Try me."

I described the clothing. By the time I was down to where the dead man hadn't been wearing socks, Grandfils had lost interest. He said coldly, "The man was obviously some tramp. None of my people would be seen on the street in such condition. The coat was stolen and the man deserved what happened to him. Frayed slacks! Heavens!"

I said, "Not much in his pockets, but I might as well tell you that too. A dark blue necktie with a Marshall Field label, a pair of gold-plated tweezers, several transparent envelopes about the size of a postage stamp, a pocket comb and some change . . ."

My voice began to run down. A. Cullinham Grandfils had his mouth open again, but this time there was the light of recognition in his eyes. He said crisply, "The coat was a gray flannel, Mr. Pine?"

"Yeah?"

"Carlton weave?"

"Hunh?"

"Never mind. You wouldn't know that. Quite new?"

"I thought so."

He bent across the desk to move a key on an intercom. "Harry," he snapped into the box. "That gray flannel lounge suit we made for Amos Spain. Was it sent out?"

"A week already," the box said promptly. "Maybe ten days, even. You want I should check exactly?"

"Never mind." Grandfils flipped back the key and leaned into the leather chair and went on tapping his knuckles with the knife. "Those tweezers and envelopes did it, sir. He's an enthusiastic stamp collector. Less than a month ago I saw him sitting in the outer room lifting stamps delicately with those tweezers and putting them in such envelopes while waiting for a fitting."

"Amos Spain is his name?"

"It is."

"He fits the description I gave?"

"Physically, exactly. But not the frayed slacks and dirty shirt. Amos Spain wouldn't be found dead in such clothes."

"You want to bet?"

". . . Oh. Of course. I simply can't understand it!"

"How about an address on Spain, Mr. Grandfils?"

He dug a silver-trimmed leather notebook out of a desk drawer and looked inside. "8789 South Shore Drive. Apartment 3C. It doesn't show a telephone, although I'm confident he has one."

"Married?"

He dropped the book back in the drawer and closed it with his foot. "We don't inquire into the private lives of our people, Mr. Pine. It seems to me Mrs. Spain is dead, although I may be wrong. I do know Amos Spain is reasonably wealthy and, I think, retired."

I took down the address and got up and put on my coat and said, "Thanks for your help, Mr. Grandfils." He nodded and I opened the door. As I started out, he said:

"You really should do something about your suits, Mr. Pine."

I looked back at him sitting there like one of those old Michelin tire ads. "How much," I said, "would you charge me for one?"

"I think we could do something quite nice for you at three hundred."

"For that price," I said, "I would expect two pairs of pants."

His chin began to bob and he made a sound like roosters fighting. He was laughing. I closed the door in the middle of it and went on down the hall.

V

The address on South Shore Drive was a long low yellow-brick apartment building of three floors and an English basement. A few cars were parked along a wide sweep of concrete running past the several entrances, and I angled the Plymouth into an open spot almost directly across from 8789.

The rain got in a few licks at me before I could reach the door. Inside was a small neat foyer, complete with bright brass mail boxes and an inner door. The card on the box for 3C showed the name Amos Spain.

I pressed the right button and after a longish moment a woman's voice came down the tube. "Yes?"

That jarred me a little. I hadn't actually expected an answer. I said, "Mrs. Spain?"

"This is Mrs. Monroe," the voice said. "Mr. Spain's daughter. Are you from the post office?"

"Afraid not. I'm an officer, Mrs. Monroe. Want to talk to you."

"An officer? Why, I don't believe . . . What about?"

"Not from down here, Mrs. Monroe. Ring the buzzer."

"I'll do no such thing! How do I know you're a policeman? For all I know you could be a—a—"

"On a day like this? Don't be silly."

There was some silence and then the lock began to stutter. I went through and on up carpeted steps to the third floor. Halfway along a wide cheerful hallway was a partially open door and a woman in a flowered housecoat looking out at me.

She was under thirty but not very far under. She had wicked eyes.

Her hair was reddish brown and there was a lot of it. Her skin was flawless, her cheekbones high, her mouth an insolent curve. She was long and slender. She was dynamite.

I was being stared at in a coolly impersonal way. "A policeman you said. I'm fascinated. What is it you want?"

I said, "Do I get invited in or do we entertain the neighbors?"

Her eyes wavered and she bit her lip. She started to look back over her shoulder, thought better of it, then said, "Oh, very well. If you'll be brief."

She stepped back and I followed her across a tiny reception hall and on into an immense living room, with a dinette at one end and the open door to a kitchen beyond that. The living room was paneled, with beautiful leather chairs, a chesterfield, lamps with drum shades, a loaded pipe rack, a Governor Winthrop secretary, a fireplace with a gas log. Not neat, not even overly clean, but the right place for a man who puts comfort ahead of everything else.

I dropped my coat on a hassock and sat down on one of the leather chairs. Her lips hardened. "Don't get too comfortable," she said icily. "I was about to leave when you rang."

"It's a little chilly out for a housecoat," I said.

Her jaw hardened. "Just who do you think you are, busting in here and making smart remarks? You say you're a cop. As far as manners go, I believe it. Now I think I'd like to see some real proof."

I shrugged. "No proof, Mrs. Monroe. I said officer, not policeman. A private detective can be called an officer without stretching too far."

"Private—" Her teeth snapped shut and she swallowed almost convulsively. Her face seemed a little pale now but I could have imagined that. "What do you want?" she almost whispered.

"Where's Amos Spain?" I said.

"My . . . father?"

"Uh-huh."

". . . I don't know. He went out early this morning."

"He say where?"

"No." Whatever had shocked her was passing. "Tom and I were still sleeping when he went out."

"Tom?"

"My husband."

"Where's he?"

"Still asleep. We got in late. Why do you want to know where my father is?"

I said, "I think it would be a good idea if you sat down, Mrs. Monroe. I'm afraid I've brought some bad news."

She didn't move. Her eyes went on watching me. They were a little wild now and not at all wicked. She wet her lips and said, "I haven't the slightest idea what you're talking about. Bad news about what?"

"About your father. He's dead, Mrs. Monroe. Murdered."

"I don't believe it," she said quickly. Almost too quickly.

"He's been identified. Not much chance for a mistake."

She turned away abruptly and walked stiffly over to a lamp table and took a cigarette from a green cloisonné box. Her hand holding the match wavered noticeably but nothing showed in her face. She blew out a long streamer of smoke and came back and perched carelessly on an arm of the couch across from me.

"There's been some mistake, Mr. Pine. Dad never had an enemy in the world. What do you suggest I do?"

I thought back to be sure. Then I was sure. I said, "The body's probably at the morgue by this time and already autopsied. Might be a good idea to send your husband over. Save you from a pretty unpleasant job."

"Of course. I'll wake him right away and tell him about it. You've been very kind. I'm sorry if I was rude."

She hit me with a smile that jarred my back teeth and stood up to let me know the interview was over and I could run along home now.

I slid off the chair and picked up my hat and coat. While putting them on, I moved over to the row of windows and looked down into the courtyard. Nobody in sight. Not in this weather. Rain blurred the glass and formed widening puddles in thin brown grass that was beginning to turn green.

I turned and said, "I'll be running along, Mrs. Monroe," and took four quick steps and reached for the bedroom door.

There was nothing wrong with her reflexes, I'll say that for her. A silken rustle and the flash of flowered cloth and she was standing between me and the door. We stood there like that, breathing at each other, our faces inches apart. And her face was as hard as four anvils.

"I must have made a mistake," I said. "I was looking for the hall door."

"Only two doors," she said between her teeth. "Two doors in the entire apartment. Not counting the bathroom. One that lets you out and one to the bedroom. And you picked the wrong one. Go on. Get out of here before I forget you're not a cop."

On my way out I left the inner door downstairs unlocked. In case.

VI

The rain went on and on. I sat there listening to it and wondering if Noah had felt this way along about the thirty-ninth day. Smoke from my fourth cigarette eddied and swirled in the damp air through the no-draft vent.

The Plymouth was still parked across from 8789, and I was in it, knowing suddenly who had killed Amos Spain and why Amos Spain had been wearing what he wore and why he wasn't wearing what he hadn't worn. It was knowledge built piece by piece on what I had seen and heard from the moment I walked in and found the body on the couch. It was the kind of knowledge you can get a conviction with—if you have that one key piece.

The key piece was what I didn't have.

Now and then a car came into the wide driveway and stopped at one of the entrances to let somebody out or to pick somebody up. None of them was for the rat hole to which I was glued. A delivery truck dropped off a dinette set a couple of doors down and I couldn't have cared less.

I lighted another cigarette and crossed my legs the other way and thought about hunting up a telephone and calling Lund and telling him to come out and get the knife artist and sweat the key piece out in the open. Only I didn't want it that way. This was one I wanted to wrap up myself. It had been my office and my couch and almost my client, and I was the one the cops had tromped on. Not that the tromping had amounted to much. But even a small amount of police displeasure is not what you list under assets.

Another twenty minutes floated by. They would still be up there in that apartment, wearing a path in the rug. Waiting, hanging on desperately, risking the chance that I had known more than I let on and was already out yelling for the cops.

I would have loved to know what they were waiting for.

When the break did come I almost missed it. An ancient Ford with a pleated front fender wheezed into the curb. A hatless young man in a rained-on gray uniform got out to look at the number over the entrance to 8789. He had a damp-looking cigarette pasted to one corner of his mouth and a white envelope in his left hand. The local postoffice dropping off a piece of registered mail.

And then I remembered Mrs. Monroe's first question.

I slapped open the glove compartment and got out my gun and shoved it under the band of my trousers while I was reaching for the door. I crossed the roadway at a gallop and barged into the foyer just as the messenger took a not too clean thumb off the button for 3C. I made a point of getting out my keys to keep him from thinking Willie Sutton was loose again.

He never even knew I was in town. He said, "Postoffice; registered letter," into the tube and the buzzer was clattering before he had the last word out. He went through and on up the steps without a backward glance.

The door was off the latch, the way I had left it earlier. By the time the door to 3C opened, I was a few feet away, staring vaguely at the closed door to 3B and trying to look like somebody's cousin from Medicine Hat. The uniformed man said, "Amos Spain?" and a deeper voice said, "I'm Mr. Spain," and a signature was written and a long envelope changed hands.

Before the door could close I was over there. I said, "It's me again."

He was a narrow-chested number, with a long sallow face, beady eyes, a thin nose that leaned slightly to starboard, and a chin that had given up the struggle. Hair like black moss covered a narrow head. This would be Tom Monroe, the husband.

Terror and anger and indecision were having a field day with his expression. His long neck jerked and his sagging jaw wobbled. He clutched the edge of the door, wanting to slam it but not quite daring to. The silence weighed a ton.

All this was lost on the messenger. He took back his pencil and went off down the hall, his only worry the number of hours until payday.

I leaned a hand against the thin chest in front of me and pushed hard enough to get us both into the room. I shut the door with my heel, said, "I'll take that," and yanked the letter out of his paralyzed fingers. It had sealing wax along the flap and enough stamps pasted on the front to pay the national debt.

Across the room the girl in the flowered housecoat was reaching a hand under a couch pillow. I took several long steps and stiff-armed the small of her back and she sat down hard on the floor. I put my empty hand under the pillow and found a snub-nosed Smith & Wesson .32, all chambers filled and dark red nail polish on the sight. I held it loosely along my leg and said, "Well, here we are," in a sprightly voice.

Monroe hadn't moved. He stared at me sullenly, fear still flickering in his small nervous eyes. The girl climbed painfully to her feet, not looking at either of us, and dropped down on the edge of a leather chair and put her face in her hands.

The man's restless eyes darted from me to the girl and back to me again. A pale tongue dabbed furtively at lips so narrow they hardly existed. He said hoarsely, "Just what the hell's the bright idea busting in here and grabbing what don't belong to you?"

I flapped the envelope loosely next to my ear. "You mean this? Not yours either, buster."

"It belongs to my father-in-law. I simply signed for it."

"Oh, knock it off," I said wearily. "You went way out of your league on this caper, Tom. You should have known murder isn't for grifters with simple minds."

A sound that was half wail, half sob filtered through the girl's fingers. The man said absently, "Shut up, Cora." His eyes skittered over my face. "Murder? Who's talking about murder? You the one who shoved in here a while ago and told Cora about Amos Spain?"

"I wasn't telling her a thing," I said. "She knew it long before. You told her."

"You might like to try proving that," he said.

"You bet," I said. I put the gun on the couch arm and looked at the envelope. Yesterday's postmark, mailed from New York City. Addressed in a spidery handwriting, with the return address reading: "B. Jones, General Delivery, Radio City Station, New York, N. Y." I ripped open the flap and shook out the contents. A plain sheet of bond paper wrapped around three odd-looking stamps. One was circular with a pale rose background and black letters. The other two were square, one orange and one blue, with the same crude reproduction of Queen Victoria on both. All three wouldn't have carried a postcard across the street.

Monroe was staring at the stamps and chewing his lip. He looked physically ill. The girl was watching me now, her fingers picking at the edge of the housecoat, her face white and drawn and filled with silent fury.

I said, "It would almost have to be stamps. I should have guessed as much two hours ago. How much are they worth?"

"How would I know?" Monroe said sulkily. "They weren't sent to me. I never saw them before."

I slid the stamps back into the envelope and put the envelope in my pocket. "You'd know, brother. If you'd kept a better eye on Amos Spain, you might even have gotten away with the whole thing."

"You've got nothing on us. Why don't you just shove off?"

"I've got everything on you," I said. "Not that I deserve any credit. The Army mule could have done the job. I can give you the State Attorney's case right now."

I picked up the gun and swung it lightly between a thumb and finger and sat on the couch arm. Rain beat against the windows in a muted murmur. From the kitchen came the lurch and whine of the refrigerator motor.

"Somebody named B. Jones," I said, "gets hold of some rare stamps. Illegally. Jones knows there are collectors around who will buy stolen stamps. Amos Spain is such a collector. A deal is made by phone or letter and the stamps are mailed to Spain. In some way, you two find out about it. After the stamps are in the mail, perhaps. No point in trying to get them away from Uncle Sam; but there's another way. So the two of you show up here early this morning and force your way in on old Amos, who is still in bed. You tie him up a little, let's say, and gag him, leave him on the bed and come out here in the living room to wait for the postman with the stamps.

"But Amos isn't giving up. He gets loose, dresses and goes down the fire escape. He can't be sure when you're going to open the door and look in on him, so he puts on just enough clothes to keep from being pinched for indecent exposure. That's why he wasn't wearing socks, and why his clothes were mismatched.

"But by the time he's going down the fire escape, you look in. No Amos, and the window is open. You look out, spot him running away without topcoat or hat, and out you go after him. Tackling him on the street wouldn't do at all; your only hope is to nail him in some lonely spot and knock him off. How does it sound so far, neighbor?"

"Like a lot of words," Monroe growled.

"Words," I said, "are man's best friend. They get you fed, married, buried. Shall I tell you some more about words?"

"Go to hell."

I put down the gun and lit a cigarette and smiled. "Like I told you," I said, "you've got a simple mind. But I was telling you a story. I wouldn't want to stop now, so let's get back to Amos. You see, Amos had a big problem at this stage of the game. He couldn't go to the boys in blue and tell them about you and Cora, here. Doing that could bring out the business about the stamps and get him nailed for receiving stolen property. He had to get the two of you thrown out of his apartment before the envelope showed up.

"How to do it? Hire a strong-arm boy who won't ask questions. Where do you find a strong-arm boy on a moment's notice? The phone book's got half a column of them. Private detectives. Not the big agencies; they might ask too many questions. But one of the smaller outfits might need the business bad enough to do it Amos's way. At least it's worth trying.

"So Amos gets my address out of the phone book, the nearest one to him, and comes up to hire me. He has no idea you're following him, which means he's not too careful about keeping out in the open where nothing can happen to him. He comes up to my office and I'm not in yet. He sits down to wait. You walk in and leave a switch knife in him. But that's only part of your job. You've got to fix it so there'll be a delay in identifying him—enough of a delay, at least, to keep the cops away from here until the mailman comes and goes. Lifting his papers may slow things down, but you want more than that. Being a crook, you make a habit of carrying around phony identification cards. You substitute these for his own, lift whatever cash Amos had on him, slip out quick and come back here. Right so far?"

The fear had gone out of Monroe's eyes and there was the first faint signs of a smirk to his thin bloodless lips. He said airily, "If this is your idea of a way to kill a rainy afternoon, don't let me stop you. Mind if I sit down?"

"I don't care if you fall down," I said. "There's a little more and then we can all sit around and discuss the election until the cops arrive. A little more, like Cora knowing my name the first time I was here this afternoon. I hadn't told her my name, you see; just that I was a private dick. But to Cora there was only one private detective—the one whose office you'd killed Amos Spain in."

Behind me a quiet voice said, "Raise your hands."

I froze. Cora Monroe's .32 was on the couch arm, no more than six inches from my hand. I could have grabbed for it—and I could get buried for grabbing. I didn't grab.

A slender stoop-shouldered man in his early forties came padding on stocking feet in front of me. He had bushy graying hair, a long intelligent face and a capable-looking hand containing a nickel-plated Banker's Special revolver. The quiet voice belonged to him and he used it again, saying, "I won't tell you again. Put up your hands."

I put them up.

He went on pointing the gun at me while knocking the .32 off the couch with a single sweep of his other hand. It bounced along the carpet and hit the wall. He said gently, "I'll take those stamps."

"You will indeed," I said. "I guess I should have looked in the bedroom, after all. I guess I thought two people should be able to lift three little stamps."

"The stamps, Mr. Pine." The voice wasn't as gentle this time.

"Sure," I said. I put my hand in my coat and took out the envelope. I did it nice and slow, showing him I was eager to please. I held it out and he reached for it and I slammed my shoe down on his stocking foot with every pound I could spare.

He screamed like a woman and the gun went off. Behind me a lamp base came apart. I threw a punch, hard, and the gray-haired man threw his hands one way and the gun the other and melted into the rug without a sound.

Monroe was crouched near the side wall, the girl's .32 in his hand and madness in his eyes. While he was still bringing up the gun I jerked the Police Special from under the band of my trousers and fired.

He took three wavering steps before he hit the floor.

Cora Monroe hadn't moved from the leather chair. She sat stiff as an ice floe off Greenland, her face blank with shock, her nails sunk in her palms. I felt a little sorry for her. I bent down and picked the envelope off the floor and shoved it deep into a side pocket. I said, "How much were they worth, Cora?"

Only the rain answered.

I found the telephone and said what had to be said. Then I came back and sat down to wait.

It was ten minutes before I heard the first wail of distant sirens.

THE THEFT
OF THE OVERDUE
LIBRARY BOOK

EDWARD D. HOCH

The man on the telephone was named Fingers O'Toole, and Nick Velvet had done a few jobs for him over the years. "How are you, Fingers? How's business?"

"Frankly, it could be better, Nick. I'm in a bit of a bind."

"Can I help you out?"

There was hesitation on the other end of the line. "Is this phone safe?"

"If your end's safe, my end's safe," Nick assured him.

"Look, I want you to steal a person for me."

"That sounds like kidnapping. I don't do anything like that."

"Come on, Nick, you stole a whole baseball team once! And a jury!"

"Groups of people are different," Nick explained. "It doesn't seem like kidnaping when there are a dozen people involved. But tell me a little more. Who do you want stolen?"

"Tony Wilde."

"The restaurant owner?"

"That's him. Can you do it?"

62

"You're going to hold him for ransom, right?"

"Well, I'm going to hold him till I get something out of him, sure."

"Sorry, Fingers. Count me out. First of all, I don't steal anything of value and Tony Wilde is something of value. Secondly, he's an old friend of mine."

"If you won't do it, someone else will, Nick."

"Tony Wilde can take care of himself. It would be next to impossible to kidnap him."

"I know somebody who specializes in impossible things. Sure you won't give it a try, Nick?"

"Sorry, Fingers," he said and hung up.

It was a warm afternoon in May and Nick went went out in the backyard where Gloria was planting some new rose bushes. "Who was on the phone, Nicky?" she asked.

"Business."

"A job?"

"No. I turned him down."

She stood up, brushing the dirt from her hands. "You look worried."

"Not really. It was just something he said, something about knowing a person who specializes in impossible things. I heard that once before."

Gloria remembered, too. "Sandra Paris, the White Queen."

He nodded. *"Impossible things before breakfast.* That was her motto."

"Do you think she's out of prison?"

"I guess I'd better find out."

Nick telephoned a politician he knew in southern New Jersey. "Marty, this is Nick Velvet. I've got a question for you."

"Good to hear from you, Nick. What's the question?"

"How much time do you get for stealing a roulette wheel in your state?"

Marty chuckled. "Thinking of coming down to Atlantic City?"

"I was already there—last year. Someone I know got into a little trouble."

"Well, a roulette wheel would be grand larceny. It would depend on their previous record, prior convictions and such. Give me a name and I'll check it for you."

"Sandra Paris. Atlantic City, about thirteen months ago."

"I'll call you back, Nick."

Thirty minutes later he phoned to report that Sandra Paris had drawn a one-year sentence and had been paroled after eight months.

"She's out," Nick told Gloria.

"Stay away from her, Nicky. She's trouble."

"I just don't like her taking my clients away."

"You didn't want the job anyway."

"Of course not! Tony Wilde is an old friend. I might even take a run out to see him and drop him a friendly warning."

"He lives in Chicago!"

"I can fly out tomorrow and be back the next day. It would be good to see Tony again."

"Can't you just phone him?"

"Not after all these years, Gloria. I just want to have dinner with him and give him a casual warning about Fingers O'Toole."

"Well, if you're flying to Chicago so am I," she decided. "There's an old school chum in Oak Park I've been dying to visit. She lives in a house designed by Frank Lloyd Wright."

There was no talking her out of it. The following afternoon they were both on a plane to Chicago.

Tony Wilde was delighted to hear Nick's voice and immediately invited him to dinner at his downtown supper club, The Wilde Spot. "Is Gloria with you?" he asked.

"Yes, but she's dining with an old friend."

"Pity. Give her my love, Nick."

Seeing Tony after such a long time brought back memories of Nick's Army days when they were both kids just out of school, catching the tail end of the Korean War and making plans for a future they hoped they'd live to see. It hadn't turned out exactly as planned for either of them, Nick decided, remembering how Tony had wanted to be a lawyer.

He was a stocky man with steel-grey hair. As he greeted Nick at the entrance to The Wilde Spot, he had the familiar twinkle in his eye. "Damn, good to see you, Nick! What brings you to Chicago?"

"I thought I'd just stop off and see you after all these years." His gaze took in the lobby fountain and the subdued, candlelit dining room beyond. "I couldn't afford this place if I didn't know the owner."

Tony gave him a friendly pat on the shoulder. "Go on, Nick. I hear you're pretty successful in your line of work." He led the way to a secluded table where a waiter quickly appeared to take their drink order.

Nick motioned toward a piano and microphone. "You have entertainment, too?"

"A singer comes on at eight. It's atmosphere, you know?" He smiled a bit. "Her voice isn't very good, but she looks great."

They chatted over drinks and the meal that followed—an excellent veal concoction that was one of the house specialties. Nick noticed that the couple at the next table had it, too—and cleaned their plates. Tony told Nick about his recent divorce. Finally, when they were relaxing over dessert, Nick asked, "Do you know a fellow named Fingers O'Toole?"

"O'Toole?" Tony's reply was carefully measured. "I may have heard the name. Why do you ask, Nick?"

"I don't want to involve myself in your personal affairs, Tony, but I'd be a little careful these days if I were you. Just call it a tip from an old friend."

"What is it? Did Fingers put out a contract on me?" Wilde asked, apparently decided to treat Nick's warning as a joke.

"Not exactly, but you're close. Would it be to his advantage if you were to disappear for a time?"

Tony Wilde stopped smiling. "How much do you know, Nick?"

"Very little. Just that O'Toole tried to hire me."

"To steal what?"

"You."

Tony was silent for a time. Nick watched the waiter bring the check and a doggie bag to the couple at the adjoining table. Finally, Wilde said, "Thank you for telling me, Nick. I've often said that old friends are the best."

"I think he'll hire someone else for the job. If I'm right, you might be especially vulnerable in the morning, before breakfast. What's your daily routine?"

"I assure you I'm quite safe before breakfast. I walk my dog in the park across from my apartment. Bruno's a mean German Shepherd who loves to bite people. He's far more effective than a human bodyguard."

"Still—"

"Look, Nick, I appreciate the warning. But I can take care of myself. As a matter of fact, if you and Gloria are free tomorrow morning I'd like to invite you over for breakfast. You can even walk Bruno with me if you'd like."

"I don't—"

"I may have some business to throw your way."

"I deal only in objects without value," Nick reminded him.

Tony Wilde nodded. "Come by in the morning, and bring Gloria. I'd like to see her again."

Later that evening, back at their hotel, Nick told Gloria about the invitation. "I suppose I should go," she agreed. "How was dinner?"

"The food was excellent, and his restaurant is certainly interesting."

"How do you mean interesting, Nicky?"

"It's the only place I ever saw where the customers take home doggie bags even after they've cleaned their plates."

In the morning they took a cab to Tony Wilde's condominium in a swank section of the city not far from The Wilde Spot. The building was across the street from a large park that covered several acres with tree-shaded paths and a small pond. It was here, Wilde explained after meeting Gloria with an affectionate kiss, that he walked Bruno every morning before breakfast.

The dog started to growl deep in his throat at the first sign of Nick and Gloria. Wilde slid his fingers beneath the dog's collar and scratched him soothingly. "There, there, boy. These are friends."

Once on his leash, Bruno calmed down a bit, and as they entered the park Wilde even allowed Gloria to take over and walk with him. Wilde himself dropped back to talk with Nick. "I told you last night I might have a job for you. Could you steal a library book for me?"

"You hardly need to pay me twenty-five thousand for that, Tony. You just stick it under your coat and walk out of the place. Unless they've got one of these new alarm systems with a magnetic strip inside the book."

"My problem is that the book isn't in the library. It's overdue and I have no way of finding out who has it."

"If it's a valuable first edition or something like that—"

"Lord knows it's not valuable, Nick. It's a cheap hardcover reprint of Hammett's *The Thin Man,* the sort they used to publish back in the 1930s before paperbacks became popular. The paper's beginning to turn brown and I suppose the library will simply discard it before long."

"There are diamonds hidden in the binding," Nick speculated.

"Nothing's hidden in it at all. You can take my word for it. But I need it, and I'll pay you your fee to get it for me."

Gloria and Bruno rounded a curve in the path and the German Shepherd turned his head to make certain his master was still behind him. It was obvious he never let Wilde out of his sight on these morning walks, but Nick decided to test it by pulling Tony off the path and behind a tree. Immediately, the dog broke free from Gloria's grip and bounced back, seeking them out and almost bowling Nick over with the ferocity of his charge. Wilde had to call him off as his powerful jaws were about to settle on Nick's wrist.

"Satisfied?" Tony asked.

"I guess so."

"He's the best bodyguard I ever had."

"But not much protection against a bullet fired at you from twenty yards away."

"No one wants to kill me, Nick. They just want a piece of my money."

Gloria joined them as Wilde retrieved the dog's leash. "That beast is a *beast!*" she announced.

Wilde chuckled and calmed the dog down once more. "He's just a loyal friend."

"Tell me more about this book," Nick urged.

"It belongs to our neighborhood branch library across the park. They only have one copy, and none of the other branches or the main library have this particular edition. It's more than a month overdue and the library says there's nothing they can do about it except send overdue notices. They have people who go out and collect overdue books, but that's not going to happen with this one for several more months. I need the book now."

"It should be simple enough, once I find out who has it."

"There's the problem. The library records are computerized. It's not as simple as looking in a file drawer." The path had led them to a small cubical building without windows. The sign on the door read

MEN. "If this is unlocked, I usually stop here," Wilde explained. Then, turning to the dog, he commanded, "Sit, Bruno!"

"He's a good dog," Nick observed, following Tony into the men's room. The grey cinder-block building contained a single urinal, a toilet stall, and a sink in a space perhaps ten feet square. The walls were marked with the usual graffiti but otherwise the place was reasonably clean.

"I told you so. Man's best friend. He'd wait out there for me all day."

Nick turned on the faucet and washed his hands. "How soon do you need the book?"

"I'd like it by tomorrow night. What do you think?"

"I'll let you know. If I can do it at all I should have it by then."

They emerged to find Gloria and Bruno eyeing each other with mutual distrust. But as soon as he saw Wilde, the dog was on his feet once more, tagging along at his side. "Is there a ladies' restroom in this park somewhere?" Gloria asked.

"Straight ahead." Wilde pointed, indicating a second cinder-block building about a hundred feet ahead of them on the path.

"Go ahead, we'll wait," Nick told her. He glanced around from where they strolled, noting a single telephone booth at the side of a park road about fifty feet directly behind the men's room. It was a good thing to remember.

When Gloria rejoined them, they circled around and left the park from the point where they'd entered it, across the street from Tony Wilde's condominium. He took them upstairs for breakfast, and over scrambled eggs Nick agreed to go after the overdue book. "I can do it," he said with assurance. "It'll just mean staying here a bit longer than we planned."

"Do you want a retainer now?"

"Your money's good," Nick said. "You can pay me on delivery."

Back at their hotel Gloria said, "You're not staying here just to do the job for him, are you, Nicky? You still think the White Queen's going to turn up."

"I don't know if she is or not, but a job's a job. Stealing things like overdue library books is what people pay me to do."

"Why do you think he wants that book, especially if there's nothing hidden in it?"

"We'll probably find out sooner or later."

"What am I supposed to do while you're out finding that book?"

"I have a job for you," Nick said. "I want you to follow Tony Wilde."

"What for? I'm certainly no bodyguard!"

"I just want to make sure nothing happens to him—because he's an old friend and because he's going to owe us twenty-five thousand dollars very shortly."

"If it's the White Queen, she'll go after him in the morning. Remember? Impossible things before breakfast?"

"I know," Nick agreed. "But I want you to be seen. If there's anyone else watching him I want them to know you're around. It might just be enough to scare them off, at least while we're in town."

Gloria took some persuading, but finally she agreed to keep an eye on Tony. "But what if something *does* happen? What'll I do?"

"Phone me. I'll manage to let you know where I can be reached most of the time."

He spent the rest of the day at the library branch, watching the operation of the computerized checkout system. When he first arrived there shortly before noon, he'd taken the direct approach, asking for the book in the hope it had been returned. But it was still overdue. Next he asked if its location could be traced. It was very important, he insisted, and offered the girl behind the counter a five-dollar tip. She promised to see what she could do, and returned in five minutes with a triumphant smile. "Here you are, sir. We have another edition of *The Thin Man,* in large print. I'm sure it will serve your purpose."

Nick started to protest, then he saw it was hopeless and accepted the book, taking it to a corner of the reading room.

As he studied the library's operations, he learned that each book now carried a barcode, much like those on food items at the supermarket. When a patron checked a book out, it was checked with a light pen, which registered the book's identification number along with the number of the borrower's library card. Nick thought about this for some time, then finally went to the card catalogue to look up the number assigned to *The Thin Man* in the edition he needed. But it was an up-to-date library and instead of a card catalogue he found himself confronted by a microfiche reader.

In a moment, however, he had what he wanted. And he thought he knew how he could discover the location of the book he'd been hired to steal.

That evening after dinner, Gloria reported that Tony Wilde had gone down to his supper club around noon and stayed till two o'clock, then driven to the Chicago public market, apparently to buy some choice cuts of beef for the restaurant. When he'd returned to The Wilde Spot for the evening, Gloria decided it was safe to abandon the tail.

"So that was my day," she concluded. "Boring. How about you? Did you get the book?"

"Not yet. Tomorrow."

"Do you still want me to watch him in the morning?"

"Of course. As you said yourself, if it's the White Queen, she'll go after him in the morning."

"While he's walking his dog."

"Exactly." He copied down a phone number from his notebook. "Here's what I want you to do. I'll be at the library at seven-thirty—"

"Do they open that early?"

He ignored the question and went on. "This is their phone number. I want you to call me there from the park. You'll see a pay phone by the road behind the men's restroom where Wilde stopped this morning. Today we reached there at just about seven-thirty, and I assume he walks the dog at the same time every day. Call me whether or not Wilde stops in the restroom, and I'll cross over from the library and meet you in the park."

"Why do I need to phone you if you're so sure of the time I'll be there?"

"Trust me," Nick said.

In the morning he was up early, shaking Gloria awake and reminding her she should be at Wilde's place by seven in case he walked the dog a bit earlier than usual. It was six-thirty when he left the hotel and drove his rented car to an all-night supermarket in one of the residential sections near the library. There he walked quickly up and down a couple of aisles, inspecting the barcode labels on the items until he found three that would serve his purpose. Happily, most barcodes included a digital translation directly beneath. He paid for the items and returned to his car.

It was growing light as he worked, though the dawn sky was cloudy with the threat of rain. The microfiche catalogue-listing for Hammett's *The Thin Man* in the edition Wilde needed gave its number as 4-2222-00003-3522. Nick cut away at the barcodes on the products he'd purchased and taped them together to form the number he needed. Then he drove on to the library.

It was a modern building, open only a few years, and he was stunned that a place with the latest in computers should have such a primitive alarm system. He was inside within five minutes, moving across the familiar carpeting of the main reading room to the book-return desk. He seated himself at the computer terminal and flipped the switch to turn it on. Then he picked up the light pen which served as the machine's optical scanner and passed it over the homemade barcode strip.

At once the terminal screen came alive with the book's author, title, publisher, edition, and publication date, followed by a call number and self location. Below this was a list of borrowers, identified by a number. Nick studied the final number for some time, wondering what he should do next. He decided he needed help.

In a desk drawer, he found a printed instruction-sheet giving the proper access code for identifying library borrowers. He typed in the necessary words and followed them with the borrower's number. At once the screen supplied the information he needed: Norman Wells, 503 Scott Street.

"What in hell are you doing here?" a gruff voice asked in surprise.

Nick froze at the computer terminal. He'd been so intent on the machine he hadn't heard anyone enter the library. He glanced quickly at his watch as he turned with a smile. It was 7:32. "I'm checking out all the computer terminals for the manufacturer," he explained. "We've had some malfunctions."

The man had a face that went well with his voice. "Nobody told *me* about it. We're not having any trouble. How'd you get in here, anyway, and what are you doing here at seven-thirty in the morning?"

"I've got a lot of terminals to check today. I had to get an early start. This is the first one."

"A lot of terminals? There are only two branches automated so far in the entire city!"

"Not just libraries. The commodities exchange uses this same model."

"Well, I'd just better check up on this."

"If you'll wait a few minutes, the director's secretary will be phoning me here. You know Miss Fritz, don't you?"

"Who? Yes, yes, I guess I know her," the man answered.

At that moment the telephone rang. Nick scooped it up before the man could reach it. "Nicky? This is Gloria. I'm at the booth in the park. Tony Wilde just went into the men's room and that beast is waiting outside."

"Yes, Miss Fritz, I'm glad you phoned."

"What? Nicky, it's me—Gloria!"

"I know, Miss Fritz. I have a gentleman here who wants to speak with me. Can you tell him that I'm authorized to be here, checking the computer terminals for malfunctions?"

"Oh! Sure," she said, finally catching on. Nick passed the receiver to the gruff-voiced man.

He accepted the phone gingerly. "Hello? Miss Fritz? This man— Yes, I see. But it's a bit early in the day— All right, I just want to make sure everything's in order."

He hung up and Nick turned off the terminal. "This machine's perfect. I hope all the rest work as well. Thanks for your cooperation, Mr.—"

"Jennings," the man supplied. "But I still don't understand how you got in here."

"Miss Fritz gave me a key."

"Oh."

"Goodbye now." Nick hurried toward the front door.

"What was she doing at work so early?"

"She came in early to phone me," Nick said, and then he was through the front door and out of there before Jennings could think of another question.

* * *

He drove into the park and left his car a short distance from the men's restroom. Even at a distance, he could see Gloria and Bruno eyeing each other again and he wondered why she'd gotten that close. "Where's Tony?" he asked when he joined her.

"Still inside. What was that business on the phone? You almost got caught, didn't you? Is that why you had me call?"

"It was a safety measure in case I needed it. And I did." He glanced at the dog. "How long has Wilde been in there?"

"About ten minutes. He went in just before I phoned you."

"I think I'll see what's keeping him."

The dog glanced up at him as Nick walked past him and opened the door of the cinder-block building. "Tony?" he called out. "Are you in there?"

Silence.

He stepped inside and looked around the tiny space. There was no one at the urinal or sink. He pushed open the door of the toilet stall and that was empty, too. He glanced up at the solid wooden ceiling, as unbroken as the slab of concrete beneath his feet. One door and no windows. Yet Tony Wilde had vanished.

Then he saw the little calling card propped against one of the faucets on the sink. It read simply:

THE WHITE QUEEN
Impossible Things Before Breakfast

It wasn't until Gloria had a look inside the place herself that she was willing to accept Nick's report that Tony Wilde had truly vanished. Then she simply stood there shaking her head. "It's impossible, Nicky, he can't be gone!"

"It's not impossible at all. He probably never entered this place to start with. You were off to one side—you thought he came in here, but he didn't."

"I didn't *think* anything!" she snapped, her temper up. "I was right outside. I saw him tell Bruno to sit, just like yesterday morning, and then push the door open and come in. I saw the door close after him."

"You couldn't be mistaken?"

"Not a chance. I was only on the phone with you for about two minutes, and Tony was in here all that time. Then I went back out and stood not twenty feet from the door. He never came out."

"Well, he certainly didn't get out through the plumbing. And the ceiling, floor, and walls are all solid. There's no place to hide in here, except maybe behind the door of the toilet stall, and he's not there. He wasn't behind the outside door when I entered, either. I felt it hit the wall when I pushed it open. And you were still outside—you would have seen him."

"Should we call the police?" Gloria asked.

"And tell them what? That a lady thief called the White Queen stole a man from a men's room in the park while you and his faithful dog were on guard outside? They'd laugh in our faces, not to mention ask a lot of embarrassing questions about my business with him."

"Then what do we do? What do we do with Bruno, to start with?"

Nick reached out and carefully picked up the German Shepherd's leash. "We'll leave him with the doorman in Tony's building."

The doorman, a white-haired man named Fred, was willing to take the dog when Nick told him they'd found Bruno alone in the park. "He must have gotten separated from his master," Nick said. "We saw the name and address on his collar, so we brought him back."

"I can't understand that," Fred told them. "The dog never ran away from him before. What's the matter, Bruno?" He carefully patted the dog's neck. Bruno let out a sudden bark. "Collar too tight?" Fred loosened the dog's collar and Bruno quieted down. "Good dog," the doorman said.

"You'll keep him for Mr. Wilde?" Nick asked. "He's a friend of ours."

"Sure, I remember seeing him with you yesterday. Don't worry, I'll take care of Bruno."

They left him and walked back to where Nick had left the car in the park. "What now?" Gloria asked.

"We look for Sandra Paris. And we look for Fingers O'Toole because that's who she's working for."

"What about the book you're supposed to steal?"

"First I'd better find my client. The book can come later."

They spent the rest of the day checking local hotels, but neither O'Toole nor Sandra Paris were registered under their own names. Every hour Gloria tried calling Wilde at his apartment and at the supper club, but he hadn't returned.

Nick called O'Toole's New York number but there was no answer there, either. "What do you think they want him for?" Gloria wondered.

"I don't know. I don't even know if O'Toole wanted his presence or merely his absence. Maybe Tony was going to do something or be somewhere and they wanted to stop him."

In the afternoon they went back to the park, back to the men's restroom where it had happened. But there was nothing to be found. Nick had Gloria inspect the ladies' restroom as well, though it was some distance down the path. "Are you sure there's nothing you forgot?" he asked her. "Is it possible he came out the roof somehow while you were phoning me?"

"You think I wouldn't have seen him? You think the dog wouldn't have caused an uproar? Nicky, he walked through the door—that one and only door—and he never came out."

"Come on," Nick said, depressed. "I'll take you out to dinner."

"Where?"

"Where else? The Wilde Spot, of course."

At the restaurant Nick was simply told that Tony Wilde was away. The waiters were as efficient as they had been on the first night, but there was an undertone of uncertainty about the place.

"The food is great," Gloria said, finishing her veal. "Tony must make a fortune here."

"I suspect he does," Nick murmured. He called the waiter over and said, "We'd like a doggie bag, please."

The waiter gestured at their plates. "But you have nothing to put in a doggie bag, sir."

"You know what I mean." Nick winked as he said it.

The waiter hesitated and then said, "You must mean the special-dessert menu, sir. It's not available tonight. You must come when Mr. Wilde himself is here."

"But I'm a close friend of Mr. Wilde. I dined with him here two nights ago. We sat at that corner table."

"I remember you, sir, but—"

"He told me to be sure to ask for the special-dessert menu the next time I was in."

"Well, I suppose it would be all right." The waiter went off and returned after a few moments with a menu. Nick opened it and looked down the list of cakes, pies, and ice creams, thinking for a moment there had been some misunderstanding. Then he found it, on a separate page, in light type, clinging to an end paper:

Not for Consumption on Premises
(Please order by number)
101. Famous marijuana brownies (serves two), $25
102. Hashish cake (full size), $75.
103. Apple custard pie, dusted with cocaine, $100
104. Frozen ginger cream with dilute LSD, $80
105. Marijuana mousse, $50
106. Gingerbread with powdered opium, $65

There were twenty-five items on the list in all, and Nick read them with growing astonishment. He had to admit that Tony Wilde had a great imagination when it came to finding new marketing techniques for tried-and-true products. "Just number 101," he told the waiter, handing back the menu.

"Very good, sir."

"What are you getting now?" Gloria asked.

"A take-out surprise for later."

It was eight o'clock, and as Nick accepted the doggie bag and paid the bill, the piano started playing. A slightly husky female voice began singing an old Cole Porter melody. He turned in his chair to look at her. She had platinum-blonde hair and was wearing a sequined evening gown. As Tony had said, her voice wasn't very good but she looked great.

It was Sandra Paris, the White Queen.

Nick gave Gloria the doggie bag and the key to the car. "I'll see you at the hotel," he said. "I have to speak with her."

"Nicky, remember the last time!"

"The last time she went to jail and I collected my fee. I'd like this to be a repeat performance."

"I don't trust any woman who looks like that."

"Don't worry. I'll be back in an hour."

He waited until Sandra Paris took her break and then approached the piano. "Remember me?"

She turned her head just a trifle and he saw again at close range the pale innocence of her face. "Nick Velvet, all the way out here in Chicago!"

"I get around. But then, so do you. I never thought you'd be frequenting men's rooms in public parks."

She smiled as she gathered up her music. "Oh, you found my card."

"Where's Tony Wilde?"

"In a safe place. He won't be harmed."

"How did you do it, Sandra?"

"Professional secret, Nick."

"How long is O'Toole holding him?"

She didn't answer right away. Instead she started to walk away and Nick tagged along. "How much do you know?" she asked at last.

"Enough. Fingers wanted me for the job first."

"I always seem to get your cast-offs, don't I?"

"How was prison, Sandra? Want to go back again?"

She shook her head. "I won't be going back again. I learned a few things since Atlantic City."

"Let me buy you a drink and we'll talk about it."

"I have another set in fifteen minutes."

"That's time enough. How'd you land this job, anyway?"

"The regular girl was persuaded to be sick for a week. I'm filling in."

"Why?"

She shrugged. "To keep an eye on Tony. I figured he'd rather be kidnaped by a familiar face."

They slid onto padded bar stools and she ordered white wine. "You know what he does here?" Nick asked.

"Sure. Have you tried the mousse? It's great."

"O'Toole wants a cut of it, doesn't he?"

"The damn fool wants to franchise the idea! Can you believe it? He says if all his restaurant-owner friends started offering it, with a percentage off the top to him, he could retire."

Nick shook his head. "Fingers is going to end up dead."

"Sure, but I don't question my clients. I just take the money and do the job."

"How much are you getting for this one, Sandra?"

"Fifty, plus my pay for singing here this week. I always wanted to be a singer."

"That's twice as much as I get for a job."

She shrugged her bare shoulders. "I have people to pay out of my share."

"So Fingers is holding him till he agrees to this crazy scheme?"

"Not exactly. Wilde has a big shipment of his raw material coming in any day now. Fingers plans to intercept it. Then it really won't matter if Tony agrees or not."

"Then why did he need to kidnap him?"

"Fingers intercepted a message about the shipment, but it's in some sort of code, he can't read it. That's why he needs Tony—when Tony tells him what it says, he'll be a free man."

Nick was remembering the library book. "I think I might have something you want," he said slowly. "When can we get together?"

"You mean with Tony Wilde?"

Nick nodded. "I want him free."

"That's Fingers' business, not mine."

"Get Fingers and get Wilde, and we'll meet tomorrow morning— around eleven. O.K.?"

"I'm not promising anything, Nick." She finished her wine and stood up. "I have to get back to the piano."

"That was just grandstanding this morning," he said. "You could have taken Tony right off the path, without any impossibilities."

She smiled at him. "I saw you and Gloria with him yesterday morning. I knew one of you would be back today, so I thought I'd show you how the pros do it."

"Call me tomorrow morning, Sandra, or I'll try a bit of grandstanding myself."

She smiled and strolled back to the piano. As he left, she was starting to sing another song.

When he got back to the hotel Gloria was already in bed. "Nicky, what was in those brownies?"

"Go to sleep. I'll tell you in the morning."

*   *   *

Norman Wells lived in a small, single-family house a few blocks from the library. It was shortly after nine o'clock when Nick arrived and rang his bell. A pleasant middle-aged woman answered.

"I'm looking for Norman Wells."

"That's my son. He's in school. What's he done now?"

"Nothing serious, Mrs. Wells—just kept a library book overdue."

"His room is full of books. I'm surprised it's only one."

"Well, there may be more, but the one I was sent after is *The Thin Man* by Dashiell Hammett. Do you think you could find it for me?"

"Oh, I couldn't find anything in that room of his. You'll have to come back when he's home."

"It's very important. Do you think I could just have a peek in his room to see if I could spot it?"

"Well, I don't know—"

"I'd hate to have the library turn it over to the police."

"The police! Oh, I suppose we could take a look."

His room on the second floor was cluttered with football pennants, old and new sneakers, and an assortment of books from the public and high-school libraries. "He likes mysteries," Nick observed.

She agreed. "Those and horror stories. He reads them all the time, but right now it's the baseball season and he doesn't get so much reading done. That's probably why he forgot to return the books."

A few minutes later, Nick held up the book in triumph. "Here it is!"

"Well, I'm really sorry about this," Mrs. Wells said.

"Don't worry. Just tell him to get any other overdue books back to us as soon as possible."

"He'll have them back tonight, believe me."

At the door, Nick stopped and handed her a ten-dollar bill. "Tell Norman this is for his library fines. I know how it is. I was young once, too."

"Why, what a sweet thing!"

Back at the hotel, Gloria told him, "She called about ten minutes ago. Here's her number."

"Good. We're rolling now."

"Did you get the book?"

"Right here."

"Why do you think it's so valuable to him?"

"Book code. His contacts used a copy of this edition. Something happened to his and he was using the library's one and only copy. Then it got borrowed and never returned, and Tony was in trouble. The other editions have the pages numbered differently, and he couldn't use them to read the message. He was getting desperate because the stuff's due in any day now."

"Drugs?"

Nick grinned at her. "Couldn't you tell from those brownies?" He dialed the number Sandra Paris had left and heard her familiar voice on the other end. "Nick Velvet here. You called?"

"I called, but it's no dice. Fingers won't trade him for anything you have, unless it's the shipment."

"Look, meet me in the park in thirty minutes. By the men's room."

"What for?"

"I still think we can work this out."

When he hung up, Gloria asked, "Where are you going now?"

"To meet the White Queen."

He was at the park in twenty minutes, but Sandra Paris was there ahead of him, seated on a bench halfway between the two restrooms. She looked at the book he carried in one hand. "What's that?"

"The key to the code. Want it?"

Sandra tossed her blonde mane. "It means nothing to me. I've been paid and tonight is my last as a singer, whatever happens."

"Tell me where Fingers is hiding him."

"Not a chance."

"Then tell me how he disappeared from that men's room."

Her eyes twinkled with something like pride in her work. "That's got you bothered, hasn't it? He walked through that door, the only door, and Gloria and his faithful pet waited outside. He never came out and yet there's nowhere he could have gone."

"Suppose I could figure out how you did it. Then would you tell me where he was?"

"Forget it. You'll never figure this one out in a hundred years."

"I thought you were a gambler after Atlantic City, Sandra. Give me a crack at solving it. If I'm right, you take me to him. If I'm wrong, I give you this book and you can sell it to Fingers for another fifty."

Her eyes dropped to the book, weighing the possibilities. His mention of cash had obviously interested her. "How much time would I have to give you?"

"Ten seconds."

She laughed and slapped his hand to seal the bet. "You're on! All right, ten seconds—how did I do it?"

Nick smiled and said five words . . .

When Fingers O'Toole turned, startled at his sudden entrance, Nick held up his hand.

"No gunplay, Fingers. I don't want trouble."

"How the hell did you find me? Did Sandra—?"

Nick could see Fingers was determined to make trouble. He crossed the room quickly and hit him on the jaw, sending him backward over a low coffee table. He knelt to remove the holstered revolver on Fingers' belt, then went into the back bedroom to find Tony Wilde handcuffed to a brass bed. "Hello, Tony," Nick said. "Sorry to have taken so long. I'll get the key to those cuffs."

That evening, Nick was once again Tony's guest at The Wilde Spot. Gloria was with them, demanding explanations. "How did you disappear from that restroom when I was outside watching?" she asked Tony.

He smiled. "Since the White Queen isn't here to tell you, I think Nick should explain."

"I told Sandra I could solve it—and I did, in just five words. We had a sort of bet—the book against Tony's hiding place. She was quite gracious about it—took me right to the door of O'Toole's house before she headed for the airport."

"What were the five words?" Gloria asked.

"*It was a different dog.*"

"What?"

"It was a different dog. The first time we saw Tony with Bruno, I remember he calmed the dog by sliding his fingers beneath the collar and rubbing him. But yesterday, after Tony's disappearance, the doorman wondered if his collar was too tight. Had Bruno's neck gotten bigger in a single night? No, Sandra Paris saw the dog with Tony, probably even took instant photographs of him, and obtained an identical German Shepherd with the same coloring."

"But Tony must have known the difference," Gloria insisted.

"It was still Bruno when Tony left the house with him. It was still Bruno when Tony told him to wait outside the restroom. But then Tony stepped through the door and found the White Queen waiting for him, dressed as a man in case someone else entered. She knocked him out with a quick injection and then opened the door, firing a tranquilizer dart into Bruno. A couple of hired cohorts brought in the substitute German Shepherd to take Bruno's place and carried Tony and Bruno away.

"You were on the phone to me. Remember, the booth was directly behind the restroom and so for two minutes you couldn't see what was happening out front. That was all the time they needed. Sandra removed Bruno's collar and put it on the new dog, getting it a bit tight rather than risk buckling it into a different hole that might be noticed. Then they all vanished into the trees while you came back to wait with the dog."

"What if I hadn't phoned you, Nicky?"

"I asked Sandra that. She was prepared to kidnap you, too, if necessary—along with any other early-morning strollers who happened along. But the whole thing went off exactly as she'd hoped, creating a nice impossible disappearance. We should have realized it wasn't the same dog, of course. Bruno was far less aggressive than he'd been the previous day."

"What happened to Fingers O'Toole?"

"I told Nick to let him go," Wilde said. "He's made a lot of enemies in organized crime, and this caper won't help him any."

"What about the book?" Gloria asked.

"My contacts telegraphed me about shipments using a book code from this edition of *The Thin Man*," Wilde explained. "My copy got left with my ex-wife when we divorced, and I was temporarily using the library copy. I wish Nick hadn't been so generous in offering it to Sandra Paris as a gambling stake."

Nick chuckled. "I put the library jacket on the bible from our hotel room. Sandra might have gotten religion, but she wouldn't have gotten the message."

"I decoded it just in time. The shipment's due tomorrow."

"Watch yourself, Tony. You're in a dangerous business."

He waved away the words of advice. "Anyway, you've earned your fee, Nick. More than earned it! You stole the book, rescued me, and even rescued Bruno from O'Toole's basement."

"Give him a bone for me."

"I'll do that," Wilde said with a smile. "Now how about some dessert?"

THE PLAY'S THE THING

ROBERT BLOCH

You ask the impossible, gentlemen. I cannot name the greatest Hamlet.

In fifty years as a drama critic, I've seen them all—Barrymore, Gielgud, Howard, Redgrave, Olivier, Burton and a dozen more. I've seen the play in cut and uncut versions, in modern dress, in military uniform. There's been a black Hamlet, a female Hamlet, and I shouldn't be surprised to learn of a hippie Hamlet today, but I wouldn't presume to select the greatest portrayal of the role, or the greatest version of the play.

On the other hand, if you want to know about the most memorable performance *in* Hamlet, that's another story . . .

The Roaring Twenties are only a murmuring echo in our ears now, but once I heard them loud and clear. As a young man I was in the very center of their pandemonium—Chicago; the Chicago of Hecht and MacArthur, of Bodenheim, Vincent Starrett and all the rest. Not that I traveled in such exalted company; I was only the second-string theatrical critic for a second-string paper, but I saw the plays and the players, and in that pre-depression era there was much to see. Shakespeare was a standby with the stars who travelled with their own repertory companies—Walter Hampden, Fritz Leiber, Richard Barrett. It was Barrett, of course, who played Hamlet.

If the name doesn't ring a bell today, it's not surprising. For some years it had evoked only the faintest tinkle in the hinterlands, where second-rate tragedians played their one-night stands "on the road," but then, for the first time, Richard Barrett brought his production to the big time, and in Chicago he really rang the bell.

He didn't have Hampden's voice, or Leiber's theatrical presence, and he didn't need such qualities; Barrett had other attributes. He was tall, slender, with a handsome profile, and although he was over thirty he looked leanly youthful in tights. In those days, actors like Barrett were called matinee idols, and the women adored them. In Chicago, they loved Richard Barrett.

I discovered that for myself during my first meeting with him.

Frankly, I hadn't been much taken with his performance when I saw it. To me, Barrett was, as they said of John Wilkes Booth, more acrobat than actor. Physically, his Hamlet was superb, and his appearance lent visual conviction to a role usually played by puffy, potbellied, middled-aged men. But his reading was all emotion and no intellect; he ranted when he should have reflected, wailed when he should have whispered. In my review I didn't go so far as to say he was a ham, but I admit I suggested he might be more at home in the stockyards than the theatre.

Naturally, the ladies weren't pleased with my remarks. They wrote indignant letters to the editor, demanding my scalp or other portions of my anatomy by return mail, but instead of firing me, my boss suggested I interview Richard Barrett in person. He was hoping, of course, for a follow-up story to help build the paper's circulation.

I wasn't hoping for much of anything except that Barrett wouldn't punch me in the jaw.

We met by appointment for luncheon at Henrici's; if I was to have my jaw punched I might at least get a good meal on the expense account before losing the ability to swallow. As it turned out, I needn't have worried. Richard Barrett was most amiable when we met, and highly articulate.

As the luncheon progressed, each course was seasoned by his conversation. Over the appetizer he discussed Hamlet's father's ghost. With the salad he spoke of poor Ophelia. Along with the entree he served up a generous portion of opinion regarding Claudius and Gertrude, plus a side-order of Polonius. Dessert was topped with a helping of Horatio, and coffee and cigars were accompanied by a dissertation on Rosencrantz and Guildenstern.

Then, settling back in his chair, the tall Shakespearean actor began to examine the psychology of Hamlet himself. What did I think of the old dispute, he demanded. Was it true that the Prince of Denmark, the melancholy Dane, was mad?

It was a question I was not prepared to answer. All I knew, at this point, was that Richard Barrett himself was mad—quite mad.

All that he said made sense, but he said too much. His intensity of interest, his total preoccupation, indicated a fanatic fixation.

Madness, I suppose, is an occupational hazard with all actors. "Realizing" the character, "losing oneself" in a role, can be dangerous, and of all the theatrical roles in history, Hamlet is the most complex and demanding. Actors have quit in the midst of successful runs rather than run the risk of a serious breakdown by continuing. Some performers have actually been dragged offstage in the middle of a scene because of their condition, and others have committed suicide. *To be or not to be* is more than a rhetorical question.

Richard Barrett was obsessed by matters extending far beyond the role itself. "I know your opinion of my work," he said, "but you're wrong. Completely wrong. If only I could make you understand . . ." He stared at me, and beyond me, his vision fixed on something far away—far away and long ago.

"Fifteen years," he murmured. "Fifteen years I've played the part. Played it? I've lived it, ever since I was a raw youngster in my teens. And why not? Hamlet was only a youngster himself—we see him grow to maturity before our very eyes as the play goes on. That's the secret of the character."

Barrett leaned forward. "Fifteen years." His eyes narrowed. "Fifteen years of split-weeks in tank towns; vermin in the dressing rooms, and vermin in the audiences too. What did they know of the terrors and the triumphs that shake men's souls? Hamlet is a locked room containing all the mysteries of the human spirit. For fifteen years I've sought the key. If Hamlet is mad, then all men are mad, because all of us search for a key that reveals the truth behind the mysteries. Shakespeare knew it when he wrote the part. I know it now when I play it. There's only one way to play Hamlet—not as a role, but as reality."

I nodded. There was a distorted logic behind what he said; even a madman knows enough to tell a hawk from a handsaw, though both the hawk's beak and the saw's teeth are equally sharp.

"That's why I'm ready now," Barrett said. "After fifteen years of preparation, I'm ready to give the world the definitive Hamlet. Next month I open on Broadway.''

Broadway? This prancing posturing nonentity playing Shakespeare on Broadway in the wake of Irving, Mansfield, Mantell and Forbes-Robertson?

"Don't smile," Barrett murmured. "I know you're wondering how it would be possible to mount a production, but that's all been arranged. There are others who believe in the Bard as I do; perhaps you've heard of Mrs. Myron McCullough?''

It was an idle question; everyone in Chicago knew the name of the wealthy widow whose late husband's industrial fortune had made her a leading patron of the arts.

"She has been kind enough to take an interest in the project," Barrett told me. "With her backing—''

He broke off, glancing up at the figure approaching our table; a curved, voluptuously slender figure that bore no resemblance to that of the elderly Mrs. Myron McCullough.

"What a pleasant surprise—'' he began.

"I'll bet," said the woman. "After you stood me up on our lunch date.''

She was young, and obviously attractive; perhaps a bit too obviously, because of her heavy makeup and the extreme brevity of her short-skirted orange dress.

Barrett met her frown with a smile as he performed the introductions. "Miss Goldie Connors," he said. "My protégée.''

The name had a familiar ring, and then, as she grinned at me in greeting, I saw the glint of her left upper incisor—a gold tooth.

I'd heard about that gold tooth from fellow reporters. It was well known to gentlemen of the press, and gentlemen of the police force, and gentlemen of Capone's underworld, and to many others, not necessarily gentlemen, who had enjoyed the pleasure of Goldie Connors' company. Gold-tooth Goldie had a certain reputation in the sporting world of Chicago, and it wasn't as a protégée.

"Pleased to meetcha," she told me. "Hope I'm not butting in.''

"Do sit down." Barrett pulled out a chair for her. "I'm sorry about the mix-up. I meant to call.''

"I'll bet." Goldie gave him what in those days was described as a dirty look. "You said you were gonna rehearse me—''

Barrett's smile froze as he turned to me. "Miss Connors is thinking of a theatrical career. I think she has certain possibilities."

"Possibilities?" Goldie turned to him quickly. "You promised! You said you'd give me a part, a good part. Like what's-her-name—Ophelia?"

"Of course." Barrett took her hand. "But this is neither the time nor the place—"

"Then you better make the time and find a place! I'm sick and tired of getting the runaround, understand?"

I didn't know about Barrett, but I understood one thing. I rose and nodded. "Please excuse me. I'm due back at the office. Thank you for the interview."

"Sorry you have to leave." Barrett wasn't sorry at all; he was greatly relieved. "Will there be a story, do you think?"

"I'm writing one," I said. "The rest is up to my editor. Read the paper."

I did write the story, stressing in particular the emphasis Barrett placed on realism. BARRETT PROMISES REAL HAMLET FOR BROADWAY was my heading, but not my editor's.

"Old lady McCullough," he said. "That's your story!" And he rewrote it, with a new heading: MRS. MYRON MCCULLOUGH TO FINANCE BARRETT'S BROADWAY BOW.

That's how it was printed, and that's how Richard Barrett read it. He wasn't the only one; the story created quite a stir. Mrs. McCullough was news in Chicago.

"Told you so," said my editor. "That's the angle. Now I hear Barrett's closing tomorrow night. He's doing a week in Milwaukee and then he heads straight for New York.

"Go out and catch him at his boardinghouse now. Here's the address. I want a follow-up on his plans for the Broadway opening. See if you can find out how he managed to get his hooks into the old gal so that she'd back the show. I understand he's quite a ladies' man. So get me all the gory details."

The dinginess of Barrett's quarters somewhat surprised me. It was a theatrical boardinghouse on the near North Side, the sort of place that catered to second-rate vaudeville performers and itinerant carny workers. But then Barrett was probably pinched for funds when he'd come here; not until he met Mrs. McCullough did his prospects improve. The meeting with his wealthy patroness was what I'd come to find out about—all the gory details.

I didn't get them. In fact, I got no details at all, for I went no farther than the hallway outside his door. That's where I heard the voices; in that shabby hallway, musty with the smell of failure, the stale odor of blighted hopes.

Goldie Connors' voice: "What are you trying to pull? I read the paper, all about those big plans of yours in New York. And here you been stalling me along, telling me there was no job because you couldn't get bookings—"

"Please!" Richard Barrett's voice, with an edge to it. "I intended to surprise you."

"Sure you did! By walking out on me. That's the surprise you figured on. Leaving me flat while you went off with that rich old bag you been romancing on the side."

"You keep her name out of this!"

Goldie's answering laugh was shrill, and I could imagine the glint of the gold tooth accompanying it. "That's what you tried to do—keep her name out of this, so I'd never know, or so she'd never know about me. That would queer your little deal in a hurry, wouldn't it? Well, let me tell you something, Mr. Richard Hamlet Barrett! You promised me a part in the show and now it's put up or shut up."

Barrett's voice was an anguished pleading. "Goldie, you don't understand! This is Broadway, the big chance I've waited for all these years. I can't risk using an inexperienced actress—"

"Then you'll risk something else. You'll risk having me go straight to your great lady and tell her just what's been going on between you and me!"

"Goldie—"

"When you leave town tomorrow night I'm going with you—with a signed contract for my part on Broadway. And that's final, understand?"

"All right. You win. You'll have your part."

"And not just one of those walk-on bits, either. It's got to be a decent part, a real one."

"A real part. I give you my word."

That's all I heard, and that's all I knew, until five days after Richard Barrett had left Chicago behind.

Sometime during the afternoon of that day, the landlady of the run-down boardinghouse scented an addition to the odors mingling in the musty hallway. She followed her nose to the locked door of what had been Barrett's room. Opening the door, she caught a glimpse of Barrett's battered old theatrical trunk, apparently abandoned upon his departure the day before. He'd shoved it almost out of sight under the bed, but she hauled it out and pried it open.

What confronted her then sent her screaming for the police.

What confronted the police became known in the city newsrooms, and what I learned there sent me racing to the boardinghouse.

There I confronted the contents of the trunk myself—the de-capitated body of a woman. The head was missing. All I could think of, staring down at it, was my editor's earlier demand. "The gory details," I murmured.

The homicide sergeant glanced at me. His name was Emmett, Gordon Emmett. We'd met before.

"What's going on?" he demanded.

I told him.

By the time I finished my story we were halfway to the Northwestern Depot, and by the time he finished questioning me, we had boarded the eight o'clock train for Milwaukee.

"Crazy," Emmett muttered. "A guy'd have to be crazy to do it."

"He's mad," I said. "No doubt about it. But there's more than madness involved. There's method, too. Don't forget, this was to be his big chance, the opportunity he'd worked and waited for all these years. He couldn't afford to fail. So that knowledge, combined with a moment of insane impulse—"

"Maybe so," Emmett muttered. "But how can you prove it?"

That was the question hanging over us as we reached Milwaukee at ten o'clock of a wintry night, and no cab in sight. I whistled one up on the corner.

"Davidson Theatre," I said. "And hurry!"

It must have been ten-fifteen when we pulled up in the icy alley alongside the stage door, and twenty after ten by the time we'd gotten past the doorkeeper and elbowed our way backstage to the wings.

The performance had started promptly at eight-fifteen, and now a full house was centering its attention upon the opening of Act Five.

Here was the churchyard—the yawning grave, the two Clowns,

Horatio, and Hamlet himself; a bright-eyed, burning Hamlet with feverish color in his cheeks and passionate power in his voice. For a moment I didn't even recognize Richard Barrett in his realization of the role. Somehow he'd managed to make the part come alive at last; this was the Prince of Denmark, and he was truly mad.

The First Clown tossed him a skull from the open grave and Hamlet lifted it to the light.

"Alas, poor Yorick," he said. "I knew him, Horatio—"

The skull turned slowly in his hand, and the footlights glittered over its grinning jaws in which a gold tooth gleamed . . .

Then we closed in.

Emmett had his murderer, and his proof.

And I? I had seen my most memorable performance in Hamlet: Goldie's . . .

HIS HEART COULD BREAK

CRAIG RICE

As I passed by the ol' state's prison,
Ridin' on a stream-line' train——

John J. Malone shuddered. He wished he could get the insidious melody out of his mind—or, remember the rest of the words. It had been annoying him since three o'clock that morning, when he'd heard it sung by the janitor of Joe the Angel's City Hall Bar.

It seemed like a bad omen, and it made him uncomfortable. Or maybe it was the cheap gin he'd switched to between two and four a.m. that was making him uncomfortable. Whichever it was, he felt terrible.

"I bet your client's happy today," the guard said cordially, leading the way towards the death house.

"He ought to be," Malone growled. He reminded himself that he too ought to be happy. He wasn't. Maybe it was being in a prison that depressed him. John J. Malone, criminal lawyer, didn't like prisons. He devoted his life to keeping his clients out of them.

Then the warden told me gently——

That song again! How did the next line go?

"Well," the guard said, "they say you've never lost a client yet."

It wouldn't do any harm, he thought, to get on the good side of a smart guy like John J. Malone.

"Not yet," Malone said. He'd had a close call with this one, though.

"You sure did a wonderful job, turning up the evidence to get a new trial," the guard rattled on. Maybe Malone could get him a better appointment, with his political drag. "Your client sure felt swell when he heard about it last night, he sure did."

"That's good," Malone said noncommittally. It hadn't been evidence that had turned the trick, though. Just a little matter of knowing some interesting facts about the judge's private life. The evidence would have to be manufactured before the trial, but that was the least of his worries. By that time, he might even find out the truth of what had happened. He hummed softly under his breath. Ah, there were the next lines!

> *Then the warden told me gently,*
> *He seemed too young, too young to die,*
> *We cut the rope and let him down—*

John J. Malone tried to remember the rhyme for "die." By, cry, lie, my and sigh. Then he let loose a few loud and indignant remarks about whoever had written that song, realized that he was entering the death house, and stopped, embarrassed. That particular cell block always inspired him with the same behavior he would have shown at a high class funeral. He took off his hat and walked softly.

And at that moment hell broke loose. Two prisoners in the block began yelling like banshees. The alarms began to sound loudly, causing the outside siren to chime in with its hideous wail. Guards were running through the corridor, and John J. Malone instinctively ran with them toward the center of disturbance, the fourth cell on the left.

Before the little lawyer got there, one of the guards had the door open. Another guard cut quickly through the bright new rope from which the prisoner was dangling, and eased the limp body down to the floor.

The racket outside was almost deafening now, but John J. Malone scarcely heard it. The guard turned the body over, and Malone recognized the very young and rather stupid face of Paul Palmer.

"He's hung himself," one of the guards said.

"With me for a lawyer?" Malone said angrily. "Hung himself,——" He started to say "hell," then remembered he was in the presence of death.

"Hey," the other guard said excitedly. "He's alive. His neck's broke, but he's breathing a little."

Malone shoved the guard aside and knelt down beside the dying man. Paul Palmer's blue eyes opened slowly, with an expression of terrible bewilderment. His lips parted.

"It wouldn't break," Paul Palmer whispered. He seemed to recognize Malone, and stared at him, with a look of frightful urgency. *"It wouldn't break,"* he whispered to Malone. Then he died.

"You're damned right I'm going to sit in on the investigation," Malone said angrily. He gave Warden Garrity's wastebasket a vicious kick. "The inefficient way you run your prison has done me out of a client." Out of a fat fee, too, he reminded himself miserably. He hadn't been paid yet, and now there would be a long tussle with the lawyer handling Paul Palmer's estate, who hadn't wanted him engaged for the defense in the first place. Malone felt in his pocket, found three crumpled bills and a small handful of change. He wished now that he hadn't got into that poker game last week.

The warden's dreary office was crowded. Malone looked around, recognized an assistant warden, the prison doctor—a handsome grey-haired man named Dickson—the guards from the death house, and the guard who had been ushering him in—Bowers was his name, Malone remembered, a tall, flat-faced, gangling man.

"Imagine him hanging himself," Bowers was saying incredulously. "Just after he found out he was gonna get a new trial."

Malone had been wondering the same thing. "Maybe he didn't get my wire," he suggested coldly.

"I gave it to him myself," Bowers stated positively. "Just last night. Never saw a man so happy in my life."

Dr. Dickson cleared his throat. Everyone turned to look at him.

"Poor Palmer was mentally unstable," the doctor said sadly. "You may recall I recommended, several days ago, that he be moved to the prison hospital. When I visited him last night he appeared hilariously—hysterically—happy. This morning, however, he was distinctly depressed."

"You mean the guy was nuts?" Warden Garrity asked hopefully.

"He was nothing of the sort," Malone said indignantly. Just let a hint get around that Paul Palmer had been of unsound mind, and he'd never collect that five thousand dollar fee from the estate. "He was saner than anyone in this room, with the possible exception of myself."

Dr. Dickson shrugged his shoulders. "I didn't suggest that he was insane. I only meant he was subject to moods."

Malone wheeled to face the doctor. "Say. Were you in the habit of visiting Palmer in his cell a couple of times a day?"

"I was," the doctor said, nodding. "He was suffering from a serious nervous condition. It was necessary to administer sedatives from time to time."

Malone snorted. "You mean he was suffering from the effect of being sober for the first time since he was sixteen."

"Put it any way you like," Dr. Dickson said pleasantly. "You remember, too, that I had a certain personal interest."

"That's right," Malone said slowly. "He was going to marry your niece."

"No one was happier than I to hear about the new trial," the doctor said. He caught Malone's eye and added, "No, I wasn't fond enough of him to smuggle in a rope. Especially when he'd just been granted a chance to clear himself."

"Look here," Warden Garrity said irritably. "I can't sit around listening to all this stuff. I've got to report the result of an investigation. Where the hell did he get that rope?"

There was a little silence, and then one of the guards said, "Maybe from the guy who was let in to see him last night."

"What guy?" the warden snapped.

"Why——" The guard paused, confused. "He had an order from you, admitting him. His name was La Cerra."

Malone felt a sudden tingling along his spine. Georgie La Cerra was one of Max Hook's boys. What possible connection could there be between Paul Palmer, socialite, and the big gambling boss?

Warden Garrity had recognized the name too. "Oh, yes," he said quickly. "That must have been it. But I doubt if we could prove it." He paused just an instant, and looked fixedly at Malone, as though daring him to speak. "The report will read that Paul Palmer obtained a rope, by means which have not yet been ascertained, and committed suicide while of unsound mind."

Malone opened his mouth and shut it again. He knew when he was licked. Temporarily licked, anyway. "For the love of mike," he said, "leave out the unsound mind."

"I'm afraid that's impossible," the warden said coldly.

Malone had kept his temper as long as he could. "All right," he said, "but I'll start an investigation that'll be a pip." He snorted. "Letting a gangster smuggle a rope in to a guy in the death house!" He glared at Dr. Dickson. "And you, foxy, with two escapes from the prison hospital in six months." He kicked the wastebasket again, this time sending it halfway across the room. "I'll show you from investigations! And I'm just the guy who can do it, too."

Dr. Dickson said quickly, "We'll substitute 'temporarily depressed' for the 'unsound mind.'"

But Malone was mad, now. He made one last, loud comment regarding the warden's personal life and probably immoral origin, and slammed the door so hard when he went out that the steel engraving of Chester A. Arthur over the warden's desk shattered to the floor.

"Mr. Malone," Bowers said in a low voice as they went down the hall, "I searched that cell, after they took the body out. Whoever smuggled in that rope smuggled in a letter, too. I found it hid in his mattress, and it wasn't there yesterday because the mattress was changed." He paused, and added, "And the rope couldn't of been there last night either, because there was no place he could of hid it."

Malone glanced at the envelope the guard held out to him—pale grey expensive stationery, with "Paul Palmer" written across the front of it in delicate, curving handwriting.

"I haven't any money with me," the lawyer said.

Bowers shook his head. "I don't want no dough. But there's gonna be an assistant warden's job open in about three weeks."

"You'll get it," Malone said. He took the envelope and stuffed it in an inside pocket. Then he paused, frowned, and finally added, "And keep your eyes open and your mouth shut. Because there's going to be an awful stink when I prove Paul Palmer was murdered."

The pretty, black-haired girl in Malone's anteroom looked up as he opened the door. "Oh, Mr. Malone," she said quickly. "I read about it in the paper. I'm so sorry."

"Never mind, Maggie," the lawyer said. "No use crying over spilled clients." He went into his private office and shut the door.

Fate was treating him very shabbily, evidently from some obscure motive of personal spite. He'd been counting heavily on that five thousand buck fee.

He took a bottle of rye out of the filing cabinet marked "Personal," poured himself a drink, noted that there was only one more left in the bottle, and stretched out on the worn red leather davenport to think things over.

Paul Palmer had been an amiable, stupid young drunk of good family, whose inherited wealth had been held in trust for him by an uncle considered to be the stingiest man in Chicago. The money was to be turned over to him on his thirtieth birthday—some five years off—or on the death of the uncle, Carter Brown. Silly arrangement, Malone reflected, but rich men's lawyers were always doing silly things.

Uncle Carter had cramped the young man's style considerably, but he'd managed pretty well. Then he'd met Madelaine Starr.

Malone lit a cigar and stared dreamily through the smoke. The Starrs were definitely social, but without money. A good keen eye for graft, too. Madelaine's uncle was probably making a very good thing out of that political appointment as prison doctor.

Malone sighed, wished he weren't a lawyer, and thought about Madelaine Starr. An orphan, with a tiny income which she augmented by modelling in an exclusive dress shop—a fashionable and acceptable way of making a living. She had expensive tastes. (The little lawyer could spot expensive tastes in girls a mile away.)

She'd had to be damned poor to want to marry Palmer, Malone reflected, and damned beautiful to get him. Well, she was both.

But there had been another girl, one who had to be paid off. Lillian Claire by name, and a very lovely hunk of girl, too. Lovely, and smart enough to demand a sizable piece of money for letting the Starr-Palmer nuptials go through without a scandalous fuss.

Malone shook his head sadly. It had looked bad at the trial. Paul Palmer had taken his bride-to-be night-clubbing, delivering her back to her kitchenette apartment just before twelve. He'd been a shade high, then, and by the time he'd stopped off at three or four bars, he was several shades higher. Then he'd paid a visit to Lillian Claire, who claimed later at the trial that he'd attempted—unsuccessfully—to talk her out of the large piece of cash money, and had drunk up all the whiskey in the house. She'd put him in a cab and sent him home.

No one knew just when Paul Palmer had arrived at the big, gloomy apartment he shared with Carter Brown. The manservant had the night off. It was the manservant who discovered, next morning, that Uncle Carter had been shot neatly through the forehead with Paul Palmer's gun, and that Paul Palmer had climbed into his own bed, fully dressed, and was snoring drunk.

Everything had been against him, Malone reflected sadly. Not only had the jury been composed of hard-working, poverty-stricken men who liked nothing better than to convict a rich young wastrel of murder, but worse still, they'd all been too honest to be bribed. The trial had been his most notable failure. And now, this.

But Paul Palmer would never have hanged himself. Malone was sure of it. He'd never lost hope. And now, especially, when a new trial had been granted, he'd have wanted to live.

It had been murder. But how had it been done?

Malone sat up, stretched, reached in his pocket for the pale grey envelope Bowers had given him, and read the note through again.

> My dearest Paul:
>   I'm getting this note to you this way because I'm in terrible trouble and danger. I need you—no one else can help me. I know there's to be a new trial, but even another week may be too late. Isn't there *any* way?
>
> Your own
>
> M.

"M," Malone decided, would be Madelaine Starr. She'd use that kind of pale grey paper, too.

He looked at the note and frowned. If Madelaine Starr had smuggled that note to her lover, would she have smuggled in a rope by the same messenger? Or had someone else brought in the rope?

There were three people he wanted to see. Madelaine Starr was one. Lillian Claire was the second. And Max Hook was the third.

He went out into the anteroom, stopped half across it and said aloud, "But it's a physical impossibility. If someone smuggled that rope into Paul Palmer's cell and then Palmer hanged himself, it isn't murder. But it must have been murder." He stared at Maggie without seeing her.

"Damn it, though, no one could have got into Paul Palmer's cell and hanged him."

Maggie looked at him sympathetically, familiar from long experience with her employer's processes of thought. "Keep on thinking and it'll come to you."

"Maggie, have you got any money?"

"I have ten dollars, but you can't borrow it. Besides, you haven't paid my last week's salary yet."

The little lawyer muttered something about ungrateful and heartless wenches, and flung himself out of the office.

Something had to be done about ready cash. He ran his mind over a list of prospective lenders. The only possibility was Max Hook. No, the last time he'd borrowed money from the Hook, he'd got into no end of trouble. Besides, he was going to ask another kind of favor from the gambling boss.

Malone went down Washington Street, turned the corner, went into Joe the Angel's City Hall Bar, and cornered its proprietor at the far end of the room.

"Cash a hundred dollar check for me, and hold it until a week from,"—Malone made a rapid mental calculation—"Thursday?"

"Sure," Joe the Angel said. "Happy to do you a favor." He got out ten ten-dollar bills while Malone wrote the check. "Want I should take your bar bill out of this?"

Malone shook his head. "I'll pay next week. And add a double rye to it."

As he set down the empty glass, he heard the colored janitor's voice coming faintly from the back room.

> *They hanged him for the thing you done,*
> *You knew it was a sin,*
> *You didn't know his heart could break——*

The voice stopped suddenly. For a moment Malone considered calling for the singer and asking to hear the whole thing, all the way through. No, there wasn't time for it now. Later, perhaps. He went out on the street, humming the tune.

What was it Paul Palmer had whispered in that last moment? *"It wouldn't break!"* Malone scowled. He had a curious feeling that there was some connection between those words and the words of that damned song. Or was it his Irish imagination, tripping him up again? *"You didn't know his heart could break."* But it was Paul Palmer's neck that had been broken.

Malone hailed a taxi and told the driver to take him to the swank Lake Shore Drive apartment-hotel where Max Hook lived.

The gambling boss was big in two ways. He took in a cut from every crooked gambling device in Cook County, and most of the honest ones. And he was a mountain of flesh, over six feet tall and three times too fat for his height. His pink head was completely bald and he had the expression of a pleased cherub.

His living room was a masterpiece of the gilt-and-brocade school of interior decoration, marred only by a huge, battle-scarred roll-top desk in one corner. Max Hook swung around from the desk to smile cordially at the lawyer.

"How delightful to see you! What will you have to drink?"

"Rye," Malone said, "and it's nice to see you too. Only this isn't exactly a social call."

He knew better, though, than to get down to business before the drinks had arrived. (Max Hook stuck to pink champagne.) That wasn't the way Max Hook liked to do things. But when the rye was down, and the gambling boss had lighted a slender, tinted (and, Malone suspected, perfumed) cigarette in a rose quartz holder, he plunged right in.

"I suppose you read in the papers about what happened to my client, Palmer," he said.

"I never read the papers," Max Hook told him, "but one of my boys informed me. Tragic, wasn't it."

"Tragic is no name for it," Malone said bitterly. "He hadn't paid me a dime."

Max Hook's eyebrows lifted. "So?" Automatically he reached for the green metal box in the left-hand drawer. "How much do you need?"

"No, no," Malone said hastily, "that isn't it. I just want to know if one of your boys—Little Georgie La Cerra—smuggled the rope in to him. That's all."

Max Hook looked surprised, and a little hurt. "My dear, Malone," he said at last, "why do you imagine he'd do such a thing?"

"For money," Malone said promptly, "if he did do it. I don't care, I just want to know."

"You can take my word for it," Max Hook said, "he did nothing of the kind. He did deliver a note from a certain young lady to Mr. Palmer, at my request—a bit of nuisance, too, getting hold of that admittance order signed by the warden. I assure you, though, there was no rope. I give you my word, and you know I'm an honest man."

"Well, I was just asking," Malone said. One thing about the big gangster, he always told the truth. If he said Little Georgie La Cerra hadn't smuggled in that rope, then Little Georgie hadn't. Nor was there any chance that Little Georgie had engaged in private enterprises on the side. As Max Hook often remarked, he liked to keep a careful watch on his boys. "One thing more, though," the lawyer said, "if you don't mind. Why did the young lady come to you to get her note delivered?"

Max Hook shrugged his enormous shoulders. "We have a certain—business connection. To be exact, she owes me a large sum of money. Like most extremely mercenary people she loves gambling, but she is not particularly lucky. When she told me that the only chance for that money to be paid was for the note to be delivered, naturally I obliged."

"Naturally," Malone agreed. "You didn't happen to know what was in the note, did you?"

Max Hook was shocked. "My dear Malone! You don't think I read other people's personal mail!"

No, Malone reflected, Max Hook probably didn't. And not having read the note, the big gambler probably wouldn't know what kind of "terrible trouble and danger" Madelaine Starr was in. He decided to ask, though, just to be on the safe side.

"Trouble?" Max Hook repeated after him. "No, outside of having her fiancé condemned to death, I don't know of any trouble she's in."

Malone shrugged his shoulders at the reproof, rose and walked to the door. Then he paused, suddenly. "Listen, Max. Do you know the words to a tune that goes like this?" He hummed a bit of it.

Max Hook frowned, then nodded. "Mmm—I know the tune. An entertainer at one of my places used to sing it." He thought hard, and finally came up with a few lines.

> *He was leaning against the prison bars,*
> *Dressed up in his new prison clothes——*

"Sorry," Max Hook said at last, "that's all I remember. I guess those two lines stuck in my head because they reminded me of the first time I was in jail."

Outside in the taxi, Malone sang the two lines over a couple of times. If he kept on, eventually he'd have the whole song. But Paul Palmer hadn't been leaning against the prison bars. He'd been hanging from the water pipe.

Damn, and double damn that song!

It was well past eight o'clock, and he'd had no dinner, but he didn't feel hungry. He had a grim suspicion that he wouldn't feel hungry until he'd settled this business. When the cab paused for the next red light, he flipped a coin to decide whether he'd call first on Madelaine Starr or Lillian Claire, and Madelaine won.

He stepped out of the cab in front of the small apartment building on Walton Place, paid the driver, and started across the sidewalk just as a tall, white-haired man emerged from the door. Malone recognized Orlo Featherstone, the lawyer handling Paul Palmer's estate, considered ducking out of sight, realized there wasn't time, and finally managed to look as pleased as he was surprised.

"I was just going to offer Miss Starr my condolences," he said.

"I'd leave her undisturbed, if I were you," Orlo Featherstone said coldly. He had only one conception of what a lawyer should be, and Malone wasn't anything like it. "I only called myself because I am, so to speak and in a sense, a second father to her."

If anyone else had said that, Malone thought, it would have called for an answer. From Orlo Featherstone, it sounded natural. He nodded sympathetically and said, "Then I won't bother her." He tossed away a ragged cigar and said, "Tragic affair, wasn't it."

Orlo Featherstone unbent at least half a degree. "Distinctly so. Personally, I cannot imagine Paul Palmer doing such a thing. When I visited him yesterday, he seemed quite cheerful and full of hope."

"You—visited him yesterday?" Malone asked casually. He drew a cigar from his pocket and began unwrapping it with exquisite care.

"Yes," Featherstone said, "about the will. He had to sign it, you know. Fortunate for her," he indicated Madelaine Starr with a gesture toward the building, "that he did so. He left her everything, of course."

"Of course," Malone said. He lighted his cigar on the second try. "You don't think Paul Palmer could have been murdered, do you?"

"Murdered!" Orlo Featherstone repeated, as though it was an obscene word, "Absurd! No Palmer has ever been murdered."

Malone watched him climb into a shiny 1928 Rolls Royce, then started walking briskly toward State Street. The big limousine passed him just as he reached the corner, it turned north on State Street and stopped. Malone paused by the newsstand long enough to see Mr. Orlo Featherstone get out and cross the sidewalk to the corner drug store. After a moment's thought he followed and paused at the cigar counter, from where he could see clearly into the adjacent telephone booth.

Orlo Featherstone, in the booth, consulted a little notebook. Then he took down the receiver, dropped a nickel in the slot, and began dialling. Malone watched carefully. D-E-L—9-6-0——It was Lillian Claire's number.

The little lawyer cursed all sound-proof phone booths, and headed for a bar on the opposite corner. He felt definitely unnerved.

After a double rye, and halfway through a second one, he came to the heartening conclusion that when he visited Lillian Claire, later in the evening, he'd be able to coax from her the reason why Orlo Featherstone, of all people, had telephoned her, just after leaving the late Paul Palmer's fiancée. A third rye braced him for his call on the fiancée herself.

Riding up in the self-service elevator to her apartment, another heartening thought came to him. If Madelaine Starr was going to inherit all the Palmer dough—then it might not be such a trick to collect his five thousand bucks. He might even be able to collect it by a week from Thursday.

And he reminded himself, as she opened the door, this was going to be one time when he wouldn't be a sucker for a pretty face.

Madelaine Starr's apartment was tiny, but tasteful. Almost too tasteful, Malone thought. Everything in it was cheap, but perfectly correct and in exactly the right place, even to the Van Gogh print over the midget fireplace. Madelaine Starr was in exactly the right taste, too.

She was a tall girl, with a figure that still made Malone blink, in spite of the times he'd admired it in the courtroom. Her bronze-brown hair was smooth and well-brushed, her pale face was calm and composed. Serene, polished, suave. Malone had a private idea that if he made a pass at her, she wouldn't scream. She was wearing black rayon house-pajamas. He wondered if they were her idea of mourning.

Malone got the necessary condolences and trite remarks out of the way fast, and then said, "What kind of terrible trouble and danger are you in, Miss Starr?"

That startled her. She wasn't able to come up with anything more original than "What do you mean?"

"I mean what you wrote in your note to Paul Palmer," the lawyer said.

She looked at the floor and said, "I hoped it had been destroyed."

"It will be," Malone said gallantly, "if you say so."

"Oh," she said. "Do you have it with you?"

"No," Malone lied. "It's in my office safe. But I'll go back there and burn it." He didn't add when.

"It really didn't have anything to do with his death, you know," she said.

Malone said, "Of course not. You didn't send him the rope too, did you?"

She stared at him. "How awful of you."

"I'm sorry," Malone said contritely.

She relaxed. "I'm sorry too. I didn't mean to snap at you. I'm a little unnerved, naturally." She paused. "May I offer you a drink?"

"You may," Malone said, "and I'll take it."

He watched her while she mixed a lot of scotch and a little soda in two glasses, wondering how soon after her fiancé's death he could safely ask her for a date. Maybe she wouldn't say *yes* to a broken-down criminal lawyer, though. He took the drink, downed half of it, and said to himself indignantly, "Who's broken-down?"

"Oh, Mr. Malone," she breathed, "you don't believe my note had anything to do with it?"

"Of course not," Malone said. "That note would have made him want to live, and get out of jail." He considered bringing up the matter of his five thousand dollar fee, and then decided this was not the time. "Nice that you'll be able to pay back what you owe Max Hook. He's a bad man to owe money to."

She looked at him sharply and said nothing. Malone finished his drink, and walked to the door.

"One thing, though," he said, hand on the knob. "This—terrible trouble and danger you're in. You'd better tell me. Because I might be able to help, you know."

"Oh, no," she said. She was standing very close to him, and her perfume began to mingle dangerously with the rye and scotch in his brain. "I'm afraid not." He had a definite impression that she was thinking fast. "No one can help, now." She looked away, delicately. "You know—a girl—alone in the world——"

Malone felt his cheeks reddening. He opened the door and said, "Oh." Just plain Oh.

"Just a minute," she said quickly. "Why did you ask all these questions?"

"Because," Malone said, just as quickly, "I thought the answers might be useful—in case Paul Palmer was murdered."

That, he told himself, riding down the self-service elevator, would give her something to think about.

He hailed a cab and gave the address of the apartment building where Lillian Claire lived, on Goethe Street. In the lobby of the building he paused long enough to call a certain well-known politician at his home and make sure that he was there. It would be just as well not to run into that particular politician at Lillian Claire's apartment, since he was paying for it.

It was a nice apartment, too, Malone decided, as the slim mulatto maid ushered him in. Big, soft modernistic divans and chairs, panelled mirrors, and a built-in bar. Not half as nice, though, as Lillian Claire herself.

She was a cuddly little thing, small, and a bit on the plump side, with curly blonde hair and a deceptively simple stare. She said, "Oh, Mr. Malone, I've always wanted a chance to get acquainted with you." Malone had a pleasant feeling that if he tickled her, just a little, she'd giggle.

She mixed him a drink, lighted his cigar, sat close to him on the biggest and most luxurious divan, and said, "Tell me, how on earth did Paul Palmer get that rope?"

"I don't know," Malone said. "Did you send it to him, baked in a cake?"

She looked at him reprovingly. "You don't think I wanted him to kill himself and let that awful woman inherit all that money?"

Malone said, "She isn't so awful. But this is tough on you, though. Now you'll never be able to sue him."

"I never intended to," she said. "I didn't want to be paid off. I just thought it might scare her away from him."

Malone put down his glass, she hopped up and refilled it. "Were you in love with him?" he said.

"Don't be silly." She curled up beside him again. "I liked him. He was much too nice to have someone like that marry him for his money."

Malone nodded slowly. The room was beginning to swim—not unpleasantly—before his eyes. Maybe he should have eaten dinner after all.

"Just the same," he said, "you didn't think that idea up all by yourself. Somebody put you up to asking for money."

She pulled away from him a little—not too much. "That's perfect nonsense," she said unconvincingly.

"All right," Malone said agreeably. "Tell me just one thing——"

"I'll tell you this one thing," she said. "Paul never murdered his uncle. I don't know who did, but it wasn't Paul. Because I took him home that night. He came to see me, yes. But I didn't put him in a cab and send him home. I took him home, and got him to his own room. Nobody saw me. It was late—almost daylight." She paused and lit a cigarette. "I peeked into his uncle's room to make sure I hadn't been seen, and his uncle was dead. I never told anybody because I didn't want to get mixed up in it worse than I was already."

Malone sat bolt upright. "Fine thing," he said, indignantly and a bit thickly. "You could have alibied him and you let him be convicted."

"Why bother?" she said serenely. "I knew he had you for a lawyer. Why would he need an alibi?"

Malone shoved her back against the cushions of the davenport and glared at her. "A'right," he said. "But that wasn't the thing I was gonna ask. Why did old man Featherstone call you up tonight?"

Her shoulders stiffened under his hands, "He just asked me for a dinner date," she said.

"You're a liar," Malone said, not unpleasantly. He ran an experimental finger along her ribs. She did giggle. Then he kissed her.

All this time spent, Malone told himself reprovingly, and you haven't learned one thing worth the effort. Paul Palmer hadn't killed his uncle. But he'd been sure of that all along, and anyway it wouldn't do any good now. Madelaine Starr needed money, and now she was going to inherit a lot of it. Orlo Featherstone was on friendly terms with Lillian Claire.

The little lawyer leaned his elbows on the table and rested his head on his hands. At three o'clock in the morning, Joe the Angel's was a desolate and almost deserted place. He knew now, definitely, that he should have eaten dinner. Nothing, he decided, would cure the way he felt except a quick drink, a long sleep, or sudden death.

He would probably never learn who had killed Paul Palmer's uncle, or why. He would probably never learn what had happened to Paul Palmer. After all, the man had hanged himself. No one else could have got into that cell. It wasn't murder to give a man enough rope to hang himself with.

No, he would probably never learn what had happened to Paul Palmer, and he probably would never collect that five thousand dollar fee. But there was one thing that he could do. He'd learn the words of that song.

He called for a drink, the janitor, and the janitor's guitar. Then he sat back and listened.

> *As I passed by the ol' State's prison,*
> *Ridin' on a stream-lin' train——*

It was a long, rambling ballad, requiring two drinks for the janitor and two more for Malone. The lawyer listened, remembering a line here and there.

> *When they hanged him in the mornin',*
> *His last words were for you,*
> *Then the sheriff took his shiny knife*
> *An' cut that ol' rope through.*

A sad story, Malone reflected, finishing the second drink. Personally, he'd have preferred "My Wild Irish Rose" right now. But he yelled to Joe for another drink, and went on listening.

> *They hanged him for the thing you done,*
> *You knew it was a sin,*
> *How well you knew his heart could break,*
> *Lady, why did you turn him in—*

The little lawyer jumped to his feet. That was the line he'd been trying to remember! And what had Paul Palmer whispered? *"It wouldn't break."*

Malone knew, now.

He dived behind the bar, opened the cash drawer, and scooped out a handful of telephone slugs.

"You're drunk," Joe the Angel said indignantly.

"That may be," Malone said happily, "and it's a good idea too. But I know what I'm doing."

He got one of the slugs into the phone on the third try, dialled Orlo Featherstone's number, and waited till the elderly lawyer got out of bed and answered the phone.

It took ten minutes, and several more phone slugs to convince Featherstone that it was necessary to get Madelaine Starr out of bed and make the three-hour drive to the state's prison, right now. It took another ten minutes to wake up Lillian Claire and induce her to join the party. Then he placed a long-distance call to the sheriff of Statesville County and invited him to drop in at the prison and pick up a murderer.

Malone strode to the door. As he reached it, Joe the Angel hailed him.

"I forgot," he said, "I got sumpin' for you." Joe the Angel rummaged back of the cash register and brought out a long envelope. "That cute secretary of yours was looking for you all over town to give you this. Finally she left it with me. She knew you'd get here sooner or later."

Malone said "Thanks," took the envelope, glanced at it, and winced. "First National Bank." Registered mail. He knew he was overdrawn, but——

Oh, well, maybe there was still a chance to get that five thousand bucks.

The drive to Statesville wasn't so bad, in spite of the fact that Orlo Featherstone snored most of the way. Lillian snuggled up against Malone's left shoulder like a kitten, and with his right hand he held Madelaine Starr's hand under the auto robe. But the arrival, a bit before seven a.m., was depressing. The prison looked its worst in the early morning, under a light fog.

Besides, the little lawyer wasn't happy over what he had to do.

Warden Garrity's office was even more depressing. There was the warden, eyeing Malone coldly and belligerently, and Madelaine Starr and her uncle, Dr. Dickson, looking a bit annoyed. Orlo Featherstone was frankly skeptical. The sheriff of Statesville County was sleepy and bored, Lillian Claire was sleepy and suspicious. Even the guard, Bowers, looked bewildered.

And all these people, Malone realized, were waiting for him to pull a rabbit out of his whiskers.

He pulled it out fast. "Paul Palmer was murdered," he said flatly.

Warden Garrity looked faintly amused. "A bunch of pixies crawled in his cell and tied the rope around his neck?"

"No," Malone said, lighting a cigar. "This murderer made one try—murder by frame-up. He killed Paul Palmer's uncle for two reasons, one of them being to send Paul Palmer to the chair. It nearly worked. Then I got him a new trial. So another method had to be tried, fast, and that one did work."

"You're insane," Orlo Featherstone said. "Palmer hanged himself."

"I'm not insane," Malone said indignantly, "I'm drunk. There's a distinction. And Paul Palmer hanged himself because he thought he wouldn't die, and could escape from prison." He looked at Bowers and said, "Watch all these people, someone may make a move."

Lillian Claire said, "I don't get it."

"You will," Malone promised. He kept a watchful eye on Bowers and began talking fast. "The whole thing was arranged by someone who was mercenary and owed money. Someone who knew Paul Palmer would be too drunk to know what had happened the night his uncle was killed, and who was close enough to him to have a key to the apartment. That person went in and killed the uncle with Paul Palmer's gun. And, as that person had planned, Paul Palmer was tried and convicted and would have been electrocuted, if he hadn't had a damn smart lawyer."

He flung his cigar into the cuspidor and went on, "Then Paul Palmer was granted a new trial. So the mercenary person who wanted Paul Palmer's death convinced him that he had to break out of prison, and another person showed him how the escape could be arranged—by pretending to hang himself, and being moved to the prison hospital—*watch her, Bowers!*"

Madelaine Starr had flung herself at Dr. Dickson. "Damn you," she screamed, her face white. "I knew you'd break down and talk. But you'll never talk again——"

There were three shots. One from the little gun Madelaine had carried in her pocket, and two from Bowers' service revolver.

Then the room was quite still.

Malone walked slowly across the room, looked down at the two bodies, and shook his head sadly. "Maybe it's just as well," he said. "They'd probably have hired another defense lawyer anyway."

"This is all very fine," the Statesville County sheriff said. "But I still don't see how you figured it. Have another beer?"

"Thanks," Malone said. "It was easy. A song tipped me off. Know this?" He hummed a few measures.

"Oh, sure," the sheriff said. "The name of it is, 'The Statesville Prison.'" He sang the first four verses.

"Well, I'll be double-damned," Malone said. The bartender put the two glasses of beer on the table. "Bring me a double gin for a chaser," the lawyer told him.

"Me too," the sheriff said. "What does the song have to do with it, Malone?"

Malone said, "It was the crank on the adding machine, pal. Know what I mean? You put down a lot of stuff to add up and nothing happens, and then somebody turns the crank and it all adds up to what you want to know. See how simple it is?"

"I don't," the sheriff said, "but go on."

"I had all the facts," Malone said, "I knew everything I needed to know, but I couldn't add it up. I needed one thing, that one thing." He spoke almost reverently, downing his gin. "Paul Palmer said *'It wouldn't break'*—just before he died. And he looked terribly surprised. For a long time, I didn't know what he meant. Then I heard that song again, and I did know." He sang a few lines. *"The sheriff took his shiny knife, and cut that ol' rope through."* Then he finished his beer, and sang on, *"They hanged him for the thing you done, you knew it was a sin. You didn't know his heart could break, Lady, why did you turn him in."* He ended on a blue note.

"Very pretty," the sheriff said. "Only I heard it, *'You knew that his poor heart could break.'*"

"Same thing," Malone said, waving a hand. "Only, that song was what turned the crank on the adding machine. When I heard it again, I knew what Palmer meant by *'it wouldn't break.'* "

"His heart?" the sheriff said helpfully.

"No," Malone said, "the rope."

He waved at the bartender and said, "Two more of the same." Then to the sheriff, "He expected the rope to break. He thought it would be artfully frayed so that he would drop to the floor unharmed. Then he could have been moved to the prison hospital—from which there had been two escapes in the past six months. He had to escape, you see, because his sweetheart had written him that she was in terrible trouble and danger—the same sweetheart whose evidence had helped convict him at the trial.

"Madelaine Starr wanted his money," Malone went on, "but she didn't want Paul. So her murder of his uncle served two purposes. It released Paul's money, and it framed him. Using poor old innocent Orlo Featherstone, she planted in Lillian Claire's head the idea of holding up Paul for money, so Paul would be faced with a need for ready cash. Everything worked fine, until I gummixed up the whole works by getting my client a new trial."

"Your client shouldn't of had such a smart lawyer," the sheriff said, over his beer glass.

Malone tossed aside the compliment with a shrug of his cigar. "Maybe he should of had a better one. Anyway, she and her uncle, Dr. Dickson, fixed it all up. She sent that note to Paul, so he'd think he had to break out of the clink. Then her uncle, Dickson, told Paul he'd arrange the escape, with the rope trick. To the world, it would have looked as though Paul Palmer had committed suicide in a fit of depression. Only he did have a good lawyer, and he lived long enough to say *'It wouldn't break.'* "

Malone looked into his empty glass and lapsed into a melancholy silence.

The phone rang—someone hijacked a truck over on the Springfield Road—and the sheriff was called away. Left by himself, Malone cried a little into his beer. Lillian Claire had gone back to Chicago with Orlo Featherstone, who really had called her up for a date, and no other reason.

Malone reminded himself he hadn't had any sleep, his head was splitting, and what was left of Joe the Angel's hundred dollars would just take him back to Chicago. And there was that letter from the bank, probably threatening a summons. He took it out of his pocket and sighed as he tore it open.

"Might as well face realities," Malone said to the bartender. "And bring me another double gin."

He drank the gin, tore open the envelope, and took out a certified check for five thousand dollars, with a note from the bank to the effect that Paul Palmer had directed its payment. It was dated the day before his death.

Malone waltzed to the door, waltzed back to pay the bartender and kiss him good-bye.

"Do you feel all right?" the bartender asked anxiously.

"All right!" Malone said. "I'm a new man!"

What was more, he'd just remembered the rest of that song. He sang it, happily, as he went up the street toward the railroad station.

> *As I passed by the ol' State's prison,*
> *Ridin' on a stream-lin' train*
> *I waved my hand, and said out loud,*
> *I'm never comin' back again,*
> *I'm never comin' back a—gain!*

DEAD RINGER

JAMES M. ULLMAN

At 8:35 on a Tuesday night a car veered crazily down a Chicago street and hit a man stepping off the curb. The vehicle didn't even slow down. It squealed around a corner and out of sight. The first witness to reach the victim ascertained immediately that he was dead. Credentials identified the victim as William Starwood.

An hour later a cruising photographer for the *Chicago Express*, responding to a radioed request from his City Room, stopped at the home of Starwood's mother in suburban Park Ridge, where he obtained a faded picture of the dead man.

The *Express* art department did its best to retouch the picture. The result was so bad, however, that the desk held it back until a hole opened up in the racing edition, the final edition of the day, which was shipped to newsstands at 7:30 A.M. for the dubious benefit of horse players anxious to peruse the morning line. Then it ran as a one-column cut adjoining the story of Starwood's death on a back page.

That might have been the end of it—except that when the original photograph was returned to the City Room from the composing room, the picture editor tossed it face up on a stack of other photographs. And a police reporter named Barney Lear happened by . . .

It was Lear's day off. He had lumbered into the City Room to collect his pay check. An immense bearlike man, Barney strolled down an aisle exchanging pleasantries with rewritemen, for whom Lear entertained a vast respect. In his 18 years with the *Express*, Lear had

113

never written a word. Everything he learned, he telephoned or told in person to rewritemen, who transformed Lear's notes into the crisp, succinct, journalistic prose that appeared in print under Lear's byline.

As Lear passed the picture desk, he gazed down at the fuzzy likeness of the late William Starwood. Something about the photograph made Lear pause. He picked up the photograph and studied it.

"Yeah," he said slowly, "it could be."

Photo in hand, Lear walked to Leo Moran, the city editor.

"Leo, who is this guy?"

"William Starwood, a bachelor. Lived alone in an apartment on the Near North Side. Last night he sat around a bar for a few hours and then started home. But a hit-and-run killed him as he crossed a street. Know him?"

"I might. Where'd we get this?"

"From his mother, in Park Ridge. She said her son was an 'investor', whatever that is. What's bugging you?"

"You remember the Abbott case?"

"Sure. Five years ago a society woman named Elvira Abbott was murdered in an apartment hotel. She was found tied to a chair, a bullet in her head, and her wall safe empty."

"Right. Well, you know my memory for faces. And Starwood's face rings a bell. I think this Starwood was a desk clerk at that apartment hotel. And at the time his name wasn't William Starwood. It was William Stull." Lear paused. "Leo," he asked, "will you authorize overtime for me today? And let me return this picture to Starwood's mother, to see if Starwood and Stull are the same man?"

"Go ahead. If a desk clerk at a hotel where an unsolved murder took place has changed his name and blossomed out as an 'investor,' we might have one helluva story. But if you're wrong," Moran added, "your overtime ends as soon as you radio in here to me."

Lear drove out to Park Ridge on the Northwest Expressway. The more he had studied the photograph, the surer he'd become that the man had been William Stull. Lear had particular reason to recall Stull. The day after the murder, Stull had tried unsuccessfully to throw Lear and some other reporters out of the hotel.

Elvira Abbott, the murdered woman, had lived in the hotel alone.

She was estranged from her husband, Harry, who occupied the family mansion in a North Shore suburb. Infidelity had been rumored on both sides of the marriage, but neither party had sought divorce.

Mrs. Abbott was last seen alive at four o'clock on a Sunday afternoon, when she walked outside and dropped a letter into a mailbox on the corner. She could have used a mail chute on her hotel floor, but that had a later pickup. Police surmised that her haste to have the letter delivered was what had led to her death. A gang of hotel burglars had been active in the neighborhood. Elvira Abbott was known to keep a large amount of jewels in her safe. It was theorized that the thieves saw her leave the hotel and assumed she would be gone for some time; and that she surprised the thieves in her apartment when she returned almost immediately.

Her body was found shortly before 10:00 P.M. by her two nieces, Irene and Alice Abbott. Alice was twenty then; Irene was twenty-two. The tired cliché "madcap heiresses" had been applied to them in headlines more than once.

The girls, diminutive and deceptively demure blondes, collected traffic tickets the way some people collect stamps. They thrived on wild champagne parties and formed romantic liaisons with band leaders, athletes, and other minor celebrities. But their Aunt Elvira was fond of the girls; she had given them a key to her apartment, so they could spend a night in town with her whenever they wished.

The coroner reported that Elvira Abbott, shot in the head at close range with a .22, had died between four and five P.M. She had kept a weapon of that caliber in the apartment, but it was missing. Also missing were the jewels in the safe. Elvira had made the job easy for the thieves. An absent-minded woman, she had written the combination on a slip of paper and left it in a desk drawer. Some furniture was overturned, and Elvira had been bound to the chair with belts. The apartment's back door, which led to an alley service entrance, was found open.

The two Abbott girls were questioned and sent home. All members of the Abbott family had alibis for the time of the murder. Alice and Irene had been with a yachting party on Lake Michigan until 9:00 P.M. Elvira's husband, Harry, had been entertaining guests in the suburbs. Elvira died without a will, and Harry inherited her estate. And John

Abbott, father of the girls, was in New York on business. John and Elvira had quarreled many times, mostly because of the way Elvira indulged his daughters when he tried to discipline them by cutting off their allowances.

Of course the Abbott girls had no need for allowances any more. Each on reaching the age of twenty-four had inherited one million dollars from their late paternal grandfather.

Starwood's mother lived in an old but well kept brick bungalow which Lear appraised at about twenty thousand. He parked in the driveway, got out, and rang the front bell.

The woman who answered was tall, thin, and gray-haired.

"Mrs. Starwood? I'm from the *Express*. I've come to return your son's picture."

"Of course." She opened the door. Lear stepped inside and handed her the print.

"Sorry to bother you. But it's our job," Lear said.

"I understand."

"You hear any more from the police about the hit-and-run car?"

"They found it parked a few miles from the accident. They said some juveniles probably stole it for a joy ride." She shook her head. "How terrible . . ."

"This will be hard on you, won't it? If the house is mortgaged—"

"Oh, I'm all right. My son bought the house for me a year ago and paid cash for it. And I have my social security."

"That's good. Sorry, but I have to ask. Was your son ever an apartment hotel desk clerk named William Stull?"

Surprised and angry, the woman snapped, "You have your nerve! Get out, right now."

"Whatever you say. But if you throw me out, I'll come back with detectives. They'll ask the same question. I remember William Stull from the Abbott murder case. That picture looks like Stull to me. And if your name's Stull, your social security records will prove it."

The woman didn't reply for a few moments. She sat on a chair and clenched her fists. Then she said, "I was afraid someone would recognize him, after I gave your man my son's picture. I was upset, I wasn't thinking. A photographer from another paper, the *Journal*, came a few minutes later, but I didn't give him a picture. He asked some questions too. Why can't you reporters leave people alone?"

"Because the Abbott case is still unsolved. People will want to know why your son changed his name—and where he got his money."

"Well, I can't help you. My son was with me the entire afternoon of the murder and we had company. The police checked that at the time. And after he made some money, my son changed his name so he'd never be associated with the Abbott murder again."

"When did he make this money?"

"About six months later. Through an investment. But Bill never discussed his business with me. And when he said he wanted to buy me a house, I just accepted it. At my age, why shouldn't I?"

"Where did your son bank?"

"He didn't. He handled his financial affairs through a stockbroker, Peter Donnell. He's with Darby & Sons. I've never met Mr. Donnell, but he called this morning to express his sympathy. My attorney will go to his office tomorrow, to check on my son's account."

"Your son have any close friends?"

"No man friends. He did have plenty of girls—Bill always was popular with women. But he never stayed with the same girl for long. And he never brought them home to meet me. I think he was serious about a woman only once. He kept her letters, with a ribbon around them, in a little black box. I guess it's still in his apartment. I'll go over there tomorrow and look around."

"When did you last see those letters?"

"About the time," Stull's mother said, "the Abbott woman was murdered."

When Lear walked outside, he found another car parked in the driveway behind his own. The driver, a chunky, bald, middle-aged man, was puffing on a cigar. Lear walked to the second car and said, "Hi, Chester. What brings you here?"

Chester Moon, crime reporter for the *Chicago Journal*, winked and replied, "Come off it, Barney. I'm not blind. I saw that picture in your paper. It's true, isn't it? The so-called William Starwood is really William Stull? The desk clerk at the hotel where Elvira Abbott got hers?"

"There was a resemblance," Lear admitted, "but it's a false lead.

The dead guy was really named Starwood. His mother just showed me his birth certificate. She's all broken up, though, so if I were you I wouldn't disturb her now. If you insist on seeing her, why don't you drop around tomorrow, when she feels better?"

"That's considerate of you. But if you don't mind, I'll check now. Our paper, you know, offered a five-grand reward for the Abbott killer. I'd sure be in trouble if *you* collected that reward." Moon started his car's engine. "I'll back up, pal, so you can pull out. And then I'm going inside."

As Lear's car swung down a ramp and back onto the expressway, Lear reached under the dashboard for a microphone. He made contact with Leo Moran at the *Express* city desk.

"Leo? The mother confirmed that Starwood was William Stull. But we have competition. Chester Moon of the *Journal* spotted the picture too. He walked in to see the mother as I walked out."

"Bad break. Where you going now?"

"First, to Stull's apartment in town. Then I'll call on a stockbroker named Peter Donnell. After that I'll head back to the office. I should check in by twelve thirty."

"Okay. That'll give us plenty of time before deadline. And while you're on the prowl, I'll call the hit-and-run squad again. Anything else?"

"Yeah. If our financial editor's around, let me talk to him."

A moment later the financial editor drawled, "Hi, Barney. How can I help in the war against crime?"

"Can you find out where the Abbott family does its banking?"

"No problem. Harry and John are both stockholders and directors of the Midwest National. No Abbott would dare bank anywhere else."

"Swell. Now, could you get some friend of yours at the bank to do a little snooping?—to see if any of the Abbotts have been making unexplained withdrawals?"

"That request," the financial editor said, "is irregular, immoral and probably illegal. But a vice president over there does owe the *Express* a favor. So I'll see what I can do."

Lear squeezed his car into a parking place on a Near North Side street and entered the vestibule of Stull's apartment building. He pushed the button marked "Superintendent."

The super, a scowling, potbellied man in dungarees and a blue shirt, emerged from a basement apartment. He opened the inner door. Lear displayed his press pass.

"I'm from the *Express*. I wanted to ask about this man Starwood, who was killed by a car last night."

The super said, "Listen, fella. I'm sick and tired of talking about Starwood. You're the fourth guy to come around."

"No kidding. Who were the others?"

"Last night, a detective from hit-and-run. An hour ago, a reporter from the *Journal* named Moon. And after him, an investigator from an insurance company. The investigator talked me into letting him in Starwood's apartment, so why don't you go up to 205 and talk to him? I got other things to do."

Lear hiked up to the second floor. The door to 205 was open. Lear walked in. A dark-haired, broad-shouldered man, about 35 years old, was reclining in a chair, thoughtfully smoking a cigarette. He looked up and smiled.

"Hello, Barney. The super told me Moon had been here earlier. So I figured you'd be along any minute."

The man was Mike O'Brien, investigator for a group of insurance companies that had held policies on Elvira Abbott's life and on the jewels stolen from her safe. For years Lear had been cultivating O'Brien as a source for crime news.

"Hi, Mike. So you saw the picture too."

"Yep. This morning I stole what was left of my *Express* from my six kids, opened it over the breakfast table, and there he was—a dead ringer for William Stull. I'd questioned all the hotel employees at the time and figured this was worth checking. I see you and Moon figured the same."

"Learn anything?"

"From Starwood's papers, only that he did a lot of business with a broker named Peter Donnell. But the super told me that while Starwood had no apparent source of income, he never lacked for cash. And Starwood was highly secretive about his past. Which makes me damn curious to know more about him."

"Well, Starwood *was* Stull. His mother admitted it to me. Mike, when you poked around here, did you spot a black strongbox? Supposedly, Stull had love letters in it."

"No. But the super said this apartment was burglarized a few days ago. The rear door was forced. The super discovered it. Then Starwood walked in, looked around, and said nothing was missing. He told the super not to bother calling the police. But the super said Starwood seemed upset. And isn't *that* a funny set of circumstances?"

O'Brien stubbed out his cigarette. "Our companies," he went on, "took a real beating on the Abbott case. Elvira had a two-hundred-and-fifty thousand dollar policy on her life. Her husband paid the premiums, but Elvira got sore at him and made Alice and Irene her beneficiaries. We can't do much about *that*. But we also insured the missing jewels for two hundred grand more. And from the way things are shaping up, I'm beginning to think Stull knew who got those jewels. His way of life since the murder hints strongly of blackmail."

"It sure does. You talked to the police yet?"

"No, but I will. Also, to the Abbotts. And I want a few words with this stockbroker, Donnell."

"So do I. Let's hit him together." Lear winked. "When we see him, just introduce me as Mr. Lear. That way if he assumes I'm another insurance investigator, it won't be anyone's fault. I have a hunch he'll talk more freely if he doesn't know I'm a reporter."

Nervously, Peter Donnell tapped a cigarette against his wrist. He lit it and leaned back. He was a thin, bespectacled, dapper man, with blond hair and a hairline mustache. Lear and Mike O'Brien sat across Donnell's desk in the Loop brokerage office of Darby & Sons.

"I'm afraid," Donnell confessed, "I knew all along that William Starwood was William Stull. I've known Bill casually since the Korean War. We were in the same outfit. He looked me up after the war and opened a small account. Then a few years ago he walked in here with a bank draft for ten thousand dollars made out to William Starwood. He said he'd received an inheritance and had changed his name."

O'Brien asked, "Didn't that make you suspicious?"

"Of what? I'm a broker, not a policeman. If a man wants to change his name, that's his business. Bill had told me he worked at the hotel where the Abbott woman was murdered. But I had no reason to suspect him of any connection with the crime. And apparently," he added, "neither did you, or the police."

"Stull's mother," Lear said, "claims her son transacted all his personal financial business through your firm."

"That's right. When he needed cash, he'd go to the cashier and draw some from his account. The cash balance varied, of course, depending on how much stock he bought or sold. But after the original ten-thousand deposit, he walked in here the second of each month with another one thousand dollars; so he has deposited twelve thousand each year for the past five years. The only unusual activity occurred when he sold a lot of stock and withdrew a large sum to buy a house for his mother."

"How much in the account now?"

"About two thousand in cash and nine thousand in stocks." Donnell paused. "Bill did say, a few weeks ago, that he hoped to increase his income in the near future. But I have no idea what he meant."

"Well, thanks," Lear said. He rose.

"I'm quite willing to cooperate with you gentlemen," Donnell added. "And with the police. But whatever you do, please don't give my name to the newspapers!"

Lear went back to the *Express*. He sat down with Leo Moran and told the city editor all he had learned to date.

Moran nodded. "We're on to something, all right. The financial editor's pal at the bank just called. He said Irene Abbott has been withdrawing two thousand in cash from her checking account each month. Ever since the time you say Stull began giving his broker a thousand a month. Incidentally, the financial editor told me to warn you. The Abbott girls are developing a reputation in business circles for being pretty sharp with a buck. Apparently, since inheriting their first millions, they've quietly backed several successful ventures."

"Well, we can't admit to the Abbotts that we've been prying into their bank accounts. We'll have to give the tip to the police and then move in."

"It's ticklish, Barney. The Abbotts are an important family. And they all had alibis for Elvira's murder. We checked hit-and-run, by the way. The cops still think a juvenile delinquent drove that car. Their only lead is, the driver tore his right hip trouser pocket on a spring that stuck out of the front seat. It was an old heap and the upholstery was worn. The crime lab found a button and a hunk of cloth on the spring."

"While you sit here and decide how we'll play this," Lear said, "I'll grab lunch."

Lear took his time eating. He returned to his desk and made a few routine phone calls. He was about to dial a friend at Homicide when Leo Moran walked up and said, "Hey, Barney, the managing editor wants to see both of us in his office. Right now."

"What's wrong?"

"The Abbotts are in there with him. The whole clan. They know we're investigating the late William Starwood. And they have some kind of statement to make."

Harry Abbott, the dead woman's husband, chewed stolidly on a dead cigar. He was lean, short, white-haired, and middle-aged, with bushy brows and jutting jaw. His brother John, taller, heavier, and balding, stood beside the managing editor's desk. The Abbott girls, Alice and Irene, sat on a sofa. Irene, the older girl, pulled lazily on a cigarette; Alice, seemingly bored, studied her fingernails.

Lear and Moran took chairs. The managing editor looked at John Abbott, who cleared his throat and said, "Gentlemen, we're here to volunteer information about Elvira Abbott and a desk clerk named William Stull. And then to ask you, in good conscience, not to print it. We've just come from the *Journal*. Mr. Moon and some executives there said they'd abide by your decision."

Lear said, "We are investigating William Stull. But how did you know?"

"I read about his death in your newspaper," Irene put in coolly. "I knew he'd changed his name to Starwood. Later, I called his apartment. The manager said two reporters and an insurance investigator had already been there, asking questions. So Alice and I called our father and Uncle Harry and told them the truth. And we all decided to come up here and tell you."

"What is the truth?"

"Irene and I," Alice said, "have been paying blackmail to Stull for years."

"Your father and your uncle had no knowledge of this?"

"No."

"What hold did Stull have on you girls?"

"I'll explain that," Harry Abbott said. "My wife Elvira and William Stull were lovers." He paused. "I knew that at the time of the murder. Private detectives watched my wife for me, so if she ever sued for divorce I'd have evidence of my own. Elvira's affair with Stull broke up just before the murder. But apparently, Elvira wrote Stull some letters—the usual passionate effusions, plus a lot of intimate information about our whole family, including Alice and Irene. Stull threatened to sell those letters to scandal magazines if the girls didn't pay him off."

"Stull," Irene added, "was shrewd about it. He didn't ask for much. Just a twenty-thousand down payment, when we got the insurance settlement, and two thousand each month thereafter. It might seem a lot to most people, but Alice and I could afford it easily. So to protect the family name, we decided to pay him and not even tell our father or Uncle Harry."

"Stull," Lear said, "only deposited one thousand a month with his broker."

"We gave him two. We don't know what he did with the money."

"If you knew Stull had been your wife's lover," Moran asked Harry Abbott, "why didn't you tell the police?"

"I should have. And after we leave here today I will. But after the police found Stull had no connection with the crime, I saw no reason to expose their relationship. Elvira had become an unstable woman. She drank too much. She developed a string of infatuations for people like Stull—bellboys, lifeguards, and so on. She took an overdose of sleeping pills over one of those affairs. Other times, she had to pay blackmail money herself. John and I hushed most of those incidents up. If her relationship with Stull had been disclosed, it would have opened a Pandora's box of scandal, and dragged all our names through the mud."

John Abbott said, "We can't stop you from printing that William Starwood was actually William Stull, a desk clerk at Elvira's hotel. But we were sure you'd learn Stull was blackmailing the girls. And now that we've told you why they paid him, we ask you to keep that out of your story. If you print it, all you'll do is dirty the name of a woman who has been dead five years, and sell a few extra papers by cashing in on our family troubles."

"I might add," Harry Abbott said genially, "that if you print it, I'll sue you for invasion of privacy, since this has no bearing on my wife's murder whatsoever."

The managing editor looked at Moran. "Well, Leo?"

"It's a reasonable request," Moran conceded. "Despite what you might think, we don't print scandal for scandal's sake. But if there's more to this than you've told us, we'll print the story and risk a suit."

"If that happens," Harry Abbott said, "there won't be a suit."

Lear and Moran rose.

"Incidentally," Lear said, "there's one other possibility. Namely, that the hit-and-run driver who killed Stull did so deliberately."

Irene Abbott looked startled. She asked, "Is there any evidence to support that?"

"Not yet. But if it turns up, all bets we just made here are off."

Lear found Chester Moon in a newspaperman's bar. Moon stared philosophically at a half-empty glass of beer. Lear took a seat beside him and ordered a drink.

"Well, Chester," Lear said, "it looks as if the Abbott family headed us off at the pass."

"Doesn't it, though."

"I see both our papers just printed the same story in the early edition. Three short paragraphs saying Starwood was really Stull. And the cops are checking for a connection with the Abbott murder, but don't expect to find one."

"What," Moon asked guardedly, "did *you* think of the yarn the Abbotts palmed off on our bosses this afternoon?"

"I have reservations."

"So do I. 'Family name,' indeed. Since when did Alice or Irene give a damn about their family name? But then, maybe they've reformed."

"Yeah. I suppose you talked to that stockbroker."

"I did. Boy, did he jump when I told him you were a reporter. But he told me how Stull deposited a grand a month to the account, instead of the two grand Irene admitted paying. You ruined my interview with Stull's mother, by the way. When you left, she was so upset that she wouldn't talk. She hollered yes, her son was Bill Stull; no, she didn't know where he got his money; and if I wanted to find out I should see Donnell. Then she slammed the door."

Lear drained his glass. "I got to hand it to you, Chester. Recognizing that fuzzy halftone in our paper. *I* didn't peg Stull until I saw the original print."

"Class will tell. It was nice of your desk to get a picture, so I could make the indentification in *your* sheet. I don't subscribe to your home delivery edition, but I stop at my newsstand for your racing final every morning."

"Your desk didn't send a photographer to Park Ridge last night?"

"No. As soon as I saw the picture, I checked. But we didn't have a man anywhere near there." Moon paused. "Got any new ideas about the Abbott murder? I have a few. Since we're temporarily blocked by collusion among our respective editors, maybe we can put our heads together and come up with something."

"I do have an idea." Lear paid for his drink and rose. "The next time we get together, we'll kick it around and see if it yelps."

Thoughtfully, Lear walked back to the *Express*. In the photo lab he asked the chief photographer, "You have any guys getting off duty soon who live near Park Ridge?"

"Sam lives near there. He's off at six. Why?"

Lear scrawled a name on a slip of paper. "This is important. I'll send this slip to the library. The library will send you a picture of the man whose name is on here. Make a head-and-shoulders blowup of the guy. Then let Sam off a few minutes early. On his way home have him take the print to a Mrs. William Starwood in Park Ridge. Have her look at it and tell him if she's ever seen the man face-to-face before, and under what circumstances. Then ask Sam to call me at Gus's. I'll be eating supper there."

Lear returned to the City Room. He dialed Mike O'Brien at the insurance investigator's home.

"Mike? Barney Lear. How'd you like to recover a lot of money for your insurance companies. In exchange for an exclusive break on all actions your companies take, assuming my theory is correct."

"It's a deal. I'm in the mood for some good news. I talked to the Abbotts this afternoon, and I guess that William Stull lead is a bust. I see by your first edition that the Abbotts talked to you, too."

"They did. But don't give up yet. I'll stop at your place about eight. And have your hat ready. After we talk, we'll take a little trip."

O'Brien lived in a southern suburb an hour's drive from the Loop. As Barney Lear parked, five of O'Brien's youngsters were romping in the green, treeless yard. O'Brien's wife, holding the sixth child, opened the door for the reporter.

Lear found Mike in a rumpus room partly lined with filing cabinets. O'Brien handed Lear a cold can of beer and settled behind a desk. Lear pulled up a rattan chair.

"What's your theory, Barney?"

"I think," Lear said, taking a swig of beer, "Elvira Abbott committed suicide."

"You're kidding."

"No, I'm not. It makes sense. Mike, when you saw the Abbotts today, did any of them mention that Elvira had tried suicide before? Over a love affair?"

"No," O'Brien replied thoughtfully. "And we had no record of any incident of that sort."

"Naturally. Harry and John Abbott hushed it up. But Elvira and Stull had an affair, and it had just broken up. So suppose Elvira tried suicide again, and this time succeeded? And suppose the Abbott girls went to her apartment that night, found the body, and then rigged everything to make it look like murder? So they could collect Elvira's insurance? Because in Illinois most insurance companies won't pay off on a suicide unless there's a suicide clause in the policy."

"That's true. The policy didn't have a suicide clause, and *our* company certainly wouldn't have paid off. But why would the girls do it? They were due to inherit millions."

"Yeah, but at the time they were still on allowances. And the Abbott girls were smart about money. It would be another year or two before they'd get big dough from the Abbott family. With the insurance settlement they'd get more than a hundred grand each right then and there."

The reporter drank more beer. "It would have been easy, Mike. The girls could have done it in just a few minutes, and then called the cops. Knocked furniture around, tied Elvira's body to the chair, opened the safe, and removed the jewels. The girls stayed in the apartment often enough to know that the combination was in the desk. They could have put the jewels in envelopes addressed to themselves, and dropped them down the mail chute. Or hidden the jewels in their purses. The cops wouldn't subject *them* to a search. That's how I think they got the gun out—in a purse, or hidden on one of their persons."

"It's conceivable," O'Brien admitted. "But how does William Stull fit in?"

"What's the last thing Elvira did? She went out to mail a letter. I think she wrote Stull a suicide note. Then she went back upstairs and shot herself. And once Stull got that note, he figured out quick enough what the Abbott girls had done. That gave him a hold over the girls, something a lot more substantial than supposed slurs on the family name."

"Okay. If it's true, how do we prove it?"

"Simple. We find the suicide note. I think that's what the burglar who broke into Stull's apartment stole. If we find the burglar, your insurance company might get *all* its money back. And I think I know where to find him"

O'Brien rose. "I'll get my hat. Where are we going?"

Lear gazed at the ceiling. "To the detective bureau," he said. "Where you'll be booked for suspicion of William Stull's murder."

O'Brien took a step forward. Lear set the beer can down and hunched his immense shoulders.

"You wouldn't try anything, would you, Mike? With your wife upstairs? And the kids in the yard?"

The insurance investigator didn't reply.

Lear relaxed. "Of course not. Stull went to you with the note, didn't he? He figured it was worth plenty to the insurance companies. But you saw its potentialities for perpetual blackmail. You talked Stull into going along with your scheme. So you and Stull blackmailed the Abbott girls together. That's why Stull got only half the payments. But recently he got greedy; he asked for more. So you stole the suicide note from his apartment first. Then you ran him down with a car. And your plan would have worked, if our photographer hadn't picked up Stull's picture."

Casually, the reporter lit a cigarette. "That," he went on, "scared you. So you went to Stull's apartment this morning to see if anyone would show up, checking the resemblance between Stull and Starwood. Moon beat you there, and then I came along. After we left the broker's, you must have called the Abbott girls and told them Moon and I were on the trail. You ordered them to call their father and their uncle immediately with the fake yarn about being blackmailed over Elvira's love letters, so they could all rush to the newspapers and try to kill the probe before matters got out of hand. You figured that after the cops made a routine check, you'd be free to go on blackmailing the girls."

"You can't prove any of that, Barney."

"Can't I? How come, Mike, you knew the *Express* ran Starwood's picture? You said you saw the picture over breakfast at home. But Chester Moon reminded me this evening that the racing final, the only edition in which the picture appeared, is obtainable only at newsstands."

"I made a mistake. It must have been the racing final I saw it in."

"You sure did make a mistake. Mike, you knew as early as last night that the *Express* had Stull's picture. After you killed Stull, you drove out in your own car to his mother's house in Park Ridge. You posed as a *Journal* photographer. One of our guys just showed her your picture. She made a positive identification. I think you drove out there to learn if Stull had told her anything about you. If he had, you probably intended to murder her too. Lucky for her that she didn't know anything. But she did tell you a man from the *Express* had obtained her son's photograph."

Lear rose. "You'll have a tough time explaining your presence in Park Ridge *before* the story of Stull's death was even out. As for proof—those pants you tore while you drove the murder car are probably in this house somewhere. I think we'll find Elvira's love letters and suicide note here too. Some guys from Homicide are parked down the street, waiting for us to walk out, so they can begin their search. Anyhow, I don't think the Abbott girls will cover for you once they learn you're a murderer. So let's go."

Twenty minutes later Lear called his city desk on his car radio.

"Leo? All wrapped up. O'Brien began confessing as soon as we walked outside and the cops moved in. He even dug up the suicide note—he'd buried the strongbox in the back yard. I'll stop at the nearest drug store and telephone the details to rewrite. We'll make the three-star edition easy."

"Great. You plan to claim the reward the *Journal* offered for Elvira Abbott's killer?"

"I could try." Lear chuckled. "But since it was suicide, not murder, the *Journal* will probably renege on the reward. But I told the cops to put in a claim anyhow. And if the *Journal* pays off, the money will go to O'Brien's wife and six kids. They'll need it a lot more than I will."

MALICE AT
THE MIKE

JON L. BREEN

If you ever lived in the Middle West, I know you'd remember Buzz Rizzleston. Certainly his name, and probably his high, rather screechy voice—that is, if you ever listened to the radio, even if you didn't care about baseball. Because if you ever turned the dial on your radio, looking for Amos 'n' Andy or whatever, hearing Buzz's voice would be sure to make you pause for a moment.

You might have said, how'd a guy who sounds like that ever get to work in radio, the medium of Milton Cross and Lowell Thomas and Harry Von Zell? But then you'd stop a minute to marvel, and there was something about that voice that would get a hold on you, make you want to listen, even if as far as you were concerned Babe Ruth sounded like a candy bar.

Yeah, it was quite a voice, and you could always hear him, because his home station, WBB in Chicago, was a 50,000-watter, and his baseball broadcasts were on a dozen other smaller stations scattered all over the Midwest.

Buzz Rizzleston was an acquaintance of mine and today I want to tell you about sitting in a radio booth with him one day in the late 1960's, during the last season he worked the games on WBB, though he didn't know at the time it was his last year. My name is Ed Gorgon and I'm a major-league umpire of some years' standing. But at that particular time I wasn't doing any umpiring because I had a badly sprained ankle and wasn't getting around too well.

Buzz called me up and invited me to sit in the booth with him for a Saturday afternoon game—first he invited me, then he begged me.

"I need your help, Ed," Buzz said. "Somebody's trying to kill me."

Under the circumstances I could hardly turn him down.

How many people do you think it takes to broadcast a baseball game? Let me set that day's scene for you, and maybe you'll be surprised.

The broadcast booth is a sort of partitioned-off area of the press box, containing a long table with folding chairs. The Chicago Hoggers have a three-man broadcasting team: there's old Buzz himself, a skinny, bald, and by this time rather frail-looking guy of seventy (remember he dates back to the days of Graham MacNamee), a real loud but at the same time super-casual dresser. Today he's wearing a blood-red sweatshirt, baggy denim trousers with paint stains on them, and comfortable-looking brown sandals with bright Day-Glo orange socks.

Then there's Alex Rhodes, a crew-cut three-hundred pounder who has been Buzz's Number Two man for about twenty years. Alex dresses more conventionally but still more for comfort than appearance (how much can you do at 300 pounds in that direction anyway?). Alex is a very smooth and very professional announcer, though his deep and beautifully modulated bass seems more likely to lull fans to sleep than to fire them up to get out to the ball park.

The third member of the team is Billy Conover, until a couple of years ago the star second baseman of the Chicago Hoggers. I know what they say about ex-athletes turning sportscasters, but this kid is really taking it seriously: a brief case full of preparation, an on-the-air delivery that would make Howard Cosell jealous, and, perhaps most important, a smart junior-executive wardrobe. I might mention here that the owner of the Chicago Hoggers owns a chain of clothing stores, which must have made it hard for him to put up with Buzz Rizzleston and Alex Rhodes all those years.

But that's not all. There's Doug Peck, the engineer, and Ross Bodgner, a kid whose job is to get late scores of other games off the Western Union teletype, and Doc Spoon, an old crony of Rizzleston's (and his personal physician), who keeps score for Buzz and also keeps a body between him and his announcing partners.

All the broadcasters, you see, hate each other. Buzz thinks one of his play-by-play men is probably the author of the anonymous notes, which he showed me before the game when he asked me to watch for the threat on his life which he is sure will take place at any moment.

As the game is about to commence, we are seated in this order along the table, overlooking the field:

```
D   R   E   B   D   A   E   B
O   O   D   U   O   L   M   I
U   S       Z   C   E   M   L
G   S       Z       X   A   L
                            Y
```

I haven't mentioned Emma. She's Alex Rhodes' wife, an angular, stern-faced battle-ax who keeps score for Alex. Billy Conover keeps his own scorecard. That's right, sports fans, they hate each other so much they won't even use the same scorecard. Fortunately, Emma, Doc, and Billy are on good enough terms to get together on things, so their three scorecards agree.

Billy Conover is last one into the booth, because he has to do the pregame interview. He comes rushing in just as Alex Rhodes is announcing the lineups for the game between the Hoggers and the L.A. Surfers. He pours himself a quick cup of coffee from the pot sitting on a little hotplate. Billy drinks it black.

At the end of the lineups we stand for the National Anthem. It's quite an engineering feat for Alex to heave himself out of his chair, but he makes it in time for "what so proudly we hailed." I notice out of the corner of my eye that Billy fidgets during the anthem—Billy's a very nervous, high-strung type. And a hungry one, just as he was as a ballplayer.

Baseball announcers guard their innings like they were the crown jewels. Under the setup used by the Chicago Hoggers this year, Buzz Rizzleston opens, doing innings one and two; Alex Rhodes has innings three and four; Buzz comes back for five; Billy Conover gets the sixth, his one chance to shine; Alex does seven; and Buzz does eight and nine. In case of extra innings Buzz goes on till he gets tired and then gives it to Alex. Billy is out of the picture by now, waiting in the clubhouse to do his postgame interview.

And I should add that Buzz is allowed to jump in on the other guys' innings to put in whatever sage comment happens to occur to him, but no one can open his mouth during Buzz's innings, unless it's something really important. Like if the press box is on fire.

So Alex, with his eyelids looking sleepy, says into his mike, "Pitcher Crib Jagger takes the last of his warmups, and here for the play-by-play, in his thirty-ninth year as voice of the Hoggers, the old philosopher himself, Buzz Rizzleston." That's a set introduction, written into his contract.

Alex leans back into his chair, ready to shut up for two innings, and Buzz leans forward, looks lovingly at the microphone, and goes to work. I wonder if the folks who listened to Buzz back in 1930 thought it was possible his voice could ever get worse. It was possible.

"Hi, folks. It's a great day for baseball, sun's high in the sky, and a fine pitching duel's in prospect. Crib Jagger is five and one on the year so far. First batter's up there now, Denny Judson, his name, shortstop of the Surfers. A .249 hitter. First pitch low for ball one.

"Guest in the booth with us today, Ed Gorgon, a great umpire. How's the ankle, Ed?"

I don't answer. Even a guest in the booth doesn't encroach on Buzz Rizzleston's innings.

"Hey, that's great. Be out there again any day. One of the great umps. Ball two. Doc Spoon here with us today, keeping the stats for us, doing a fine job, as always. Doc's been with us since 1944. Little grounder to short. Up with it little Jose what's-his-name, throws him out. One down.

"Marty Marion used to make that play. All the great infielders used to make that play. Make it look easy. Heck, it is easy. I coulda made that one myself, right, Doc?

"Smith the batter. What's he hitting? .300, huh? Way over his head. He'll be .240 by July fourth. We've seen some great morning glories in our day, haven't we, Doc? Spring phenoms, can't take the guff. Holds that bat like he knew what it was, what it can do. A confident grip. Lou Gehrig used to hold his bat that way, all the great hitters. But this guy's fooling. He's no hitter. First pitch a ball.

"Wowee! The next one's a line drive to Crane at second. What a play! What a second baseman! Best guy at second sack the Hoggers have had in twenty years. I think my broadcast partner Billy Conover will be the first to agree he couldn't have made that play with a fishnet. Billy Conover never saw the day he could make that play. Two down.

"It's a great day for baseball, fans. Eddie Gorgon here beside me, one of the great umps. Better not second-guess the arbiters today, not with Ed here. You tell me if it's a bum call, Ed, and I'll lay it on 'em, but you say the word first. For the Hoggers, against the Hoggers, whatever. They blow one, Ed, and you tell me, and I'll tell the world. We respect you, Ed. We all respect you. A man who's done his job long and well deserves our respect. Many of the young have no respect today, Ed Gorgon, and that's the trouble with this world.

"The third guy gets a base hit to right. First hit of the ball game off Crib Jagger. I don't know if he has his stuff today. That was a sharply hit ball. One on, one out. What's that, Doc? That's right, two men out, the roller to Jose and the hard shot to Crane.

"What a play that was, Billy Conover. Eat your heart out, like they say. Billy knows I'm just kidding, and anyway we can't all be great glove men. When I played ball back in high school I was a crummy fielder. That's why I became an announcer, so I could be a pro at something. Some guys never get to be pros at anything.

"Has Jagger got a three-ball no-strike count on that guy? Holy mackerel, Doc! Where's his control? I think it's pretty well recognized, even in the Hoggers' front office, that it was one crummy deal that brought Jagger to the Hoggers from St. Louis in exchange for two regulars who play every day. If we'd had those two regulars last year, Doc, it would have been a World Series check, but that's water under the dam, ain't it?

"Good greasy gravy! It's ball four. That's Hollingsworth, the Surfer first sacker going down to first. At least he can't hurt us with the long ball, but, Doc, it's two men on now with only one out. No, check that, it's two out. Roller to Jose and smash to Crane. So, let's see, it's McMillen on second now, a good runner. How many steals last year, Doc? No steals? Well, he was a good runner when he came up in '53. I remember that well.

"In sixty years of watching baseball I've seen days as nice as this, but certainly none nicer, have you, Doc? It's a great day for watching baseball.

"Well, look at that! A check-swing roller back to the box off the bat of the Surfer hitter, and Jagger makes the easy play to first. He got out of it. Dumb luck. For the Surfers, no runs, one hit, no Hogger errors, and two men left, and the Hoggers come to bat in the first. Let's get some runs, 'cause this guy gonna need all he can get!"

As I sit watching the game and listening to Buzz Rizzleston describe it, I think back to what he told me the night before. "Anonymous notes, Ed. Threats. Here, look at this one."

All in block capitals on plain white paper, it says:

> If you want to live do it away from the Hoggers.

And another:

> Hang up that mike or you're a dead man.

And a third:

> Saturday you die. Pick your inning.

"During the ball game, Buzz?"

"Yeah, I guess so. Sick, isn't it, Ed? I mean it's sick. I mean that Rhodes or Conover should want my job so badly. It's no secret that Mr. Hammond intends to cut back to a two-man team next year. And I'm not going to retire, Ed, and obviously Hammond wants me in there. So it's between Rhodes and Conover.

"One of them's going to try to kill me Saturday, Ed, during the game. Only time they could get close enough to me—that is, if it happens during the game—nobody but those two in the booth are close enough to me. Do you see?"

"But how, Buzz? How can they do it without being seen?"

"I don't know. That's what has me worried. Poison? All I'll drink during the game is coffee, and Doc makes that—and I can trust Doc. I just put a little non-dairy creamer in it. Oh, and I take my pills. I have to. But Doc has those. They can't get to 'em. So how will they do it, Ed? How could they be so small?

"I'm going to be worried during that game tomorrow, Ed. Not so you'll notice, but I'll be really worried. I'll feel better if you're there, though. Can you be there?"

So here I am. Through the early innings I notice that Buzz has taken a few pills, provided by Doc Spoon, with water out of the cooler next to Ross Bodgner's teletype. Everybody's been drinking out of that water cooler, and as I watch Ross hand Buzz the water I see no chance for slipping something in the water, water being a poor vehicle for poison anyway, unless the poison is completely tasteless and invisible.

By the end of the fifth inning only Buzz and I of the booth's occupants have abstained from the frequently replenished coffee pot. They all seem to drink it black, however, and the jar of powdered cream substitute stands unused next to Buzz's microphone.

Buzz doesn't sound like worry has affected his delivery and he could get back in the game at a half-moment's notice—during another guy's inning.

At the completion of the beer commercial between innings five and six, Alex Rhodes intones, "And now for the play-by-play of the next inning, that all-time Hogger great, Billy Conover."

"Thanks, Alex. We go to the top of the sixth, no score. Crib Jagger has held the Surfers to three hits. Crib's not the fastest we've seen him today, but he's getting beautiful action on his breaking ball. Mark Smith the batter, O for two, a line drive right to the second baseman Crane and a fly to center.

"The first pitch is a fast ball on the outside corner for strike one. Mark Smith told me before the game he's using a lighter bat for quickness, but giving up some control that way. You have to give up something to get something.

"The next pitch, a breaking ball low for ball one. One and one. Jagger gets it back, looks in to get the sign. Working quickly now, he winds up and here's the pitch. A smash to short, tough play for Gomez, who has to go deep. His throw's a little low, Anderson stretches . . . *SAFE*, says the umpire, as the throw pulls Anderson off the bag. Anderson is hot! He thought he got him! He and first-base umpire Fred Sims are at it nose to nose."

"What about it, Ed?" Buzz piped up. "Was he safe?"

"I can't question another umpire's judgment, Buzz."

"Well, I can. He was out! Anderson's foot was on the bag. He came off, but only after he'd made the play. That was the worst call I've ever seen!"

"Bad call or not," Billy Conover says, "the runner Smith stays at first, and it'll go as an error on Gomez, whose throw pulled Anderson off the bag."

"It didn't, it didn't! There's no justice in this world if Smith is in," Buzz screeches.

"Well, there's no justice then. I can tell you these umpires are more often right than wrong. That's my observation as a player."

"The dumb jock!" Buzz mutters, off mike.

Billy Conover tries to get on with the game. "Next up is McMillen. Singled in the first, then struck out. One for two."

"Umpires are human just like anybody else," Buzz says. "I'm sure you'd be the first to admit that, wouldn't you, Ed?"

"The first pitch is a little low—"

"If an umpire could just admit his mistakes, like the rest of us. That's the thing."

"Jagger says his breaking ball this year is—"

"I admit it when I get the count wrong, don't I, Doc? Why, I'll bet in my years of broadcasting I've made as many as half a dozen mistakes. You can attest to that, Doc."

As this goes on, Billy Conover is getting understandably nettled. I don't hear many play-by-play men work in my job, being down on the field most of the time, but he sounds like a good one to me, especially in view of the lack of support he gets from his senior colleague. This is his only inning, and he can't even talk uninterrupted.

"The count now is two balls and no strikes on McMillen. Chance for a double play here, as McMillen is slow getting down the line—"

"He could run in his day, couldn't he, Doc? Back in the fifties."

"The next pitch, swung on and tapped weakly down to second. Crane goes to Gomez for one, back to Anderson—"

"They got two! Great job by Crane starting that double play."

Fury is written all over Billy Conover's face. He picks up a press release in front of him, wads it up, throws it point-blank at Buzz Rizzleston, gets up, and stalks out of the booth.

"Ed!" Buzz screams. "Ed," he tells the whole Middle West, "he tried to kill me, Ed. You saw him! That kid tried to kill me!"

I can imagine what that must have sounded like to all the baseball fans listening, who generally go elsewhere for the kind of dramatics Buzz is providing. I also wonder what Paul Hammond, the Hoggers' clothing-store-magnate-owner, thinks of all this, if he's listening up in his box. The next question: will some little men in white coats be stealing into the booth in a moment to take the old philosopher Buzz Rizzleston away?

But Buzz recovers quickly.

He chuckles into the mike, "Well, folks, our colleague Billy Conover has retired for the day. I know you remember what a temper

Billy used to have as a player, and he never quite overcame it, isn't that right, Doc? But he'll be a fine announcer one day, improving all the time. He'll be a good one. Maybe not with the Hoggers, though."

A little chuckle. "Our apologies if we got a little excited, nerves a little on edge today, for reasons you folks wouldn't know anything about. We have to do a job no matter how we feel, no matter what's going on or what's going through our minds. Right, Doc?

"Two out, and the big tall kid up there. And it's a three-and-two count. Did I mention Ed Gorgon is with us today?"

Yeah, Ed's in the booth today and mighty uncomfortable. The engineer Doug Peck has poured himself a cup of coffee, and I decide I could use a little, too. I pour a cup and reach for the jar of cream substitute. As I reach for it, Buzz waves his arms like a damn goony bird, yelling, "Strike three! What a pitch!" He knocks the jar out of my hand and onto the floor, the powder spilling all over the desk and the floor around me.

It's at this point that a small light-bulb, invisible to the naked eye, appears over old Ed's head. When Buzz breaks for the commercial I whisper in his ear, "You know, I think that jar of creamer ought to be analyzed."

"Arsenic?" says Buzz Rizzleston.

"Yeah, mixed in with the powder. Enough to kill." I'm sitting in his apartment, high over the lakefront, that same evening, my bad ankle propped up on a footstool. He lives alone.

"Arsenic. Well, I guess I was right. You've been to the police on this?"

"Sure. I have lots of police friends."

"Arsenic. No kidding. Should I call the papers?"

"The papers?"

"I think the papers should know somebody on my own broadcasting team tried to kill me."

"Who could have got to that jar of creamer, Buzz?"

"Any of them, Ed. Any of them. But Doc is out and so are Ross and Doug. No motive there. It's got to be either Billy Conover or Rhodes or Rhodes's wife. That dame always did hate my guts. I'd pick Conover, though. I've always tried to help him, break him in, give him the benefit of my experience. But he always resented it, Ed. You saw how he acted today. I never saw such hate in a kid's face as I saw in his. It scared me, Ed.''

"But he's young and got a future, Buzz. Anybody could tell he's a natural broadcaster, and he seems to do his homework. Besides, why make a scene like that and draw attention to himself if he knew he'd poisoned the creamer and would get you that way?''

Buzz shrugs. "His temper. He's always had a terrible temper, Ed. But I suppose you're right. It was probably Alex or Emma.''

We pause for a minute. "Seems like I almost got the poison meant for you, Buzz.''

"That was sure lucky, wasn't it? You see, the one who did it knew I was the only one of that crew who didn't drink my coffee black. They didn't figure on you being in the booth. Spoiled everything for them. Lucky how it turned out.''

"Very lucky. Buzz, put yourelf in the murderer's place. If the wrong guy started to take the poison, what would you do?''

"That's a tough one, Ed. If I could, I suppose I'd—''

"Knock it out of his hand?'' I said.

"Well, yeah, right. But I knocked it out of your hand, Ed, so the murderer didn't have to.''

"Very lucky. And very convenient, wasn't it?''

"That was a great pitch Jagger threw. I got excited. After all these years the old man can still get excited about baseball, Ed. It's a great game, isn't it?''

"The greatest game in the world.''

"So what are your police friends doing about this attempt at killing me, Ed? They haven't been around to talk to me yet.''

"They won't be doing much, Buzz. I explained the whole thing to them.''

Buzz doesn't answer. He stands with his back to me.

"What were you planning, Buzz? How were you going to call attention to the arsenic in the creamer without actually taking some yourself? Certainly you didn't plan it to happen as awkwardly as it did?

"The giveaway should have been when you seemed to pass over the creamer as a possible vehicle for the poison. How could you miss it? But you knew I'd pick it up—you wanted me to. Did you think I was smart enough to figure out where the poison was and yet too dumb to figure out that you were the one who must have put it there?

"And did you really think you could save your job by writing those notes to yourself and then poisoning the creamer to throw suspicion on your fellow announcers? Did you really think that could work, Buzz?"

He finished out the year, but as I say it was his last. Now Billy Conover is the voice of the Hoggers, and Alex Rhodes is still Number Two. He doesn't seem to mind. They even use the same scorecard.

BEFORE HE KILLS

RAY RUSSELL

Although it was a typically sticky Chicago summer day, temperature in the high nineties, street asphalt melting into lava, humidity steamy enough to wilt steel, to say nothing of executive shirt collars, the sweat streaming from Dr. David Gorman was caused more by anxiety than by the heat. Moments after his patient left his air-conditioned Rush Street office, he was on the phone, hurriedly dialing the police.

Gorman was a man of small, slight build, who looked even younger than his twenty-nine years. Ordinarily, he didn't see patients on Saturday, but this had been an emergency. The man was desperate, near the edge, he had called the answering service three times before the doctor had been able to return his call and make a four o'clock appointment.

When the police station answered, Dr. Gorman calmly gave his name and address and identified himself as a psychiatrist. Then he said, "In one hour, a patient of mine is going to kill somebody."

"What's your patient's name?" asked the voice at the other end of the line.

"That's just it, I don't know."

"Do you know his address?"

"No—"

"Sir, there's really nothing much we can do. In the first place, no crime has been committed. In the second place—"

"Do you still have a man named Ross there?"

"Detective Lieutenant Ross is with the department, yes."

"I know him, he's a personal friend, please let me speak to him."

"All right, sir. I'll try to reach him if he's on duty. Hold on."

Ross was not exactly a personal friend, but Dr. Gorman felt the white lie was justified in the face of official apathy. A year before, while on duty at Wesley Memorial Hospital, the doctor had talked a teenage girl out of jumping from a ledge. She was pregnant, unmarried, and the daughter of Lieutenant Ross.

Ross came on the line; Dr. Gorman identified himself and restated his present problem.

"Of course I'll do all I can," said Ross, but his voice dripped doubt. "I can't understand why you don't know your own patient's name."

"He's been coming to me for eight weeks now, and he's been using the name Joel Grant. It never occurred to me that it wasn't his real name. But just now, as he left my office, he told me he's been using an alias all the time. I checked the phone book, and there's no Joel Grant listed. Everything he gave me at our first session, name, phone number, address, they were all false."

"But what about his checks? How do you mail his bill?"

"Look, I'm just starting to set up private practice. I'm alone here. To keep my overhead down, I don't have a receptionist and I don't use a billing procedure. My patients pay me at the end of each visit. Most of them pay by check, of course, but Grant—or whatever his name is—pays cash, and I write him a receipt."

"All right, Dr. Gorman, we'll need a description of the man, but first you better tell me who he's going to kill."

"His ex-wife. She's remarried."

"Her name?"

"Lola. He never uses her last name, and even 'Lola' may be false."

"Has he ever said where she lives?"

"No."

"You're sure?"

"Positive."

"Christ. All right, Doctor, what's his description?"

"Medium height, medium build . . ."

"Can you be a little more specific?"

"About five ten or eleven, maybe one forty."

"Age?"

"He gave his age as 37, and that could be about right."

"Color, hair, eyes?"

"I don't know."

"What?"

"He always wears a cap. Very short sideburns. The little I can see of his hair seems to be sort of brownish . . ."

"Sort of brownish."

"But for all I know he may be bald."

"Eyes?"

"Dark sunglasses. Never takes them off."

"Cap, dark glasses, isn't that a little odd? Inside?

"It's part of his *problem*. I could explain it in detail but we haven't *time!*"

"What was he wearing today, besides the cap and glasses?"

"Look, shouldn't you be *doing something?*"

"What would you suggest, Doctor? You haven't told me anything we can use yet. Now what was he wearing?"

"A checked jacket. Big loud checks, blue on green. Gray slacks. Black socks, I think. Gray suede slip-on shoes, loafers, that sort of thing."

"Shirt?"

"Kind of a pearl-gray button-down, I think. No tie."

"Any distinguishing marks? Scars? Tattoos? Broken nose? Anything?"

"Nothing like that."

"Anything about the teeth? Visible gold fillings? Dentures maybe?"

"I don't think he wears dentures."

"A cauc, I suppose?"

"What?"

"Caucasian."

"Yes, he's white."

"Mannerisms? Quirks? Tics? Habits?"

"Frowns a lot, very deep frown lines above the nose, but I can't think of anything else. Smokes non-filters, Camels I think. Seems to be a film buff . . . Listen, we've got to *stop* this man!"

"*What* man? I understand your impatience, but we don't know anything about him. Another officer is checking out other possible name combinations, but meanwhile all I can do is ask questions. What about his voice? Foreign accent? Lisp? Hoarseness?"

"Nothing along those lines. The accent—well, I'm no expert at that—but I guess you'd call it Midwestern."

"So." Ross audibly took a deep breath. "We have a male Caucasian we think is 37, five ten or eleven, one forty, name unknown, address unknown, color of eyes unknown, hair unknown, may even be bald, smokes Camels, and according to you he's going to kill a woman whose first name *may* be Lola, last name and address unknown."

"That's about it."

"What makes you think he's going to kill this woman?"

"He told me."

"You believe everything your patients tell you?"

"Of course not. But I've been working with this man for eight weeks, and I think I can detect when he's fantasizing. He told me this afternoon would be his last visit, he felt it wasn't doing him any good, the only way to solve his problem was to kill Lola."

"Did you try to talk him out of it?"

"I spent the whole *hour* trying to talk him out of it. I even told him it was within my power to have him forcibly hospitalized for seventy-two hours and held for observation. He started to talk about the doctor-patient relationship and all that, and I told him that we were not exactly under the seal of the confessional, I'm not a priest and it's not the same thing . . ."

"Go on. What happened then?"

"I started to reach for the phone to call for assistance. That's when he pulled the gun on me."

"What kind of gun?"

"How should I know? A big . . . black . . . *gun*. Told me he'd blow my head off if I touched the phone."

"What did you do then?"

"Kept my hand off the phone, of course. And that's just about when he got up and walked to the door. He smiled at me. 'You tried, Doc,' he said. 'We both tried, but it's no good. I've got to solve this my way. You can tell the police if you like, after I walk out of here, but you'll just be wasting your breath. My name isn't Joel Grant. One hour from now, that bitch will be dead. They'll never grab me in time.'"

"I'm afraid he may be right, Doctor. While we've been talking, one of our men has been checking other possible names in the phone book. Also Evanston, Oak Park, the works. Grant Joel, Joseph Grant, Grant Josephs, Grant Josephson, Joel Granville, and so on. When people use a phony name, they sometimes choose one that's a form of their own. But that seems to be a dead end. What kind of car does he drive?"

"No idea."

"He left your office how long ago, five minutes?"

"About that."

"If he's driving, he could be miles away by now, in any direction."

"I guess he could."

"Doctor, is there *anything* else you can tell me about him? Any little thing he may have said, at any time, that might give us some idea where he lives or where this Lola may live?"

"I'm trying to think . . ."

"Anything at all."

"No. No, there's nothing."

From the other end of the line came a long wordless sound of frustration.

Most people called him Mac. He hated the pompous first name his parents had saddled him with. His lack of top hair did not detract too much from the rugged good looks of his face—it may have emphasized those looks. His eyes were gray. His flashy checked jacket was now folded neatly in the trunk of his car, next to the cap, the sunglasses and the gun. In his shirtsleeves he drove at a steady thirty m.p.h. The car was a deep green four door with white sidewall tires.

He wasn't thirty-seven, he was forty-two. But he had been thirty-seven when he married her. She had been twenty-three. The fourteen-year difference didn't seem to matter—at first. But then, little by little, it started. She began calling him her "old man." He told her to stop it, he wasn't old, and anyway, "old man" meant father. She told her it didn't mean that anymore, it just meant husband or guy. He wasn't buying that. And then kidding him about his bald head, rubbing it and all that, even in public. "I think it's sexy," she insisted, but he wasn't buying that either.

And that first awful night when he had been unable to make love to her. That was bad enough, but then she had to say it was all right, don't let it bug you darling, you've got to expect that every now and then at your age.

At your age!

It began to happen more frequently. She suggested he see a doctor. He refused. There was nothing wrong with him, he'd been perfectly fine until he married her, it was her fault, she was doing it to him!

And he could prove it. By going to other women.

But even then her influence seemed to reach out and follow him into strange beds and unman him.

The divorce. Her new husband. That young creep.

And still she was doing it to him! Even now! Sending out her curse, like some witch, striking him at the core of his manhood.

But all that would stop very soon. It would stop tonight. Even she couldn't reach out to him from the grave.

Dr. Gorman, impelled by what can only be called inspiration, looked for a name in the Chicago phone directory. When he found it, his heart contracted. He sucked air into his mouth through clenched teeth and began to dial the number. He was nervous, his hands were wet, he made a mistake, hung up, began again. At the other end, the phone rang and rang. Ten times, eleven, twelve. No answer. He hung up and dialled the police once more, asking for Lieutenant Ross. There was some delay in getting through to him, and Dr. Gorman cursed under his breath.

Finally: "Homicide, Ross."

"Dr. Gorman again, Lieutenant."

"Yes, Doctor. Something new?"

"Can you get us a warrant to search an apartment?"

"Whose apartment? Why?"

"A man named—well, I think I stand a better chance of convincing you if I let you tell me his name. There's a thing we sometimes do in my profession, it's called word association. Now, I want you to tell me the first name that pops into your mind when I say *Joel.*"

"McCrea, the old time cowboy actor."

"Good. Now how about when I say *Grant*?"

"Cary Grant."

"That was my first thought, too, but it didn't work. Try again."

"Grant's Tomb?"

"Very good."

"What's very good?"

"Didn't you tell me that when people make up false names, they often select a form of their real name? I thought about that quite a lot, and then it hit me. I checked the phone book. There *is* a listing—and only one."

"Only one what?"

"Ulysses McCrea. I called his number and got no answer. He's not home. Lieutenant, I think he's our man!"

"But a judge won't sign a search warrant on a slim thing like that."

"Not even on the strength of my expert opinion, as a psychiatrist, that a man named Ulysses McCrea, looking for an alias, stands an excellent chance of choosing the name Joel Grant?"

Ross hesitated for only a second. "All right, we can try. I'll pick you up at your office in a few minutes. Now what's this Ulysses McCrea's address?"

That young headshrinker. What does he know? Fresh out of school. Wet behind the ears. Trying to get me to say it's all something in my head, something I'm doing to myself. When I know she's the one.

Her creep husband is out of town. I checked. A concert. Concert they call it. Long-haired guitar-playing creep. Like to see his creep face when he comes home and finds her with bullet holes in her, all over, in her pretty head and everywhere else.

Ulysses McCrea braked for a red light. He took the opportunity to look at his watch. Plenty of time. Fifteen minutes. No need to speed. In fifteen minutes it would be six o'clock, and she would be dead.

Six o'clock, the exact hour McCrea married her, on this very date in this very month. A quickie wedding in a Vegas marriage-mill.

The light turned green, and he drove on.

"Happy anniversary, my dear," he murmured. He repeated it over and over again as he drover closer and closer to her home.

* * *

Detective Lieutenant William Ross, fifty-one, was an enormous man, well over six-feet tall, nothing but muscle from the chin down. Hands like iron gauntlets. When he pounded on a door with one of those giant fists, the sound was thick with authority and menace. He was pounding now, on the door of McCrea's apartment.

He had picked up Dr. Gorman at his office. On their way to Judge Pierson's Lake Shore Drive home, the doctor had asked Ross about his daughter. Ross reported that she was happily married to her child's young father, now safely out of the Army, and the baby had turned out to be a large, healthy boy, named William after his grandfather.

Judge Daniel Edgar Pierson, a white-haired antique with a Mount Rushmore face, had done a poor job of concealing his distrust of psychiatry and its practitioners. His signing of the search warrant was due largely to his fanatical devotion to law-and-order-at-almost-any-price and his love affair with the romantic ideal of preventive detention. ("That's why I picked him," Ross later confided to the doctor.) Even so, his signature had been obtained only after considerable conversation, during which the clock relentlessly ticked toward the death of Lola.

"Police officers! Open up!" Ross shouted outside McCrea's Cedar Street door.

When there was no reply, his uniformed assistant sprung the lock. The two policemen and Dr. Gorman entered the apartment and clicked on the lights.

The doctor went straight for the living room telephone, in search of a personal notebook of phone numbers. He found none, but Ross and the other officer called his attention to a mound of stubbed-out Camels in an ashtray. "Looks more and more like he's your boy," Ross admitted. "That Joel-McCrea connection of yours was quite a brainstorm. Specially at your age. I'm old enough to remember Joel McCrea in pictures, but you're too young."

Dr. Gorman strode purposefully toward the bedroom, saying over his shoulder, "I put the two together because I'm a bit of a film buff, myself, like my patient. Joel McCrea wasn't only a cowboy actor, by the way. He was very good in sophisticated comedy. Ever see him in *The More the Merrier*, 1943? Or *Sullivan's Travels*, 1942?" The police officers followed him into the bedroom.

There was another phone on the bedroom night table, and, in a drawer, the little book they sought. It was bound in red imitation leather, with the initials U.M. embossed on the cover. Quickly but carefully, the doctor turned the pages, while Ross looked over his shoulder. Page after page of names and phone numbers, no addresses.

When the doctor had turned the last page, Ross said, "About six dozen names, twenty of them women, not one of them Lola. Well, give me the book and I'll phone every one of the women until I find his ex-wife." He looked at his watch. "Time is running out."

The uniformed officer said, "Lieutenant, look," and swung the bedroom door closed. It was covered by an enormous poster, one of those mail order blow-ups made from a snapshot. A beautiful blonde girl, in her twenties, displaying her fine young body in an exceptionally brief bikini. Ulysses McCrea had used the poster as a dartboard. There were darts in her face, both breasts, navel, and pubic area. "Lola," said Ross. "Your boy is a real sickie, all right. Well, let's get started calling those women. All twenty of them." He reached for the phone.

"Wait," said Dr. Gorman, who had begun to leaf through the book again. "I don't think we'll have to call all of them. Just this one."

"This Frazier woman? Why?"

"No time to explain."

"All right, your hunches have played off pretty good so far." Ross dialled the number and waited. Then his face darkened and he said, "*Damn* it!"

He handed to phone to Dr. Gorman. The doctor heard the small recorded voice in the earpiece: "You have dialled a disconnected number. Please—"

Ross slammed down the phone. "She probably got herself an unlisted number very recently, in order to shake our friend Ulysses. If I try to pry the new number out of Information, they'll give us a lot of static and probably tell me to make a personal appearance at their office with my badge hanging out. So . . ."

He picked up the phone and began dialling again.

"Who are you calling?"

"The station. We have something there called the backward book. A phone directory with the numbers listed first, followed by names and addresses. Her old number—the one written in McCrea's little red book—will probably be listed there, and that'll give us her address. I just hope she still lives there. Hello? This is Ross . . ."

* * *

The bitch. The little bitch. Refusing to talk to me. Even getting her phone number changed. Well, she'll talk to me soon. Loud and long. She'll beg for her life. She'll cry and moan. She'll go down on her knees. And then she'll scream, when I put the first slug into her. She'll scream again when I fire the second one. She'll scream and scream and scream.

She's probably in the shower right now. She always showers this time of day, just before dinner . . .

Ulysses McCrea remembered every inch of her body. His mind replayed each curve and dimple; his fingertips, though tightly gripping the wheel, tingled with the feel of her skin; the lilt of her voice was in his ears.

He approached the corner, braked briefly for a stop sign, then made a right onto her street.

He parked across the street from her apartment building. He looked at his watch. Six minutes. Just right. From the seat beside him he picked up a dark poplin jacket. He climbed out of the car and, despite the heat, donned the jacket, zipping it up. Then he unlocked the trunk of the car and took out the gun, a .455 Webley. He hid it under his jacket.

He walked casually across the street, slipped into a delivery entrance of the building, and quickly climbed three flights. At her door, he briefly noted the nameplate: *V. & M. Frazier*. The "V" stood for Virgil. Silly damn name. No sillier than Ulysses, but this creep actually used it. He methodically worked a stiff plastic credit card between door and jamb, hoping she was running true to form and had not bothered to affix the chain bolt. If she'd changed her habits and had used the chain, he would have to break it with the pliers he was carrying in his hip pocket, but that would take time and make noise. The lock sprung under the plastic card, and he slowly, carefully turned the knob. Good! The chain had not been used. The door swung open and he entered her apartment.

In the living room, he cautiously looked around. It was dead quiet. All the lights were on. "Marlie?" he called, almost with tenderness, his hand upon the gun.

From the bedroom walked Dr. Gorman. "Hello, Joel," he said gently.

Ulysses McCrea turned and looked at him with disbelief.

Behind McCrea, Ross and the uniformed officer stepped silently from their hiding place and expertly relieved him of his gun. Before he knew what was happening, the handcuffs had been snapped on his wrists.

"We have a lot to talk about, Joel," said the doctor.

"My name isn't Joel," McCrea said sullenly.

"I know. And Lola's name isn't Lola. That's the name of the girl Dietrich played in *The Blue Angel*. Lola Lola. The one who made a fool out of that older man."

"We'll take care of him, Doctor," said Ross. "You'd better take care of her."

"Yes," said Dr. Gorman, touching a folded handkerchief to his damp brow. "She could do with a sedative."

From the bedroom, they could hear the unmistakable sounds of hysteria rising from the still shower-wet Mrs. Frazier, the ex-Mrs. McCrea, otherwise known as Marlene.

BROTHER ORCHID

RICHARD CONNELL

"**B**e smart," the warden said. "Go straight."

A grin creased the leather face of Little John Sarto.

"I *am* goin' straight," he said. "Straight to Chi."

"I wouldn't if I were you, Sarto."

"Why not? I owned that burg once. I'll own it again."

"Things have changed in ten years."

"But not me," said Little John. "I still got what it takes to be on top."

"You didn't stay there," the warden observed.

"I got framed," Sarto said. "Imagine shovin' me on the rock on a sissy income tax rap!"

"It was the only charge they could make stick," the warden said. "You were always pretty slick, Sarto."

"I was, and I am," said Little John.

The warden frowned. "Now look here, Sarto. When a man has done his time and I'm turning him loose, I'm supposed to give him some friendly advice. I do it, though I know that in most cases it's a farce. You'd think men who'd done a stretch here in Alcatraz ought to have a sneaking notion that crime does not pay, but while I'm preaching my little sermon I see a faraway look in their eyes and I know they're figuring out their next bank job or snatch."

"Don't class me with them small-time heisters and petty-larceny yeggs," said Little John. "I'm a born big shot."

"You're apt to die the same way," said the warden dryly.

"That's okay, net, by me," said Little John. "When I peg out I want to go with fireworks, flowers and bands; but you'll have a beard to your knees before they get out the last extra on Little John Sarto. I got a lot of livin' to do first: I got to wash out the taste of slum with a lakeful of champagne, and it'll take half the blondes in the Loop to make me forget them nights in solitary. But most of all I got to be myself again, not just a number. For every order I've took here on the rock, I'm goin' to give two. I'm goin' to see guys shiver and jump when I speak. I've played mouse long enough. Watch me be a lion again."

The warden sighed. "Sarto," he said, "why don't you play it safe? Stay away from Chicago. Settle in some new part of the country. Go into business. You've got brains and a real gift for organization. You ran a big business once—"

"Million a month, net," put in Sarto.

"And you're only forty-six and full of health," the warden went on. "You can still make a fresh start."

"Using what for wampum?" asked Little John.

"You've got plenty salted away."

Sarto laughed a wry laugh.

"I got the ten bucks, and the ticket back to Chi, and this frowsy suit the prison gimme, and that's all I got," he said.

"Don't tell me you're broke!"

"Flat as a mat," said Little John. "I spent it like I made it—fast. A king's got to live like a king, ain't he? When I give a dame flowers, it was always orchids. My free-chow bill ran to a grand a week. They called me a public enemy but they treated me like a year-round Sandy Claws. . . . But I ain't worryin'. I was born broke. I got over it."

A prison guard came in to say that the launch was ready to take Sarto to the mainland.

"Well, goodbye, Warden," said Sarto jauntily. "If you ever get to Chi gimme a buzz. I'll throw a party for you."

"Wait a minute," said the warden. "I can't let you go till I make one last attempt to start you on the right track. I know a man who'll give you a job. He runs a big truck farm and—"

He stopped, for Sarto was shaking with hoarse laughter.

"Me a rube?" Little John got out. "Me a bodyguard to squashes? Warden, the stir-bugs has got you."

"It's a chance to make an honest living."

"Save it for some cluck that would feel right at home livin' with turnips," Sarto said. "I got other plans."

The siren on the launch gave an impatient belch.

"So long, Warden," said Little John. "I won't be seein' you."

"You're right there," the warden said.

Sarto's face darkened at the words.

"Meanin' Chi might be bad for my health?"

"I've heard rumors to that effect," replied the warden.

"I've heard 'em for years," said Little John. "They're a lotta rat spit. Plenty guys has talked about what they was goin' to do to me. I always sent flowers to their funerals—you heard about that."

He chuckled.

"A big heart of forget-me-nots with 'Sorry, Pal' in white orchids on it."

"All right, wise guy," the warden said. "Go to Chicago. The sooner you get rubbed out, the better for everybody. You're no good and you never will be."

"Atta clown," said Little John Sarto. "Always leave 'em laughin' when you say goodbye."

Laughing, he started out toward the big gray gate.

Deep in the woods in an out-of-the-world corner of Michigan, squat, unkempt Twin Pine Inn hides itself. It was silent that summer night, and dark save for a single window in the taproom. Behind the customerless bar, Fat Dutchy was drinking his fourth rock-and-rye.

"Stick 'em up. This is a heist."

The voice, low and with a snarl in it, came from the doorway behind him. Up went Fat Dutchy's hands.

"Easy with the rod," he whimpered. "There ain't a sawbuck in the joint."

"Not like the good old days," the voice said.

Dutchy turned his head. Little John Sarto was standing there with nothing more lethal in his hand than a big cigar. Dutchy blinked and goggled.

"Well, greaseball, do I look funny?" Sarto demanded.

"No—no—boss, you ain't changed a bit."

"I don't change," Sarto said. "Gimme a slug of bourbon."

Fat Dutchy sloshed four fingers of whisky into a glass. His hand trembled. Liquor splashed on the bar.

"What you got the jits about?" asked Sarto.

"You gimme a turn comin' in like you was a ghost or sumpin'," said Fat Dutchy. He wiped sweat from his mottled jowls with the bar rag. Sarto gulped his drink.

"Business bad, eh?"

"It ain't even bad, boss. It just ain't."

"Cheer up, big puss. You'll soon be scoffin' filly miggnons smothered with century notes," Sarto said. "I'm back."

Fat Dutchy rubbed his paunch and looked unhappily at the floor.

"Things is different," he said.

Sarto banged his glass down on the bar.

"If one more lug tells me that, I'll kick his gizzard out," he said. "Now, listen. I'm holin' up here till I get my bearin's. Soon as I get things set, I'm goin' to town. But first I gotta contact some of the boys."

Fat Dutchy played nervously with the bar rag.

"Gimme another slug," Sarto ordered. "I got a ten-year thirst."

Fat Dutchy poured out the drink. Again his shaking hands made him spill some of it.

"Here's to me," said Sarto, and drank. "Now, listen: I want you to pass the office along to certain parties that I'm here and want to see 'em, pronto. For a starter, get in touch with Philly Powell, Ike Gelbert, Ouch O'Day, Willie the Knife, Benny Maletta, French Frank, Hop Latzo, Al Muller and that fresh kid that was so handy with a tommy gun—"

"Jack Buck?"

"Yeah. I may need a torpedo. When I fell out, he had the makin's of a good dropper. So get that phone workin', lard head—you know where they hang out."

"Sure," said Fat Dutchy. He held up his hand and ticked off names on his thick fingers.

"Ike Gelbert and Al Muller is in the jug doin' life jolts," he said. "Philly Powell and French Frank was crossed out right at this bar. Ouch O'Day throwed an ing-bing and was took to the fit house; the G-boys filled Benny Maletta with slugs and sent Willie the Knife to the hot squat; I dunno just where Hop Latzo is but I've heard talk he's at the bottom of Lake Mich in a barrel of concrete. So outa that lot there's only Jack Buck left and I don't guess you wanna see him—"

"Why not?"

"He's growed up," said Fat Dutchy. "He's the loud noise now. What rackets there is, Jack Buck's got 'em in his pocket."

"I'll whittle him down to his right size," said Sarto.

"Jack's in strong. He's waitin' for you, boss, and he ain't foolin'. The boys tell me it's worth three G's to the guy that settles you."

Sarto snorted. "Only three grand!" he said indignantly.

"That's serious sugar nowadays," said Fat Dutchy. "I'm tellin' you times is sour. Jack Buck has cornered the few grafts that still pay. He's got a mob of muzzlers that was in reform school when you was head man. You ain't nothin' fo'em but a name and a chance to earn three thousand fish."

Sarto sipped his drink. Lines of thought furrowed his face.

"I'll stay here till I figure out an angle," he announced.

"Boss," said Fat Dutchy, "I don't wanna speak outa turn, but wouldn't it be a smart play to take it on the lam for a while?"

"Where to?"

Fat Dutchy shrugged his stout shoulders.

"I wouldn't know, boss," he said. "When the heat's on—"

"Yeah, I know," cut in Sarto. "You're smoked wherever you go."

"What are you goin' to do, boss?"

"I'm goin' to hit the sheets and dream I'm out," said Little John.

Dog-tired though he was, he could not get to sleep. His mind yanked him away from dreams, back to prison, to the death-house, where men were lying in the dark, as he was, trying to sleep.

"They got the bulge on me, at that," he thought. "They *know* when they're goin' to get it."

He felt like a man reading his own obituary, complete but for two facts: where and when.

He knew he was safe where he was, but not for long. They'd comb all the known hideouts. He tried to think of some friend he could trust to hide him. Name after name he considered and rejected. He had come to the ninety-sixth name and found no one he could count on when he fell asleep.

* * *

A light in his eyes and a voice in his ear jerked him awake.

A man was bending over him, smiling and saying:

"Wake up, dear. You'll be late for school."

He was a huge, soft-looking young man with a jovial freckled face. His suit was bottle-green and expensive. Sarto had never seen him before.

"Up, up, pet," he said, and waved at Sarto a big blue-black automatic.

A second man watched from the other side of the bed. He was younger and smaller than the first man, and his flour-white face was perfectly blank. Sarto did not know him either.

Sarto sat up in bed.

"Listen, fellas," he said, "if I get a break you get five grand."

"Got it on you, darling?" asked the freckled man.

"Nope. But I can dig it up inside a week."

"Sorry. We do a strictly cash business," the freckled man said.

"I'll make it ten grand," said Little John. He addressed the pallid man. "Wadda you say, bud? Ten G's."

The freckled man chuckled.

"He'd say 'no' if he could say anything," he said. "He doesn't hear, either. His eyes are good, though. His name is Harold, but we call him Dummy."

Sarto held his naked, flabby body very stiff and straight.

"Do your stuff," he said.

Dummy took his hand from his pocket. There was a pistol in it. The freckled man brushed the gun aside.

"We don't want to give this charming place a bad name," he explained to Sarto. "For Dutchy's sake."

"So that fat rat tipped you," said Sarto.

"Yes," said the freckled man. "For a modest fee. Come along, baby."

They were speeding through open farm country. The speedometer hit seventy-five. Sarto closed his mouth and his eyes.

"Praying?" asked the freckled man.

"Naw!"

"Better start, toots."

"I know nuttin' can help me."

"That's right," said the freckled man cheerfully. "Nothing but a miracle. But you might pray for your soul."

"Aw, go to hell."

They turned into a rutty, weed-grown road. As they bumped along through a tunnel of trees, suddenly, silently Little John Sarto began to pray.

"Listen! This is Little John Sarto of Chicago, Illinois, U.S.A. I know I got no right to ask any favors. I guess I got a bad rep up there. Well, I ain't goin' to try to lie away my record. Everything on the blotter is true. I don't claim I rate a break. All I say is I need one bad and I'll pay for it. I don't know how; but look me up in the big book. It ought to say that when I make a deal I never run out on it. If I'm talkin' out of turn, forget it. But I won't forget if—"

"Last stop. All out," sang out the freckled man. He halted the car by a thicket of thigh-high brush.

Sarto got out of the car. Dummy got out, too. He kept his gun against Little John's backbone.

"Goodbye, now," said the freckled man, and lit a cigarette.

Dummy marched Sarto off the road and into the thicket. Abruptly, like a spotlight, the moon came out. Dummy spun Sarto around. Sarto could see his face. It held neither hate nor pity. Dummy raised his pistol. As he brought it up on a level with Sarto's forehead, the breeze whipped a straggling branch of a wild rosebush across the back of his hand, and the thorns cut a wet, red line. For part of a second Dummy dropped his eyes to his bleeding hand. Sarto wheeled and dove into the underbrush. Dummy fired three quick shots. One missed. One raked across Sarto's skull. One seared his shoulder. He staggered, but kept plunging on. Dummy darted after him. Then the moon went out.

As Sarto floundered on he could hear Dummy crashing through the brush behind him. But Dummy could not hear his quarry. Dizzy and weak, the wounded man fought his frantic way through tar-black brush. Thorns stabbed him, briers clawed. A low branch smashed him on the nose, and he reeled and nearly went down. Bending double, he churned on. Then his head hit something hard, and he dropped, stunned for a moment. He reached out an unsteady hand and felt an ivy-covered wall. No sound of pursuit came to his ears.

Painfully he dragged himself up to the top of the wall. Not a sob of breath was left in him. He straddled the wall and clung to it. Then he fainted.

In the monastery of the Floratines, today was like yesterday and yesterday was like a day in the ninth century when the order was founded. Neither time nor war nor the hate of kings had changed their humble habits or their simple creed. Over the door this creed was carved: "Be poor in purse, pure in heart, kind in word and deed and beautify the lives of men with flowers."

These were the words of the Blessed Edric, their founder, and, ever since his day, Floratines in every land had lived by them, harming no one, helping man, raising flowers.

When King Henry VIII set his face against other monks, he let no hostile hand be laid on the few Floratines.

"They do much good," the monarch said, "and, in sooth, they have nothing worth the taking, these Little Brothers of the Flowers."

They kept the name, and it gave rise to a custom. When a man left the world behind to enter their ranks, he left his name, too, and took the name of a flower.

In the first light of a new day they sat in their refectory, forty-four men in snuff-hued robes, most of them growing old. Their tonsured polls were brown from the sun, their faces serene from inner peace.

"Brother Geranium is late with the milk," observed Brother Tulip, eyeing his dry porridge.

"Perhaps the cow kicked him," suggested Brother Hollyhock.

"She wouldn't. She's fond of him," said Brother Nasturtium. "I'll go down to the dairy and see if anything has happened to him," volunteered Brother Nasturtium. But as he rose from his bench, Brother Geranium, popeyed and panting, burst into the room.

"There's a naked man lying in the petunia bed," he gasped out. "I think he's dead."

Little John Sarto thought he was dead, too, when he opened his eyes in the infirmary and saw Abbot Jonquil and Brother Nasturtium at his bedside.

"I made it," he exclaimed huskily. "I beat the rap."

"Take it easy, son," said the abbot. "You've been badly hurt."

"But I ain't in hell," said Little John. Then he added, "Or if I am what are you guys doing here?"

"You're alive and in a safe place."

Sarto stared at him.

"Say, do you know who I am?" he asked.

"No."

"You musta seen my mug in the papers."

"We don't see newspapers here," the abbot said. "And we don't ask who a man is if he needs help."

Sarto touched his bandaged head.

"How long am I in for?" he inquired.

"Until you are well and strong again."

"I got no money."

"Neither have we," said the abbot. "So that makes you one of us, doesn't it?"

"That's one for the book, mister," said Little John.

"I'm Abbot Jonquil. This is Brother Nasturtium, your nurse. If you wish us to notify your friends—"

"I got no friends," grunted Little John.

"You have now," said the abbot.

"I tell you I'm broke."

"You poor fellow," said the abbot gently. "What a life you must have led!"

"I been round long enough to know you never get sumpin' for nuttin'."

"I think you have talked enough for the present," the abbot said. "Try to rest and try not to worry—about anything. You may stay here as long as you wish, as our guest."

He went to the door.

"I'll look in again this evening," the abbot said. "Meantime, if you need anything, tell Brother Nasturtium."

His sandals shuffled softly away down the stone corridor.

Sarto squinted at the bulky monk.

"Get me a slug of bourbon, Nasty," he said.

"If you don't mind, I'd rather be called Brother Nasturtium," said the other mildly.

"Whatever you say, only gimme a snort."

Brother Nasturtium brought him a glass of water.

"Try it," he said. " 'Twill give you strength."

"Water?" said Sarto disdainfully.

"Look at lions and tigers," said Brother Nasturtium.

As he drank the water, Little John studied the man. He noted the dented nose, gnarled ears, lumpy knuckles and the jaw like an anvil.

"You was a fighter, wasn't you?" said Sarto.

"We don't ask questions like that," said Brother Nasturtium. "What we were, rich or poor, big or small, good or bad, does not matter here."

"That's double jake by me," said Little John. "I think I'm going to like it here."

"I hope so."

"Say, tell me sumpin', big boy. What's your graft?"

Brother Nasturtium's eyes twinkled.

" 'Tis twenty years and more since I've heard such talk," he said. "We raise flowers and sell them in the city."

"There's a good gelt in that," said Sarto. "You boys must be cuttin' up a nice profit."

"What we clear, and it isn't much, goes to the poor."

"That's a nutsy way to run a business," observed Little John.

He closed his eyes. Presently he said:

"How does a guy join up with this outfit?"

"It's fairly easy," Brother Nasturtium told him, "if a man wants to be a lay brother—"

"A which?"

"Lay brother. I'm one. They don't take holy orders. They have few religious duties, chiefly saying their prayers. They are not permitted to go outside the walls, and they must obey their superiors. The discipline is rather severe. Some men say it's like being in prison—"

"They do, do they?" said Little John.

"Except that there are no bars."

"That might make a slight difference," conceded Little John. "What are the other catches?"

"Before a man can take his first vow as a lay brother, he must be on probation for a year. That means—"

"I know about probation," said Little John. "Where do I sign?"

"You'll have to talk to the abbot."

"Shoo him in."

"Lay brothers do not shoo abbots."

"Then tell him I wanta proposition him."

"If you're in earnest about this," Brother Nasturtium said, "you might be choosing the name we are to call you."

"Just call me 'Lucky.'"

"It must be the name of a flower."

Little John thought a moment.

"I've picked my new tag,"he announced.

"What is it?"

"Brother Orchid."

At dusk Brother Nasturtium left the sickroom to get his patient's supper.

When he had gone, Little John began to laugh. It hurt him to laugh, but he couldn't help it.

"Boy, oh, boy!" he said. "What a hideout!"

As he weeded the rose garden Brother Orchid sang softly:

> *Johnny saw Frankie a-coming,*
> *Out the back door he did scoot.*
> *Frankie took aim with her pistol,*
> *And the gun went rooty-toot-toot.*
> *He was her man—*

He turned the tune deftly into "Abide with Me" as he saw Brother Nasturtium come out of the greenhouse and head toward him.

Three nights before he had taken the vows that made him a full-fledged lay brother. As he flicked a ladybug from a leaf, he reflected that it hadn't been such a tough year. The routine didn't bother him; he was used to one far more rigid; but he was not used to men like Abbot Jonquil, Brother Nasturtium and the rest. At first he felt sure that some sly, dark purpose lay behind their kindness to him. He watched, warily, for the trap. No trap was sprung. Always they were thoughtful, patient, pleasant with him and with one another.

"Maybe I've got into a high-class whacky house," he thought.

Whatever it was, he decided, it was perfect for his plans. There he could bide his time, snug and safe, ready to strike. He was old enough to know the wonders time can work. And he was wise enough to know that while Jack Buck reigned as czar he must remain in exile. If he ventured back to his old kingdom now, he might just as well go straight to the morgue and book a slab. But czars slip, and czars fall, sometimes suddenly in this violent world. He'd wait and be ready.

"Well, Brother Orchid, your roses are doing well," said Brother Nasturtium as he came up.

"Lay you three to one they bring more than your lilies," said Brother Orchid.

"It's a hundred to one they won't bring anything," said Brother Nasturtium, somberly. Brother Orchid looked up and saw that the face, usually so benign, was grave.

"What's the gag?" he asked.

"Our market is gone."

"How come?"

"They won't handle our flowers."

"Who won't?"

"The wholesalers. We don't belong to the association."

"Why don't we join it?"

"They won't let us. Not a flower can be sold in the city that isn't grown in their own nurseries."

"I get it," said Brother Orchid. "The old chisel. Who's the wheels in this shakedown?"

"A man named Buck is behind it, I believe. So Abbot Jonquil learned when he was in town. He tried to see this Mr. Buck to plead with him not to take away our only means of livelihood. One of Buck's ruffians kicked him downstairs."

"I suppose the abbot was sucker enough to go to the coppers," said Brother Orchid.

"He did go to the police."

"What did *they* do—slug him?"

"No. They were polite enough. But they said that so far as they knew the Floral Protective Association was a legitimate business concern."

* * *

"The bulls still know the answers," said Brother Orchid. "And the D.A. said he'd like to do sumpin', but his hands is tied, because you gotta have evidence, and all the witnesses is scared to talk."

"You seem to know all about it."

"I seen movies," said Brother Orchid.

He weeded away, deep in thought.

"Have we got any jack in the old sack?" he asked suddenly.

"About four hundred dollars, the abbot told me."

"Peanuts," said Brother Orchid. "But enough for a couple of secondhand choppers. You and me could handle 'em. We'd need roscoes for the rest of the boys. But I know an armory that's a soft touch. You and me and Geranium and Lilac could charge out tonight, hustle a hot short, and knock it off. Once we was heeled we could move in on Buck and his gorillas and—"

"Man alive, what sort of talk is that?" demanded the scandalized Brother Nasturtium.

"Forget it, pal," said Brother Orchid. "I guess this sun has made me slap-happy. What are we goin' to do?"

"Be patient and pray."

"And eat what?"

"Heaven knows."

"Yeah, and they claim it helps guys that help themselves."

"Maybe Mr. Buck will see the light."

Brother Orchid plucked up a clump of sour grass.

"Maybe this weed'll turn into an American Beauty," he said.

He wrung the weed's neck and hurled it into his basket.

"That's the only way to treat weed," he said.

"But is it?" said Brother Nasturtium. "Wasn't everything put into the world for some good use, if man had the sense to find out what that use is?"

"That's a lot of words," said Brother Orchid. "Weeds is weeds."

"No," said Brother Nasturtium, as he turned away, "weeds are flowers out of place."

Hungry after their day of work, the Little Brothers of the Flowers waited in the refectory for their abbot to come in and say grace. They tried to make light talk of events in their small world. But there was a shadow over them.

Abbot Jonquil entered, walking slowly. It came to them for the first time that he was a very old man.

"I'm afraid I have more bad news," he said. "Our funds have been taken from my safe. Of course none of us took them—"

He stopped and looked down the long table.

"Where is Brother Orchid?" he asked.

"Maybe he's in his cell, praying," said Brother Nasturtium. "Shall I fetch him?"

"Yes, please."

Brother Nasturtium came back alone. His big ruddy face was twisted with trouble.

"Maybe I was wrong about weeds," he said.

In his office, Thomas Jefferson Brownlow, special prosecutor of rackets, was talking to the press. The reporters liked him. He was so earnest and so green.

"Same old story, boys," he said. "All I can tell you is that men are selfish animals, and that's not news. I know Buck is back of all these new rackets. So do you. But I can't prove it in a court of law. The men who can simply will not go before the grand jury and tell their stories. They put their skins before their civic duty. I'm not blaming them. But the fact remains I can't force them to testify. They're not afraid of *me*. I wish they were. That's all today, gentlemen."

The reporters filed out. Brownlow bent morosely over the indictment of a jobless man who had stolen a peck of potatoes.

Swerling, his assistant, bustled in. He was excited.

"Chief," he said, "they're back."

"Who?"

"Those florists and laundrymen and fruit peddlers. And they're ready to talk."

"The devil you say!"

"Better grab 'em while they're hot, Chief," urged Swerling.

"But what's got into 'em?"

"You have me there."

"It doesn't matter," said Brownlow, "if they'll talk. Send 'em in and lock all the doors."

Once they started to talk Thomas Jefferson Brownlow had a hard job to stop them. The Grand Jury was back before its seats in the box had cooled off, and shortly thereafter Jack Buck and three of his top aides were passengers on a special train that would not stop till it had carried them to a station near a big, gray gate. Most of his lesser lieutenants also took trips, accompanied by large, official-looking men, who returned alone. A few escaped, some by taking to their heels, others by wriggling through loopholes in the law.

Mr. Brownlow was walking toward his office, debating whether he should run for governor or the Senate, when he bumped into Mr. Chris Poppadoppalous, emerging from the room where witnesses are paid their fees. Mr. Poppadoppalous beamed, bowed, and handed Mr. Brownlow a large box.

"Gardenias," he said. "I brink dem for you."

"Thanks," said Brownlow. "And there's one more thing you can do for me."

"Anythink," said Mr. Poppadoppalous with another bow.

"One day you boys were afraid to talk. The next day you talked. Why?"

"We were afraid not to," said Mr. Poppadoppalous.

"Afraid of me?" asked Brownlow, rather pleased.

Mr. Poppadoppalous tittered apologetically.

"Oh, no, sir," he said. "You're a nice man. You don't say, 'Talk, you Greek so-and-so, or I'll tear out your heart and eat it before your eyes.'"

"Did somebody say that to you?"

"Yes, sir. To all us boys."

"Who?"

"The little fellow," said Mr. Poppadoppalous, and bowed, and scurried away.

From his hotel window Little John Sarto looked out over the lighted city spread at his feet. Somebody knocked on his door.

"Come in," said Sarto.

The freckled young man came in. He had on a new suit, moss-green this time, and he was still jovial.

"Hello, sweetheart," he said.

"Hello, Eddie," said Sarto.

"You know why I'm here."

"Sure," said Sarto. "Have a drink?"

"Why not?" said Eddie, and poured out a drink from a bottle of bourbon on the table. Sarto took one, too.

"Nice going, boss," said Eddie, raising his glass. "We'll run this town right."

"We?"

"You will, I mean," said Eddie. "I'll be glad to work under a man with your brains. Poor Jack didn't have many. Nerve, yes. But he never looked ahead. You do. Well, what do you say, boss? Dummy and some of the boys are waiting downstairs for the answer. They're solid for you, boss. Anything you say goes."

Sarto didn't say anything. He went to the window and looked out over the city.

"Of course, things are rather ragged right now," said Eddie. "We'll have to take it slow and easy for a while. But the boys are counting on you to work out some nice, new, juicy angles. The town's yours."

"I don't want it," said Little John.

"What do you mean?" Eddie was not jovial now.

"I got other plans."

"You can't run out on us."

"I'm walking out," said Sarto. "Right now."

"The boys won't like that."

"I'm doing what *I* like."

"That's always expensive," said Eddie.

"I know all about that."

Eddie shrugged his shoulders.

"Okay," he said, and sauntered out of the room.

Hurriedly, Little John Sarto began to strip off his loud, plaid suit.

"I'm right," said the warden to the chaplain, laying down the morning paper. "You say all men have some good in them. I say some men are all bad and nothing can change them. Take this fellow, Sarto. Last night in Chicago, as he was getting on a bus, he was filled full of lead."

"That hardly proves your point." The chaplain smiled. "Bullets are very democratic. They'll kill good men as well as bad, you know."

"There was nothing good about Sarto. Just listen to this: 'The police say Sarto plotted to return to power in the underworld. They are at a loss to explain why, at the time of his death, he was disguised as a monk.' Why, the scheming wolf! Whether there's any good whatsoever in such a man, I leave it to you to judge."

"He does sound pretty bad, I grant you," the chaplain said. "But, even so, I hate to condemn him or any man. I might be reversed by a higher Judge."

THE SPOTTED PUP

DOROTHY B. HUGHES

I

If you stand on the corner of Clark and Randolph looking eastward to
the lake, you won't see the lake. It's four blocks away and you can't feel
its blasts in winter or breezes in summer, not by the time they're filtered
through the honky-tonk that is Randolph from Clark to Dearborn. You
think Forty-second Street west of Broadway a little Coney Island? Get a
load of Randolph.

There's the glare of movie marquees and the Caligari monstrosities
hiding the lobbies. There are Chinese restaurants and hole-in-the-wall
gyp joints called night-clubs. There are white front cafeterias and greasy
hamburger stands, hat shops, pawn shops, candy shops, junk jewelry
shops, book shops, phonograph record shops; everything scribbled up
with neon, everything blaring with noise, glaring with light.

Randolph's an old street and a narrow one, the better to hear the
loudspeakers blasting the sidewalk from the so-called night-clubs, the
better to see who's watching you while you're watching them. Dokey's
watch was in front of the drugstore on the southeast corner of Clark and
Randolph.

It's an old street, Randolph, and the buildings are like the derelicts
you sometimes see on the street, old men in dirty overcoats, and broken
shoes. Ancient, scabrous buildings that don't belong in the noise and
glitter and crazy tempo. You don't see them for the false fronts; you
don't raise your eyes above street level. There's too much to attract the
eyes below.

If you're a man there are legs, bowlegs, fat legs, skinny legs, and the legs you're watching for—all of them in imitation silk, imitation nylon—hanging below dresses that switch over knees when hips move.

If you're a woman you're looking in the show windows at shiny gewgaws, even the drugstore windows with their come-ons of lipsticks and glass beads and makeup disks enameled in raw colors. You don't even know that two flights over the drugstore in that corner building, the block letters spell out Grimsley's Confidential Agency.

In six weeks few had looked up at the dirty windows of Grimsley's. Maybe in the days when Grimsley had a red neon sign titillating the magic words over the street, the Agency picked up some of the trade shuffling up and down Randolph at night. Not after Kip Scott took over. For one thing he did away with the neon.

For another thing, Grimsley's customers edged into a fade-out after a meeting with Scott. Maybe they caught on quick that he didn't want to waste his time with larcenic dodges and divorce frames. Maybe they'd been conditioned too long to a dirty fingernail like Grimsley to be at ease with someone like Scott. Six foot military build, lean jowls without a shadow of blue, clean linen every day and a suit that hadn't come from any twenty-three seventy-five take-me-home. Shoes of stout grain, polished without highlights, the kind of shoes that walked North Michigan, not Randolph. Short clean nails on long clean hands. That was Kip Scott. Grimsley's customers stopped coming to Grimsley's. It was the way Scott wanted it.

That was why his swivel chair squeaked a warning when it whirled to the outer door's creak on a Saturday night in February at nine p.m. or thereabouts. The door hadn't any business opening. Scott remained rigid, his hand against the upper right hand desk drawer, his ears peaked, waiting. The door shouldn't have opened, but he'd been waiting long arid weeks for this moment.

There was no sound in the outer office after that first creak. Whoever had entered wasn't moving. Scott didn't move either; he scarcely breathed. He couldn't pull out the drawer without breaking the quiet, a quiet made more intense by the muffled ragout of street sounds two stories below on Randolph.

He waited until he heard steps crossing the floor. Under cover of their sound he slid the drawer open so that his fingers could remove the gun with speed. He leaned back in the swivel chair then as the shadow appeared on the dirty crinkled glass of the connecting door. The door opened. What came in had no business coming to Grimsley's.

Her hair under the mink-brown hat was afire. That was the first thing he noticed. He couldn't tell much about her shape. The deep gloss of the best mink hid that. But he guessed that she was well-built. For one thing, there was the exquisite line and texture of her legs, sheathed in real nylon; for another her height and the way she carried her chin.

He relaxed and said, "Come in."

She turned her eyes on him when he spoke. They were the color of dark smoke in a gray Chicago sky. But they were alive, the way the lake was alive, changing, moving, even in seeming quiescence.

He repeated, raising his voice, "Come on in."

She stepped in, closing the door behind her. She was very deliberate in her actions. For a moment her eyes narrowed in distaste as she regarded the shabby office. Her cheeks were pink without makeup, her mouth aflame with plenty of makeup. She had come through Chicago streets into this rat trap of Grimsley's, and she didn't look as if she had any business here at all.

When she spoke, her voice was right, alive and rich. "Mr. Grimsley?"

"Scott," Kip said. He pulled the squeaking Grimsley chair closer to the battered Grimsley desk. He put his fingers together on top of it, the open and aboveboard manner of Grimsley greeting money.

A faint hesitancy touched her eyes. "This is Grimsley's?"

"Yes, Miss—" He waited for her to fill the blank but she didn't.

Her eyes went beyond Kip's shoulders. "Might I see him?"

She couldn't help but know that this was all of Grimsley's, this square, sordid room with the battered desk.

She must know this was the end of the trap. Two gray windows looking down on Randolph, one gray window looking down on Clark. But she pried beyond him as if Grimsley were standing there, a dirty little ghost looking down on Randolph—or as if the door to the corridor had been left unlocked for an intruder.

"Grimsley isn't here," Scott said brusquely. "I'm Grimsley's."

She moved forward slowly, her mink coat swinging open to show the expensive rust wool molded to her beauty, the glint of diamonds pinned below her throat. She put one expensive brown suede fingertip on the back of the client's chair.

"What can I do for you?" Scott asked suddenly. His voice surprised him, the shame in it as he asked, "Will you sit down, Miss—"

II

Again she ignored the lead, but she came around the chair and sat down, carefully crossing her shapely legs. She looked across at him and he noticed the slant of her eyes and the black fringe of her lashes. She looked at the fingertip of her glove. She spoke to it.

"I was looking for Mr. Grimsley—Grimsley's Confidential Agency."

"I've taken over Grimsley's," Kip told her as he took a Chesterfield from a clean, uncrumpled pack, and lit it. He then pushed the cigarettes across the width of desk. "Will you?"

"Thank you." She tapped out one. He gave her a light.

When she had drawn on it, he asked, "Is there something I can do for you, Miss—"

This time she answered, "Smith." It was phony, he knew. A girl like this one wouldn't give a real name. She looked at him out of her harlequin eyes. "I expected someone—"

"Older?"

"Seedier." She smiled then.

He met the smile. "What is it you want?"

It couldn't be just another divorce case. She wouldn't have come here. There were society dicks in better neighborhoods. Her lawyer would hire one for her.

Curiosity made him repeat, "What is it?"

"I want to find a man."

If they'd been looking at each other across a table in the Empire Room or the Pump Room, there would have been provocation in the remark, a smile for answer. That wasn't the cause of the remark. It wasn't a sufficient answer.

"Who is he?" Kip asked.

She didn't look at him. Her eyes were on the desk, on the *Sun* and the *News* littered on it. There were no letters, no business, but two newspapers, a lamp, a telephone, a dirty ash tray.

"Who is he?" he repeated.

She said, "Don Redhair."

Kip didn't speak for a moment. When he spoke his voice was well controlled.

"That is his real name?"

She was momentarily surprised at the question. Her lashes lifted. "Yes. That's his real name."

He gestured with impatience. "Who is he? Where is he from? Where was he when you last heard from him?"

"He was in the Army." She seemed uneasy. Her eyes moved to the cigarette, to her gloves, to her shoes.

"Why don't you write the C.O. of his outfit?"

"He *was* in the Army" she repeated. "He isn't now."

"Where is he now?"

"I don't know." Her shoulders moved almost with amusement. "That's why I came to Grimsley's."

The anger came creeping up into his voice. "How do you expect me to find him if you're not going to tell me? Start at the beginning. Is he a deserter?"

"He was mustered out." She spoke calmly. "He was supposed to meet me in Chicago, two weeks ago. He didn't."

His lip curled deliberately. "And you want me to find him before he gets that muster-out money all spent? Is that it?"

He'd flicked her. She brought her anger forward. "Do I look as if I need money? I'm worried about him." She flared, "If you don't want the case, say so."

"Hold it." Kip put his hands flat on the desk. "You think I sit up here on Saturday nights because I admire the decor? What outfit was he with?"

He pulled a scratch pad from the center drawer, slapped it on the desk. He took out a pencil.

"Go ahead," he said.

He wrote down the information she gave. She took a card from her purse, read a serial number.

"Got a photograph of him?"

"Not here."

"Can you get me one?"

She bit her lip. "Yes. Maybe."

"Make up your mind."

"I'll try."

"Describe him."

"Fairly tall, five-foot ten. Stocky. Gray eyes."

"That the best you can give?"

"Red hair." She flared up again. "I'm not an artist. He looked as if he were daring someone to knock a chip off his shoulder."

Kip glanced over the notes. "My retainer fee is fifty dollars. And expenses."

She opened the brown suede handbag again. She counted out five twenty-dollar bills. "Is that enough?"

He folded the money into his pocket. "You'll get an itemized bill, Miss Smith. Your address and phone number?"

The tortoise shell mounting on her bag clicked definitely. "I'll get in touch with you."

She stood up and he pushed to his feet. "I'll go through regular channels first. Frankly, I think you're wasting your time. He probably didn't give you his right name."

"It's his right name." Her eyes looked long into his. "It wasn't a bar pickup. I've known him all my life." Kip watched her walk to the door. She paused there and then turned. "If it will help you any," she said, "he's in Chicago now."

She went without more words. He listened to her heels cross the outer office. He sat down again at the desk.

Don Redhair was his name. But he wasn't in Chicago. He'd been killed in action in the landing at Cherbourg. When he was hit, he'd pushed his rifle into the hands of his mate, Kip Scott. And he'd said, the words coming out of his mouth with blood and sand and sea water:

"Don't let—any of them—get—my dog—" Then he had died.

III

When the footsteps were gone, Kip moved into the corridor. The door locked itself behind him. Kip moved swiftly towards the staircase, running down the two flights and pushing out on the street.

Dokey was on watch at the corner. From the doorway Kip saw the shape of his black hat pulled over his black eyes, the belted light coat, patch pockets hiding his hands, the nervous black pointed shoes.

Kip went to him. "Which way did she go?"

"Who?" Dokey's whisper was harsh.

"The girl. Which way did she go?"

Dokey whispered, "No girl."

He'd been watching Randolph. She could have hugged the building, and rounded Clark. Kip went fast around the corner. No woman was in sight. North, she'd have had to cross the street. Dokey would have noticed her. He went back to the man.

"Dokey, listen. She was wearing mink, million-dollar mink. She had red hair; bright red hair."

Dokey said huskily, "No girl, Kip. I been watching all night."

If she hadn't come out, she was somewhere in that empty, creaking building. Kip suddenly felt the cold of the bitter, damp night.

"Watch for her," he said. She knew he'd try to follow her. She was hiding in that cavernous emptiness. He shivered as he went back.

The elevator stood at the ground floor now. The dark gray face of the operator turned. "Why didn't you ring, Mr. Scott?"

"Didn't want to disturb your slumbers, Adam." He stepped in.

"Disturb 'em less with a little buzz than you do tumbling those stairs down on my head." The cage crawled up the two flights.

"What happened to the woman who went down a little while ago?"

"Didn't take no one down, Mr. Scott," Adam said. He stopped the cage at the floor. "Not tonight. Just took one up, though." He cackled. "Business must be picking up."

Kip stepped out in the dingy corridor.

"Adam—" But the cage was slithering down.

He'd talk to Adam later. His heels, clicking along the corridor floor, flung up noisy echoes in the dim stillness. Empty doors, someone hiding behind their emptiness. Dentist, Insurance, untenanted, Employment Agency. He cut the corner sharp to Grimsley's wing.

He crossed the outer office. The back of his neck was wet when he slammed the door behind him. He crossed to the desk, sat down in the swivel chair, pulled open the top right hand drawer. The gun was still there. He lifted it out, pushed it into his coat pocket before the knock sounded on the inner office door.

"Come in," he yelled. He kept his hand in his pocket as the door slowly opened.

A girl stood in the doorway, a girl in a red coat with a cluster of red roses on her polished dark hair, a girl with enormous dark eyes that looked only at his face.

"Come in," he repeated.

She came in and closed the door behind her.

"Mr. Grimsley?"

He knew what she was here for. He started all over again. "Mr. Grimsley isn't here. I'm Grimsley's."

She moved forward slowly across the room. She walked like a model, swaying from side to side, the red coat buttoned to her rounded chin. He didn't speak until she stood behind the client's chair, her white gloved hand resting on it.

Then he said, "Sit down. What can I do for you?"

She looked down at the rotting chair and slowly came around it. She sat down on the edge of it. "I want to see Mr. Grimsley," she said.

"I'm his successor. Is there something I can do, Miss—"

She ignored the lead as the other girl had, turned her great dark eyes on him. "I'm looking for a man."

He'd known it would be the same and it was the same. He knew whom she was looking for. He smiled at her and passed his cigarettes across before taking one himself. This girl didn't anger him. There was no arrogance in her. She seemed to be feeling her careful way through the dirt of Grimsley's. And she didn't know his smile was the smile of a hunter closing in on his quarry. She moved into a more comfortable position.

"Who is he, Miss—" He smiled again. "And don't say it's Miss Smith."

Her small mouth moved at the corners. "It isn't Miss Smith. I'm Hyacinthe Fouré."

At least she had imagination even if he had warned against Smith. Hyacinthe Fouré. She might be French. Small bones, those he could see.

"I am Kip Scott, Miss Fouré. Mr. Grimsley's successor. Who is this man you're looking for?"

"His name is Don Redhair."

The smile didn't move on Scott's lips. "Yes?"

She didn't know how to continue. For a long, tense interval he withheld the lead. Then he said, "Tell me about him. When did you last hear from him?"

He didn't say: "Why do you want to find him?" even as he had kept that query from Miss Smith. It was too soon for that. Let her tell him. Force her to come to him.

She moistened her lips. "He was in the Army. Private Don Redhair." Kip didn't help her. "He's in Chicago."

He pushed away the pad with a pretense of amusement. "If he's in Chicago, why hire an investigator to find him?"

She didn't know what to say.

"Why don't you just telephone him, or drop him a note?"

She spoke hurriedly, huskily. "Because I don't know where he is. I thought maybe you could find him."

"What makes you think he's in Chicago?" he asked.

She had control of her hands again, of her voice. "He's been seen."

Scott pulled the scratch pad toward him. He noticed what he had doodled earlier. A spotted dog. He began shading the spots. "Who saw him?"

"I don't know. Someone told me that he had been seen."

"Who told you?" he asked. "Put a name on someone."

Again she moistened her lips. "It was just talk at the Club. That Dokey had seen him on the street."

She knew Dokey. His eyebrows met. She belonged to Randolph Street.

"What club?"

"The Club Elegante."

The monstrosity with the blaring sidewalk loudspeaker. She sang into that thing, or she danced to the sounding brass within. He needn't ask where Dokey saw Don Redhair. Dokey hadn't seen him.

"It isn't much to go on," Kip said. "Suppose you tell me a little more about him. Before he went in the Army, where was his home?" He filled in another polka dot on the dog. "Draw me a picture." Under his eyelids, he saw fear stiffen the girl's lips. "Go on," he said. "His home?"

Her voice was unsure. "He lived in Chicago."

"Where?"

"In a hotel. The Bursley. A cheap hotel on La Salle."

He wrote down the name. "Did you meet him there?"

"No. I met him at the Club."

It was as if the Club were home to her—as if she repeated it to be warmed by its security.

"How? Who introduced you?"

"I don't believe anyone did." She was at sea. "Sometimes Peppo, the manager, if a man wants to meet you—I mean, if Peppo knows the man—"

"Did Peppo know Don Redhair?"

She said simply, "I don't know."

"Who did Don Redhair come there with?"

"I don't know," she repeated.

Scott shrugged. "All right. You met him. Now, why do you want to find this guy?"

She said, "He—he asked me to marry him."

"Did you?"

"We were—engaged." Her voice broke just a little. "Now he's back here and he hasn't come near me."

Scott tilted in his chair. It squawked. "So you're looking for him."

She nodded.

"Has he money?" Scott flung it in her face.

Her eyes burned back at him. "No. His sister got everything."

"How'd that happen?" he asked.

"That's the way it was left—" She broke off. "What has that to do with it?"

He smiled. "I'm expensive. Don't let the surroundings fool you."

She opened her purse. "How much?"

"Retaining fee, fifty dollars. That's for a week. And expenses."

She took out a smaller purse. "Will fifty dollars do for now?"

"For now." He took the five tens, crackling new. "I'll keep in touch with you at the Club Elegante?"

She hesitated. "I'd better—I'll keep in touch with you."

"Very well, Miss Fouré."

IV

Kip didn't wait until her footsteps receded before crossing to the Randolph street windows, throwing one wide. Dokey was on the corner watching. Scott banged down the window. Dokey would see her if she emerged. Dokey would know about Hyacinthe Fouré if she was Hyacinthe Fouré. And maybe Miss Smith had gone.

Scott again left the office. He put his finger on the elevator buzzer but he didn't push. The cables were motionless. Hyacinthe must have walked down. Or run. There were no steps audible. He couldn't stand here waiting for the long pull of the ancient cage.

He clattered down the two flights and on the street floor he rang the elevator bell. He could see through the street door while he waited in the semi-darkness, the endless procession of those who walked at night on Randolph street. Miss Smith could have made her exit without Dokey observing it. If she'd gone out when a group was passing the door, she could have been hidden amid it long enough to get away. What purpose? Then Dokey knew her and she knew him, or knew of him.

Adam clanged open the door. "You come down on your feet, then you ring the buzzer. What's the sense of that, Mr. Scott?"

Kip leaned against the cage. "I can come down faster than you can come up in that thing. I wanted to ask you a question about that girl you didn't bring down."

"Never laid eyes on her, Mr. Scott."

"You took her up?"

"No, sir." Adam was definite.

She hadn't wanted to be seen. She wouldn't have walked up two flights from choice, not Miss Smith.

"Who was she, Mr. Scott?"

"She said she was Miss Smith."

The old man grinned. "Lots of Miss Smiths come to Grimsley's, or used to come." He covered the grin. "Dokey'd see her."

"Dokey didn't. She slipped past him. Unless—" He raised two fingers and rushed out to the corner of Clark and Randolph. "Did she come out yet, Dokey?"

"Who?" The watcher blinked slowly.

"Minks. Red hair."

Dokey shook his head.

"Do you know Hyacinthe Fouré?"

"Peppo's joint."

"Yes. Did she come out?"

"Yeah. Rose in her hair."

"The other one didn't?" Kip insisted.

Dokey shook his head.

Kip turned back to the building. He pushed the buzzer. The cage came from above, slowly.

"How could she get out?" Kip asked.

Adam said, "The service door."

"Locked at night."

"I'll see if the bolt's off, Mr. Scott. She'd have to walk soft." His blue eyeballs turned upwards. "There's another one."

Kip frowned. "What's that?"

"I just took another one up. She asked for Grimsley's."

Kip got in the cage. He didn't say anything. He walked silently, slowly to the door of the private office.

This one hadn't waited outside: She was seated in the old leather chair.

"The door was unlocked," she said. "The lights were on."

He pushed the door shut behind him, came over to his place in the cranky swivel chair.

He said, "I suppose you're looking for Don Redhair."

"Yes, I am," she admitted quietly.

Her eyes were blue, sea blue, and they didn't waver while he studied her face and speculated about her reasons for seeking Don Redhair. Don hadn't mentioned women. Don hadn't talked about himself. Kip Scott hadn't realized that until he had come to Chicago two months ago to find out about Don Redhair, and to find out what had happened to Don Redhair's dog. Don had shot the breeze about the Cubs and the White Sox, movies, the Lake, Michigan Boulevard, the Loop, things that were outside a man. Nothing about himself. There hadn't been a lead. His mother was dead.

"Never knew my mom," he'd said. "She died when I was a baby.

My old man's dead." No more than that. A little more, one night in a slit trench under enemy bombardment. "I joined the Army because they were trying to kill me."

They? A fresh bombardment had prevented any more explanation. When you could hear talk again, Don Redhair chinned about a steak at Jonesy's.

That little scrap and the words spilled on an invasion beach—they kept coming back, over and again after being mustered out. Why would a dying kid put a rifle in your hands pointed to kill? Why would he hold fast to breath long enough to cry they mustn't get his dog? The words were gadflies, stinging Kip Scott, impelling him to do something about them.

No leads. No Redhair in the Chicago directory who had a son Don. Through the War Department, through friends of friends, a look at Don's enlistment. Next of kin was an uncle, Jake Grimsley, on Randolph Street, Chicago. Don Redhair was listed as missing in action. After that slaughter, more than one identification tag was missing. But there was always hope of a soldier's return if his death was not a corroborated fact.

There was hope in those who cared, in those who would kill. Start a whisper, drop a pebble in the lake—"Don Redhair is back in Chicago"—and not one, but three girls had heard the whisper.

This one had less business at Grimsley's than the others. She was small and ashen fair. Her navy blue hat was tailored, her navy coat with the round white collar and white pearl buttons was like that of a schoolgirl. She didn't look as if she had anything to hide and she wasn't startled because he'd known why she was here.

He asked, "Why do you want to find him?" Then he noticed the top page of his scratch pad was gone. A clean sheet faced him. Had she taken it, this girl who looked as if she should be carrying school books under her arm? Why? There was nothing on it but his scribbling. And one address. He remembered it—the Bursley Hotel, La Salle street.

She said, "Where is Mr. Grimsley?"

He answered by rote. "He isn't here any more. I've taken over Grimsley's. I'm Kip Scott, Miss—"

"Mariel Smith."

He smiled. "I've had one Miss Smith tonight."

She was matter-of-fact. "That happens to be my name."

"Very well, Miss Smith. You, too, are looking for Don Redhair?"

"Yes," she said. "Where is he?"

Kip's laugh was short and loud. "I'm an investigator, Miss Smith, not a prestidigitator."

"You don't know where he is?"

V

She wasn't like the others, feeling their separate ways to information concerning Don Redhair. She was point-blank, and she forced him to dissemble.

He said pleasantly, "I'm a stranger in Chicago. I can scarcely be expected to know where a man is whose name I heard only tonight. What about a picture?"

She said, "I didn't bring one."

She hadn't seemed surprised to learn that others were seeking Don Redhair. It didn't matter to her.

She went on, "I didn't think it would be needed. I thought you would know where Don is."

"And what made you think that?"

"I shouldn't have said you. I expected to find Mr. Grimsley. He knows where Don is." She gathered her navy blue felt pouch into her gloved fingers. "If you'll tell me where I can find Mr. Grimsley, I won't bother you, Mr. Scott."

Kip leaned back in the squeaky chair, clasping his hands behind his neck. "I don't know where Grimsley is. I took over the business."

Anxiety quickened her voice. "You don't know where he is?"

"No." He was curious. "Was Grimsley a friend of yours?" It seemed impossible. She was washed, she was neat, she appeared honest.

"No, I never met him. He didn't leave an address?"

Kip shook his head. He asked, "Do you want me to try and find Don Redhair for you?"

She gathered her pouch again. "How could you? You're a stranger. I know more about him than you ever could."

He mustn't lose Mariel Smith. She had knowledge of Don Redhair in Chicago. Unlike the others she wasn't afraid to admit that knowledge. He spoke rapidly, while his mind sought a way to hold her.

"What made you think Grimsley could find him? If he could, I could. I'm as good an operator—"

She interrupted quietly. "Mr. Grimsley was Don's friend. He would know if Don was in Chicago. When Don went into the Army, he named Mr. Grimsley as next of kin."

And how had she found this out? The hard way, through correspondence channels? Or had Don told her?

He pretended mild surprise. "Was Grimsley related to Don Redhair?"

"No. Don just called him Uncle Grim. Mr. Grimsley worked for Don's father when Don was a boy."

"Don's father was a detective?'

She raised her eyebrows. "You don't know who Don's father was?"

He checked his temper. "No, I don't know who Don's father was. I don't know anything about Don." He'd realized that prior to tonight. Knowing someone was a swell fellow to be with in a pinch or on leave or killing time didn't mean you knew him. Because she was silent, he asked, "Who was his father?"

Her face didn't change. "He was Ott Redhair." When his face didn't change, she said, "The Rackets King."

Kip let her see his reaction—everything he would have revealed at mention of the name had he been a Chicagoan. But he said, "He's dead."

"He was bumped off by a rival prince." She was as serene as if she were discussing the strawberry festival at the Episcopal church. "That was a year before Don enlisted."

He found his voice. "Miss Smith, will you have a cup of coffee with me? I don't want to keep you in this—this squalor. And I do want to talk with you."

She was shaking her head.

"Please," he begged. "I've been hired by two women tonight to find Don Redhair."

"Two?" She seemed surprised.

"You know all about him. I know nothing. I'll split the fees."

He'd give it all to her. But if he suggested that, she'd begin wondering what he was doing here. "I'll do all the leg work, if you'll just give me a little brain help."

She interrupted. "Do you think Don Redhair is in Chicago?"

He was ashamed to lie to her, afraid to be truthful. Until he knew who "they" were, no one could be trusted.

He said, "Those two gals said he'd been seen on Randolph street."

She spoke after a pause. "I can't work for you, Mr. Scott. I already have a job. I'll be glad to tell you anything I can, but I'm afraid I don't know much more."

"Yes, you do," he said quickly. "You haven't told me how you came to know him, his friends—"

The mask settled on her face.

"How about the coffee?"

"I don't care for coffee now, thank you," she refused. "I would prefer to talk here." She looked at her watch. He looked at his. It was past eleven.

"May I take you home?"

"No, thank you. It is better if you don't." She didn't explain.

Kip twisted in the chair, wincing at its sound. Her mask was still working and he had to remove it.

He began conversationally, "Miss Smith, another Miss Smith and a Miss Fouré came here tonight looking for Don Redhair. Do those names mean anything to you?"

She didn't answer until she'd thought about it. "No."

"One girl knew him all her life. One is his fiancée. They told me nothing about him. How did you happen to know him?"

She was hesitant. "Ours was a business relationship."

He pressed her. "Who introduced you? Who are his friends?"

She spoke with stiff lips. "No one introduced us. I knew who he was. He—" She was being careful. "You would say he picked me up."

"A business relationship?"

"Yes. I did some work for him."

"You're a stenographer?"

"Yes."

"Where?"

"I would prefer not to tell you that, Mr. Scott," she replied quietly.

He accepted it. "What about his friends?"

"I was not introduced to any of his friends." She looked at her watch again, frowned. "I must go. It's late."

He reached for the pad. "Will you give me your home address?"

She was up. "I'd prefer not to."

He flung down the pencil, jumped up. "Where can I reach you?"

She hesitated. "I'll get in touch with you, Mr. Scott."

VI

He had no way of knowing how to get in touch with any of them except Hyacinthe Fouré. And he had a hunch she was the least important of the three. He wanted to protest Mariel Smith's decision, but what good would that do? You couldn't argue with her, but maybe you could persuade her. Away from this den he'd look more like a human being.

He said, "If you'll wait a minute, I'll go downstairs with you."

Her refusal was as quiet as her others had been. "I'd rather not be seen with you, Mr. Scott."

He met her eyes. "Will you phone me tomorrow?"

To his surprise she answered, "Yes. Tomorrow evening?"

"You set the time."

"Between eight and nine," she said.

"I'll be in the office." He waited until she was at the door. "What did you do with my notes?" He waved the pad.

"I didn't touch your desk," she flared. The door slammed behind her. He'd probably made a mistake mentioning it. The scrap of paper wasn't as important as keeping Mariel Smith and her information at least in a state of neutrality.

He listened until the corridor was silent, without echoes. For the first time he regretted that he was attempting to handle this alone. He should have someone ready to follow her. But he didn't. No doubt she was already lost in the motion and sound of humanity surging up and down Randolph Street.

He clapped his hat on the back of his head, hunched into his overcoat, and put out the desk light. He crossed the room, walked fast down the corridor and ran down the stairs.

Adam was in the cage on the first floor. He said, "The service door wasn't bolted, Mr. Scott."

"I was afraid it wouldn't be." Kip went out into the night.

The lake breeze was slapping its way past Michigan, down to Randolph and Clark. Kip started into its tantrum but from the corner of his eyes he'd seen the chilled motionless figure under the lamp post. He swung around and walked towards Dokey.

"There won't be any more coming tonight, Dokey. It's too late and too cold." He slipped his arm through the icy coat sleeve. "Jude'll be going off duty pretty soon. Let's have a coffee with him."

Dokey said through chapped lips, "Someday—I do to them—what they did on Bataan."

"Sure." Kip coaxed, "You come back tomorrow. Someday—"

If you stood long enough at Clark and Randolph, you'd see everyone in the world.

Dokey was moving reluctantly to the bright warmness of the white front cafeteria. There weren't many customers at this hour near midnight. Behind the steam table was Jude, gaunt, tall—with Dokey's face, grown older, grown troubled—Jude, who wasn't wrapped in a hideous dream of righteous revenge.

"Go sit down," Kip urged Dokey. "I'll get the stuff." He waited until Dokey was at the table by the painted waterfall, in a chair facing the wide plate glass. Kip went to the counter.

"Two cups of coffee. Sweet rolls. Join us?"

"Take over, Shorty?" Jude asked the grizzled dwarf man.

"Sure." The dwarf winked. "No Japs tonight?"

Kip said, "No." He carried the tray back, put one set of coffee and rolls in front of Dokey, the other for himself in the place beside him.

When Jude carried his coffee cup and set it opposite, Kip warned, "Don't sit there. You obstruct my view."

"God's sake. Want me to lay on the floor?" Jude sidled his chair closer to the table. "What you looking for, Kip?"

"Women."

"God's sake."

"Girl in mink been in tonight?"

"What you think this is? The Edgewater Beach?"

"Ott Redhair ever come in here?"

Jude put his nose against the cup. "Maybe he did."

"What do you know about him?"

Jude said, "What everyone knew."

Kip smiled. "I'm an alien."

Dokey's lips moved, whispering blasphemy.

Kip's eyes went to the window pane. He said quickly, "That's Yun Li. You know Yun Li—our ally."

Dokey slowly relaxed.

Kip returned to Jude. "He was a racketeer?"

"Started with prohibition," Jude said. "They all did. After repeal some went straight." The scar on Jude's face wasn't from the war. He could go straight. He'd been too young to be important, a punk. Somebody had set him up in the eats business. "Ott Redhair was king of the rackets. He made his millions. Then he quit."

"Why did he quit?"

"He married a swell dame. North Shore society stuff. He was respectable then. He was—" Jude's scar twitched. "He was chairman of the Board of Directors, Rackets, Inc. Respectable. Ottley Rudyar."

"Rudyar?" Kip repeated the name.

"Maybe she wasn't Potter Palmer society," Jude went on, "but she was society. A beauty. Red hair."

"He quit and was bumped off."

Jude shook his head and sipped coffee. "He quit ten or eleven years before he was bumped off, Kip."

"Then why—"

"Grudge. The guy who bumped him was just paroled. It was Ott Redhair's gang who framed the guy. He got Ott, and the chair."

Kip passed his cigarettes and groped for an explanation. "She married him when he was a respectable King of Rackets. Then she made him quit."

"No. She died when Don was born."

"Then why did he quit?" Kip cried.

"Because of the kids," Jude explained patiently. "He didn't want them to know."

VII

The outline began to take shape.

When he was killed, the kids knew. Screaming from headlines. Ottley Rudyar—Ott Redhair. Don didn't talk of home and friends. Don didn't have friends. Pride and humiliation. Hand in hand. Pride in humiliation. Not Don Rudyar—*Redhair*.

"Kids," Kip repeated.

"Boy and a girl."

"Both with red hair."

"Like their mother. Red hair. Maybe that's why Ott married her. Ott had a sense of humor."

Kip scowled. "You knew I was looking for Don Redhair," he snapped. "Why didn't you tell me these things?"

Jude turned his deep sunken eyes on Kip. "I thought you knew."

"Sorry," Kip said. "What happened to the money?" In his mind he was thinking that he'd let Don's sister slip through his fingers tonight.

Jude was speaking. "There wasn't as much money as you'd think. Old Ott owned this block." His blunt fingers gestured. "Your building belonged to him, this club—lots of property. But he lived high."

So that was it. Don had gone to Princeton or Yale. He'd been a rich man's son. Perhaps then the papers had screamed, "He's the son of a racketeer!" And probably Don hadn't known it until then, because old Ott had been respectable for quite a time. Certainly the North Shore wouldn't have mentioned it, except among themselves as gossip. And the East hadn't heard about it. Yes, it must have been a jolt to Don.

"They had a swell apartment over on Lake Shore Drive," said Jude.

"What happened to the money?" Kip asked.

"The will was funny," Jude said but he wasn't laughing. "Borg got the buildings. Peppo the club. And I got a start here."

"The children?"

"Diana got the apartment, the bonds—about a quarter of a million. Donny got 'personal effects.' "

Kip's eyebrows lifted.

"That was in the will," Jude said. "I heard it read out loud."

"Why would they try to kill Don?"

"Nobody tried to kill Donny," Jude said, and he was curious. "Where did you get that idea?"

Kip didn't answer. Had Don Redhair, like Dokey, been crazed by the war? No, not the man Kip had known.

"He didn't get any money?"

Jude shook his head. "Many's the time I fed him. Grim would have helped him out, only Don didn't want help. He got a job on his own."

"What was the trouble between him and the old man?"

"There wasn't any," Jude said. "The old man was proud as a kite of Donny. That day in Wentworth's office, when he come back from college after hearing the news. Don's face—it was—like death."

Racketeer's son! He'd had that sledging blow, on top of the other. It had changed Don. He'd become Don Redhair—tough, taking nothing, starting from scratch.

Jude said, "I better get Dokey home." The boy's head was in his arms on the table.

"What about the Hotel Bursley where Don lived?"

"It was cheap," Jude said. "Nobody knew where Don was. When's Grim coming back?"

"I haven't heard from him," Kip said. He buttoned his overcoat. "Do you know Hyacinthe Fouré?"

"She sings at the Elegante." Jude bent over his brother. "Come on, son. We're going home now."

Kip didn't ask any more questions.

One o'clock and the Street still moved. Kip zigzagged with the wind, across to the noisiest place. It was just a hole in the wall where he blinked his eyes at the smoke, the dimmed lights and the roar of sound. He left his hat and coat with the check girl.

"A table," he said to the waiter, "for one."

In the small rectangle that was the Club Elegante, every table had a view of the orchestra platform. Hyacinthe Fouré was singing into the mike. She wasn't bad but she'd never make the Empire Room.

He said to the waiter, "Brandy without soda and I want to see Peppo."

The square, suave man, with the strangely handsome night-club face, was there before the brandy. Kip saw his maroon lapel carnation first.

He queried, "Signor Peppo?"

"Yes."

"I'd like to meet Miss Fouré."

Peppo wore courtesy over toughness. His might have been the

hands which mauled with tommy-guns, he might have driven a car of death, but he was respectable now, impresario of Chicago's night life.

He said, "I'm afraid you've come to the wrong club. Miss Fouré—"

Kip interrupted as courteously, "Will you tell her it's Kip Scott?"

Peppo bowed slight, blandly. "If you know Miss Fouré, Mr. Scott—"

He moved with dignity, maneuvering his way through the tables. The waiter brought the brandy. The first murkiness of the room was clearing as his eyes became accustomed to the smoke. He saw her then, the girl who must be Diana Redhair. Diana Rudyar. She was at a favored table, well down the room, at the edge of the diminutive dance floor. Two men were with her. One of them had his back toward Kip. It was a broad back, almost twice the width of a normal back. The other man, who was facing Kit, was blond. He had aristocratic narrow features, and a moustache.

Kip sipped brandy until Hyacinthe encored with another torch song and disappeared behind the curtained backdrop. He didn't see Peppo but he did see Hyacinthe slanting her way toward him. She was in red that glittered. Before he could rise to his feet, she slipped onto the bench beside him. The roses in her hair smelled of perfume.

"Why did you come here?" she queried.

"To speak with you, Hyacinthe. Have a drink?"

She said, "I'll have coffee." She twisted her slim fingers nervously. "I drink coffee to keep awake. You shouldn't have come here."

"Why not?" He looked into her eyes then and noticed the fright in them. "Ah. You don't want Peppo to know you're looking for—"

She caught his arm so tightly that he wanted to wince. "Don't mention the name. Please."

"I won't. Is that it?" The waiter came up, so he ordered coffee and another brandy. When the waiter had gone, she answered Kip's question with a nod. She was looking behind him, so he turned, following the direction of her graze. Peppo was standing back there, smiling across the room at their table. Kip's gaze returned to Hyacinthe.

"Who are the men with Diana Rudyar?" he asked her.

She turned her great, dark widened eyes upon him. "You know her?"

"We've met. Who are they?"

She said, "The one facing you is Monty Wentworth. The other is Cy Borg."

Her voice was a trifle too low for inflection. Jude had mentioned that name, Borg. "What do they do for a living?"

She said, "I don't know. Mr. Wentworth is a business man, I guess. I never asked."

He believed her.

"Mr. Borg is—he has money. I don't know if he works."

"Capitalists. You know many of them?"

"I've met some of them. They like to get around."

VIII

The coffee and brandy were set on the table. She took her coffee black.

"They come here often?"

"Quite often."

"And Diana Rudyar?"

"Sometimes." She looked over the cup at him. "Why did you come here?"

"You didn't tell me you worked for a man employed by Don's father."

"I didn't think it mattered," she said. Her eyes were enormous. "You won't tell him I came to you?"

"Confidential agency. Does Peppo know you were engaged to Don?"

"No."

"Has he seen Don?"

"Oh no."

"Did Don come here often?"

She finished her coffee. "No." She put down the cup. "Have you found out anything?"

He said slowly, "No. But I will."

She said, "I must go back. I have to rest my voice between numbers."

He waited until she was gone from sight, waited until the orchestra tooted two more numbers. Then he paid his check and moved towards the lodestone, stood in back of Cy Borg.

"Hello," he said.

Diana looked up and when she recognized him her smoky eyes darkened.

He said, "I didn't expect to find you here, Diana." He wanted her to think he had had her followed despite her trickery. She did.

She said, "I didn't expect to see you."

The men were standing. Borg had turned to observe Kip. Borg was an enormous man, with a flat, brutish face. At some time or other, his nose had been broken and he'd had it fixed up with plastic surgery. Borg was smiling now, but his eyes remained cold and gray. Wentworth, on the other hand, was a gentleman, older than he had looked from across the room. His hair was thinning out at the temples.

She was forced to introduce them.

"Mr. Wentworth, Mr. Borg, Mr. Grimsley."

"Scott," Kip said. The mistake had been deliberate.

"Grimsley's detective agency." Her lips lifted slightly.

Borg demanded, "Where's Grimsley?"

"I've taken over the agency." Kip bared his teeth. "I don't know where he is."

"He sold out?"

"Yeah." Kip hadn't come to rehash this. He wasn't going to be invited to join the party. He said, "Nice to see you, Miss Rudyar," nodded to the men and left.

He looked back from the doorway. They were watching him. Kip pushed against the wind to the corner of Clark and Randolph, the northwest corner. His eyes slid across and up to Grimsley's lightless windows, the name showing dark on the gray panes. He crossed to the old and blowsy but respectable hotel on Clark. His room was on the third floor, a corner room where he could watch Grimsley's windows at night.

He came into his room on slow feet. The room was too large, too shadowy. Anyone could be hiding here in dark corners. He made a light, flung off his coat and hat savagely. There was no one in the room but himself. No one was hunting him. It was Don Redhair they wanted. If Kip had dropped the name into the vortex of Clark and Randolph three weeks ago, he'd be three weeks nearer finding Don's pup.

Don's spotted pup. He now realized why he had blundered, at first. Don hadn't said, "Don't let them get—my dog." He'd said, "my pup—the spotted pup."

Someone had taken the page where Kip's hand penciled a spotted pup. Someone! It had to be Diana Rudyar or Mariel Smith, not Hyacinthe Fouré. Unless she'd slipped back while he was talking to Dokey. Whoever had taken the sheet knew that Kip Scott was aware of the spotted pup.

They—the cryptic "they"—might think he had the pup. If they had it, they wouldn't be interested in the whereabouts of Don Redhair.

He didn't know why a dog should be valuable. But he intended to find out. If only Grimsley hadn't died. That was rotten luck. Kip pulled off his clothes. Three women were in on it now. And two men, Cy Borg and Peppo, who'd been associated with old Redhair. Another man who couldn't have been Montgomery Wentworth. The luck had changed.

It was morning too soon. Another gray, dirty day, the chill of it dank even in the heated hotel room. There was no reason for Kip to dress, scald himself with coffee in the hotel drugstore, and go out into that cold to wait through another day. The girls wouldn't return by day. None of them wanted to be seen here. If the men were interested, they were leaving the leg work to the girls. He smiled mirthlessly. Leg work was right for these girls.

He dragged open the files; not that he hadn't been through them often enough to recite the contents from memory. It was more for something to do, on the off chance that some thread might have been overlooked. In them he had found papers—the dirty linen of divorce, evidence of malice and defamation, the poverty of little claims. But the files had failed to give up anything concerning Don Redhair or Rudyar.

There had not been a shred of information about Don in Grimsley's room either, when Kip had gone back to search it after Grimsley had died. It had been a curious room, Grimsley's—cluttered with colorless belongings which seemed to make a pathetic bid for respectability. Well, Grimsley had been given a nice funeral. In death Grimsley had achieved respectability.

Kip had paid for the funeral. He'd told the hospital authorities the sum was due Grimsley for a business deal. Grimsley hadn't had any money. He'd even owed three weeks' rent on his one-room apartment.

He'd had no friends, no letters. He'd kept his business confined to his office, but he'd left no record of it there.

They—and the "they" was pinned down this time; it was three girls and the men behind them—they didn't know Grimsley was dead. Each of the girls had been troubled over that, even the last one, the indefinable Mariel Smith. A small newspaper item of the death of Jacob Grey had meant nothing to them. Jacob Grey had kept Grimsley out of his life.

Again Kip found nothing which interested him in the files—nothing of the man, Jacob Grey—little on Jake Grimsley. He clanged the metal drawers shut, went over and stood behind the unwashed windows. Below him Randolph Street swirled with jostling crowds. They were gayer at night.

Kip sighed and turned away. The weight of his gun bothered him, so he removed it and replaced it in the top drawer of the desk. He put on his hat and coat, locked both doors to the private office, and went out.

IX

Scott turned up his overcoat collar to the cold, swung into Clark and went south to La Salle. Here stood the hotel where Don had lived when he was hiding from shame and death, before pride had rescued him.

It wasn't even a second-rate hotel. It was Grimsley's all over again, repeated by means of the rusty pen, the dull brass spittoon, the withered fern. A moist-eyed man behind the desk scanned Kip wearily.

Kip asked, "How long have you worked here?"

The man was wary then. He suspected Officialdom. Kip spoke before the man could answer. "Did you know Don Redhair?"

"You a friend of his?" The damp nose was wrinkled with suspicion.

"Yes," Kip said. "I'm a friend of his from the East." Don had gone to school in the East.

"He ain't here now."

"I know that. Do you remember when he stayed here?"

The man wouldn't say yes or no.

Kip hid his impatience. "He was a friend of mine," he repeated.

"I'd like to get in touch with other friends of his. I came to Chicago for that. Who came to see him when he lived here?"

"Nobody," the man replied.

"He must have had some friends."

The head moved. "He didn't. Nobody. He didn't want to see anybody. His old man was Ott Redhair."

"I know," Kip said.

"It was after Ott died. That's when Don lived here. He felt bad. He didn't want to see nobody. The old man didn't leave him a dime. The girl got it all. Only it wasn't as much money as you'd think."

Kip asked carefully, "If Don didn't have money, how could he live in a hotel?"

"Friend of his paid for his room at first. Then Don got a job."

Kip asked with careful casualness, "Who was the friend?"

"Fellow who used to live here. Jacob Grey, his name was. He left before Don did."

Kip showed no disappointment. He listened to the end of the tired clerk's reminiscences. Jacob Grey was the only one in this place who had ever been friendly to Don. That was all. The trail leading to the dog was as obscure here as it had been in Grimsley's office.

Outside again he caught a cab in front of the station, not realizing until he was slouched in the seat that he didn't know the address of the place he intended to visit next. He pulled the dividing glass window open.

"Lake Shore Drive," he directed, adding, as an afterthought, "You wouldn't know where Ott Redhair's apartment is?"

The cab squeaked past a light. "Sure, I know it. The Riviera. Show place. That where you want to go?"

"Yes."

"Ott's dead," the cabbie blabbed. "He was a big shot in the rackets until somebody took him for a ride."

"So I'm told," Kip said. To himself he thought, "Everyone in Chicago knows Ott Redhair. He was a big shot. His children weren't. They were small-timers and conventional."

The lake was drab under the drab sky. There was a threat of snow in the air. The cab finally stopped before the Riviera, an imposing apartment building. The solid mass of gray stone might have been patterned after some great ducal mansion in Europe. The lobby was sunken in blue velour, richer than the best velvet. It screened the windows and cushioned the great oaken chairs. It gave an air of magnificence to everything. No, old Ott Redhair would not have understood the casual décor that passes for the grand today.

The clerk was a "gentleman," too. He had on a neat striped tie and emitted a faint but penetrating aura of *eau de cologne*. When he spoke his voice was somewhat precious, as if his up-tilted nose had pinched the words just a trifle.

"What can I do for you, sir?"

Kip said, "Miss Rudyar."

"Your name, please?"

If Kip told his name, she might not see him.

"Trent," he said, and smiled widely. "She asked me to drop around for Sunday breakfast."

He was taking a chance, but she might not remember whether or not she had met a Trent and issued an invitation. That type of girl would be curious about any man. The clerk spoke into the phone, nodded to Kip.

"Twelve A," he said.

Twelve A was the penthouse. Kip rode up in a silent plushy elevator. The man who admitted him was lighter than a mulatto, and as unobtrusive as the small gray-and-silver foyer.

He took Kip's hat and coat, and said, "Will you wait in the living room, Mr. Trent? Miss Rudyar is dressing."

He left Kip in the spacious room, redecorated after old Ott's tenancy. It was a splash of the modern—fuchsia on gray, expensive, exquisite. The great front window looked out on the lake.

Kip sat down on the satin stripes of an angular chair, lighted a cigarette. Diana had spent money on this room. There must have been fourteen more rooms at least on the two floors of the penthouse. Diana wouldn't have left any remnant of what old Ott had chosen in any of them.

He heard her coming down the oak staircase behind him but he didn't move until she was standing in front of his chair, with her smoky eyes cold as the window glass.

She said, "Your name isn't Trent."

"No." He couldn't explain why he'd used the name to this angry girl in golden lounging pajamas. He merely said, "I wanted to see you."

Her flaming hair was caught in a gold metallic net. She tossed her head in defiance.

"If I'd wanted you here I'd have sent for you," she said.

He sat down. This wasn't going to be pleasant. Kip waited until she looked at him before he spoke. "You haven't asked me why I came here. Don't you want me to find your brother?"

She stopped before him. Anger was swelling in her breast. "You won't find him here."

He smiled a little. "I'm quite sure of that."

"Get out then and find him."

He made himself more comfortable. "You didn't tell me Don Redhair was your brother."

"You found it out."

"I'm a detective, remember? Why did you come to me?"

She curled herself in the corner of the couch. Her eyes narrowed. He grew uneasy. He had felt surer of himself when she was angry.

"Who told you to come to me?" he asked her.

"I didn't come to you," she said insolently.

"Whom were you looking for? Redhair or Grimsley?"

X

She didn't flinch. There was no change in her, but he'd seen fear pushed down too often on the beachheads, to be fooled now. She didn't dare show her fear lest it run away with her. She managed to control it.

"I was looking for both," she said.

He said, "You're next of kin to Don Redhair. You ought to know where he was last heard from—where he was mustered out of the Army."

"He wasn't mustered out," she said sharply. "He was missing in action. He *was* dead. But he isn't now. He's back in Chicago. You've got to find him."

"Why did the old man leave you all his dough?"

"He didn't." Her response seethed with hatred.

"I heard different."

"He left me this place, mortgaged to the roof. The banks owns it now. He left me just enough to hire a punk detective."

"What happened to the money?"

She closed her lips tight.

"Who got it? Grimsley?"

She said, "I hired you to find Don. Stop asking me questions."
She stood up. "If you want them answered, find Don."

"Maybe Grimsley could tell."

Again she winced. She was afraid of Grimsley, and she'd pushed a
bell somewhere. The servant entered.

"Mr. Trent finds he can't stay for breakfast after all, Stanton," she
said. "You will show him out?" Her eyes smouldered. "I'll call you
when I'm free, Mr. Trent."

He said, "You'll hear from me."

As the man helped him with his coat, and handed him his hat, he
wondered what Stanton knew. Nothing, probably. He was too clean.
There was nothing of the plug-ugly about him. Kip rode down to the
street and walked until he found a cab. He went back to Grimsley's and
sat there until the windows were dark.

Between six and seven the phone rang just as Mariel Smith had
said it would, although he hadn't expected it. He'd thought she would
surely forget. If she had, he wouldn't have found her again. Too many
Smiths in the city directory.

"Have you found out anything?" she inquired.

He knew her voice. "I found out a little." He was trying to hold
her.

"What is it?"

"I don't trust phones," he said. "I want to talk with you direct."

She hesitated. "I forgot this would be Sunday," she said. "I'm not
in the Loop."

"You needn't come down here. I'll come to you." He hoped she'd
give him an address.

She balked him. "No. If it's important I'll come to see you."

He didn't want her at Grimsley's. She was too good for Grimsley's.
"I was just leaving the office," he said. "I have an appointment. Could
you make it somewhere in this vicinity in about an hour?"

She said, "Yes," but she didn't suggest a meeting place.

"Club Elegante?"

"No." Her refusal was sharp.

"Where?" She, too, was known at the Club Elegante? Then
someone around here must know about her.

"Henrici's," she said after a moment. "I'll be eating dinner. Don't ask for me. Find the table."

He had to accept that. She was determined not to be seen with him, which meant she was known to Don Redhair's enemies. He was certain he was closing in on them now. He walked to the window. Dokey was standing out there on the corner. That meant Jude was in the white front. The Elegante was open on Sunday night.

Pressing against the window he could see the flicker of lights at the corner of its sign. Jude might know something. Peppo knew plenty. Kip could talk to Jude. He could also force Peppo's attention. He put on his coat and hat and clattered down the stairs. There was no elevator man on duty Sunday nights. Only a pegleg watchman playing solitaire in the basement.

Jude wasn't in the white front.

"He took off tonight," the dwarf said.

"What about Dokey?"

The dwarf slapped spaghetti on a plate. "Dokey's getting out of hand. Sometimes Jude can't do nothing with him."

"I know. Who's taking him home?"

"Jude will. He's seeing Mickey Rooney at Warner's. He'll be in later. Want some coffee?"

"Later."

Kip cut through traffic to the Elegante. It was too early but there were a few drinkers inside. Peppo was standing with Cy Borg at a table. When Peppo saw Kip, he left the table and came forward. Peppo was smooth as cream.

"You come again to see Miss Fouré?"

"I came to see you," Kip answered.

The smile vanished. "On business? I have a seven-year contract with Miss Fouré—more than five years yet to run."

"I'm not in the night-club business," Kip said. "I'm a detective."

A crafty gleam came into Peppo's restless eyes. Maybe Diana hadn't told him about Kip. Maybe he hadn't sent Hyacinthe to Grimsley's after all. Hyacinthe had said, "Don't tell Peppo." She had meant nothing much to Kip. She was only one of the gang who had tried to kill Don. But Kip tried to protect her now.

"I came to see her last night," he said. "I heard she'd been mixed up with Don Redhair."

Peppo answered, barely moving his lips. "She wasn't mixed up with anyone, if that's what you mean.'

"She knew him."

"She knew him, yes."

"He used to come here."

"Sometimes. My club is fairly popular."

"He was broke," Kip said. "Redhair didn't have the price of a meal when he came here to see Hyacinthe. She's only been working in this place a couple of years. The old man didn't leave Don anything."

Peppo spoke suavely. "Don Redhair was a guest of the club always. Because of his father."

Kip knew better than that. "The old man left you this place," Kip said.

Peppo's eyes grew murky. "In gratitude for services rendered. That is in the will. He left me no money because I needed none. I don't know what you want, Mr. Scott, but I'd advise you to see my lawyer for information on my finances. Montgomery Wentworth."

"I've been hired to find Don Redhair," Kip snapped.

The man's eyes became hooded.

"By Diana Redhair," Kip went on.

"Rudyar," Peppo muttered automatically. His expression was openly hostile. "Don Redhair is dead."

Kip thrust his hands into his pockets. "She says he's walking the streets of Chicago." He could see Cy Borg lumbering up.

"Ghosts do not walk the streets of Chicago."

"She's not the *only* one believing in ghosts," Kip countered.

XI

Cy Borg was behind them, a neolithic bulk. His voice was massive, like his frame. "Who's talking about ghosts? Who's your friend, Peppo?"

Peppo said, "He is a detective, Cy. He's looking for Don Redhair. I told him Don is dead."

Cy Borg said, "Maybe he thinks Don isn't dead."

Kip didn't like being a celluloid ball.

"Maybe I don't think one way or another," he said. "Diana Redhair heard that her brother is in town and she hired me to find him."

"You think you can do the trick?" Borg's voice sounded threatening.

"I'll earn my pay," Kip snapped. "If I don't find him, it won't be because I haven't looked around, or that I didn't ask questions."

He saw Diana Rudyar, then, coming through the door. She was glorious in brown furs, with a bit of brown on her glowing hair. With her was Montgomery Wentworth. Her face flushed with anger when she saw Kip. She came to Cy and linked her arm through his.

"What are you doing here?" she demanded of Kip.

He said, "Working."

"He is asking questions," Peppo said unpleasantly. "About your father's will."

"What's that got to do with it?" Borg stuck out his chin. "The dick says you hired him, Diana."

She didn't take her eyes off Kip. "I'm firing him now," she said. "You can forget Don Redhair."

Kip shook his head. "No, I can't forget about him."

She was uncertain for the first time. Her arm pressed into Borg's.

Smilingly Kip explained. "You see, you aren't the only one who asked me to find Don Redhair. Others—"

Wentworth said in his cultured nasal voice, "There are others looking for him?"

Diana demanded, "Who are they? Why do they want to find Don?"

Kip's eyes went from one to another of that silent waiting circle. Then he laughed, turned on his heel and walked away. But his hands were clenched in his pockets, and even when he reached the doorway, his nerve centers were all set for a quick turn. Two of that silent group behind him had been killers.

Nevertheless, Kip reached Randolph Street still a living man. He didn't cut across to the restaurant for he didn't want them to follow and see him with Mariel Smith. He couldn't explain why he felt that way about her. She could be, and probably was, just another angle of this geometric puzzle of sinister men and glamorous women.

But if she were not, if she were someone who had been kind to Don, to a desperate, despairing Don hunted by men and memory, twisting along a path into obscurity, Kip would not endanger her. Don hadn't many breaks in that year, nor after. To him the Army had been a breathing spell, though not for long. Why had Don been forced to die while Kip Scott, Cy Borg, Dokey and Peppo were allowed to go on living? The gift of life wasn't always enviable. Yet, in the final analysis, all men clung to it.

Kip walked up to State for he had no way of knowing if he were being followed through the maelstrom of night life in the Loop. His plan was to circle blocks, and eventually to duck into the side entrance of Henrici's. Then he thought of a better route, through one of the unsavory black alleys. It was dark, lonely, beset with unsavory odors.

It was not until he had cut away from State into Dearborn that he remembered about his own safety. His nerves grew as taut as fiddle-strings. At any moment he expected a bullet to seek him out, and was alert to dodge away from a skull-shattering blow. He turned into the open only when forced to do so by rubbish piles. Yet no footsteps sounded behind him, no stealthy shadows darted for cover.

It was not until he came out upon the lighted street again that he realized how great a strain he had been under. The insides of his hands were clammy with cold sweat. He was shivering. He realized now what it meant really to be afraid!

But no one had followed him. Perhaps, after all, he wasn't considered to be dangerous to the Elegantes. He wasn't going to be shot down. Not yet. Diana and her friends hadn't known about others seeking Don Redhair. They wouldn't kill Kip Scott while he had information they wanted to get.

He crossed to the restaurant, in the middle of the block. They must know about Hyacinthe Fouré. If so, they had masked their knowledge well. Seemingly she hadn't wanted them to find out. If she was holding out on Peppo and Cy Borg, she was playing a dangerous game. As for Diana Rudyar, she had claws. Hyacinthe must be aware she walked with danger. She was the only one of the three girls who had openly betrayed fear in his office. He'd have to talk with her again, away from the Elegante, away from Grimsley's, some place where she could spill everything she knew.

The restaurant was warm. It was aged, sedate and dignified. He avoided the head-waiter and went on through to the Randolph Street side. Mariel was there, in a corner, hidden from the street by the depth of the room as well as by the counters at its front. She was eating.

For the benefit of anyone who might be there by design, he said, "Hello, there. I didn't expect to find you in town tonight."

Her smile was lovely. "Hello, Mr. Scott. I've been to a movie. That's why I'm eating downtown."

"You don't mind if I join you?"

"Of course not."

He sat down beside her, ordered without caring what he chose. When the waitress had gone, Mariel spoke softly.

"What have you found out?"

He said, "I don't know."

She showed quick annoyance, as if she suspected he'd tricked her into coming here for no reason. He wanted to be her friend. Realizing it, he felt a fool. But he wanted her to accept him as Kip Scott, of Gramercy Park, New York—someone whose existence mattered.

He said, "It isn't that bad. The trouble is that I can't piece things together. Maybe you can. You knew Don in a business way, you said."

"I did."

"Then maybe you will understand. Don's father left everything to Don's sister, Diana. A few bequests to henchmen. Don got nothing. It knocked him absolutely flat at first."

"Yes." She had her face averted and he couldn't tell how she felt.

He asked, "Why was there bad blood between Don and the old man?"

"There wasn't." She turned her face and looked at him now. But her eyes betrayed nothing. "Ott Redhair was proud of Don. He was—disappointed in Diana. That's why it was such a—blow." She went back to her dinner.

XII

Kip played with a spoon until the waitress brought his dinner.

"Why does Diana Redhair want to find her brother?" he demanded. "Wait a minute. I know that's normal. But why did Don deny her existence? Why did he name Grimsley next of kin?"

She said, "I don't know. But since it was Don I'm certain he had a good reason." She was lying and he knew it.

"Sure he had a good reason." Kip began to eat angrily. "She got the dough and she didn't help him out. She let him hole up in Bursley's with Grimsley paying the room rent and Jude giving him handouts. She didn't care if he lived or died. So he got himself some new kinfolk. Then all at once she's breaking her neck to find him."

Mariel Smith wasn't going to help him. Kip realized it suddenly. Although she had made no movement, her refusal was none the less plain. Kip spoke his thought aloud.

"Don had had everything—a good life, a good father, an old man to be proud of. And then without warning, overnight, he isn't Don Rudyar, son of a financier. He's Don Redhair, son of Ott Redhair the racketeer. That isn't so bad. Don could have taken that. He wasn't afraid of getting his hands dirty. But there was something worse than any of these things. His father, the father who'd been the greatest guy in the world to Don, in death turned away from him without any explanation. That's what licked Don. That's why he hid out. That's why he ran away even from his own sister. He couldn't bear pity. The only ones he would see were grubs who didn't know the name of pity."

She interrupted him in the tone of someone making a discovery. "You knew Don!"

He hadn't meant to give it away.

"Maybe I did, maybe I didn't," he replied angrily. "The point is, what happened to him? One day he's down and out, the next day he's valuable. Who tried to kill him? Why should anyone want to kill him?" He almost had the answer, now. He unfolded his ideas slowly. "Don wasn't valuable. He had something valuable—the dog!" He grasped her arm. "What about the dog?"

She said vaguely, "Dog?"

"Don's dog. His pup."

She picked his hand from her arm as if it were a leech. Her action made him ashamed of his anger, but he didn't apologize. He couldn't then.

"It must be the dog," he insisted. "It must be valuable."

She said, "Don didn't have a dog. Diana didn't like dogs. Dogs didn't like Diana either. Don told me. He didn't ever have a dog."

He couldn't believe that. And he still didn't know which side she was on, so he couldn't talk freely. Don's mind hadn't been wandering when he'd cried out not to let them get the pup.

Kip said slowly, "There's a dog which figures in it. They don't have it. If they did, they wouldn't care about Don."

Her lips tightened. "That isn't why I want to find him. I don't care about the spotted pup. I want Don." She broke off and sucked in her breath.

He'd known it wasn't a business deal, Don and Mariel. She'd given it away. He didn't say anything. He could have told her Don was dead but didn't. She could take it. Her heart might bleed inwardly, grievously, but she would never break. Kip couldn't do it to her. He railed silently at his softness but he didn't mention Don. He began to speak again, as if talking to himself.

"There's Peppo, one of old Ott's men, and Cy Borg, another. They haven't asked me to find Don but they know Diana's looking for him. Maybe they sent her to Grimsley's. Someone sent her there. Somebody sent Hyacinthe Fouré there. They're all mixed up in it somehow. You're the only one who doesn't fit in. But you know them, because you wouldn't go to the Elegante."

She said, "I don't like night-clubs."

"You didn't want them to see me with you. They know who you are."

"You're mistaken," she said quickly. "None of them know me. And I don't know them."

"Maybe not. But there's a tie-up somewhere, just as there's a tie-up between them and Montgomery Wentworth. Only I don't know what it is. If you'd help me—"

"I can't." She used the wrong word. It should have been "won't." She shook her head. "I'm sorry." She was getting ready to go. He couldn't leave with her. She'd refuse. He was a fool to want to be with her any longer, because she was she. That she was also someone who'd hired him to do the impossible didn't matter now.

"I wish you wouldn't hurry off," he said and despised himself for saying it.

She was gentle, if surprised. "I haven't hurried." They stood up and faced each other.

"You'll call me?" he asked.

"Yes." She was hesitant. "If you hear anything from Mr. Grimsley, you'll let me know?"

He said, "I don't expect to hear from him." He watched her— straight, dark, and slim—move out of sight. She did not look back. She'd loved Don Redhair. That had been her unguarded cry, "I want Don!" And she knew he was dead. The others didn't know, but her heart knew. The others didn't care—not even Hyacinthe.

He jerked his head up. "I want Don. *I don't care about the spotted pup.''* Kip hadn't said it was a spotted pup. His chair rasped as he shoved it savagely against the table. She knew about the dog. That was what she let slip out that was important—not her love for Don. And Kip, like a wide-eyed juvenile, had sat there mooning about love. Turning, he rushed into the street, but she was long gone. There was no one on Randolph Street except the usual night herd, milling up to State, down to Clark. No one he cared about in those hundreds of people—not one person—not Mariel Smith.

He returned to the restaurant, paid his check and went out into the night. Roughly he pushed his way down to the corner, and up the stairs to the dirty empty office. He sat there alone, in the dark, until it was too late for anyone to come, even the ghost of Grimsley. . . .

Dokey wasn't on the corner. It was Jude who stood near the lamp post, in his stiff Sunday clothes, his face strained, his breath coming from his mouth in chilled vapor clouds as he scanned the passersby.

Kip said, "Jude."

The man's eyes turned. "F'God's sake, Kip."

"Where's Dokey?"

Jude said, "F'God's sake, Kip, will you find him for me? I promised Momma."

"Where is he?" Kip repeated. It wasn't his business to worry about Dokey. He had enough to worry about, for he'd known too many Dokeys, in the war and after, to take on added burdens. Boys! Their minds weren't theirs any more. They were like old men, obsessed by the past and the obscenity of war. It was not clean like death. It was the depravity of the god of war. He said to Jude, "Go on back inside before you get pneumonia. You can't take care of Dokey if you're sick. Where did he go?"

"I don't know, Kip." Jude pulled his forefinger across his moist nose. "He wasn't here at midnight when I came for him, like he ought to be. He was gone and nobody's seen him."

"Did you ask at the Chinks?"

"They haven't seen him. He never did go after them but once, but they understood how it was. Some of them were in the war. They understood about Dokey."

"Sure they did." Kip pushed Jude away. "Go on. Get inside! I'll bring Dokey back. I'll find him."

He watched Jude move stiffly up Randolph to the cafeteria with his anxiety relieved. Yeah, Kip would find Dokey for Jude. He couldn't dig up information when it hit him in the face, but he'd find Dokey.

The kid might be gone to hell and nowhere by now, following someone with slant eyes or the wrong kind of moustache. But he'd find him. Kip Scott, the great detective. The new Grimsley. He turned savagely past the drugstore into the bitter darkness of Clark. He ought to tell the police, but Momma wouldn't want her boy mixed up with the police. The cop on the corner—the cop who knew what Dokey was and how he'd got that way—that would be different.

Burzak had gone off duty hours ago. Kip shot a glance up an alley as he strode by, the sound of his feet loud on the pavement. He walked on a few steps, then stopped. Had he seen a figure up there, lying beside the ash can? Or was it a pile of dirty waste? Maybe it had been just his imagination. He was obsessed by alleys tonight, because he had skulked through one when he'd been so brave, so foolhardy.

He hesitated, then went back to the mouth of the alley, cursing himself for wanting to make sure, cursing himself for being squeamish. Already he had a queer feeling in the pit of his stomach. What nonsense. It had only been a pile of waste on greasy, dirty cobbles. Yet as he turned into the alley and walked along it, his heart began playing tricks again.

He went up the alley, part way, and halted, looking down at the waste. But it wasn't waste. It was a girl.

XIII

Kip had never seen a girl dead before. He'd seen plenty of men, slumped and grotesque in death—too many of them—but never a girl who had been flung on her face in the slime. His knees almost buckled as he bent over and half turned her, to learn who she was. As he stooped he was afraid he would know her. Because he was remembering a red dress that had glittered under cabaret lights, before it had been mauled.

There was blood on his hands as he eased her back to the paving. He took his handkerchief and wiped the blood from his fingers, sick at heart because Hyacinthe Fouré was dead. She hadn't meant anything to him but she didn't belong with death. He didn't even know if he was responsible for her death.

He stuffed the handkerchief into his pocket and his knees were strong again, from anger. Now he had more than a dog to find! A murderer!

He saw the shadow waver behind the ash can and he went lunging toward it. He had no fear as he reached for his gun. But he hadn't brought it along. It was back in the drawer at Grimsley's.

Still angry, still devoid of fear, he laid hands on the shadow, and jerked it up. Now a worse sickness came over him for it was Dokey! Dokey, with his eyes swollen from crying, his cheeks wet. The smell of cheap whiskey reeked from his coat.

Kip couldn't speak. There was nothing he could say.

Dokey's voice was hoarse and broken. "She said she was a Jap. But she wasn't a Jap. She was Hyacinthe!"

Kip took the gun out of Dokey's lax hand—Dokey's gun that was never loaded, that Jude made certain was never loaded. It had Dokey's fingerprints on it and Jude's and now Kip's. But probably not those of the man who had put real bullets in it? This had been a safe way of murder, using a weak mind that knew but one enemy. It was almost like a gag. Why had Hyacinthe played such a dangerous game? Who was behind it?

"I thought she was a Jap," Dokey mumbled again.

Kip said, "You didn't kill her." He said it coldly, beating the fact into Dokey's brain. "You didn't kill her."

He put the gun in his own pocket, with the bloody handkerchief. He said, "Come on. Jude's waiting for you."

He took Dokey's arm and led him out of the alley, back up Clark street—but not to Dokey's corner—across to the hotel. There was no blood on Dokey's coat. If there had been once it had dried now, and such stains don't show on dark blue cloth.

Kip said, "We'll go to my room. Jude's going to meet us there. Be quiet till we get upstairs. We don't want to wake anybody."

He held Dokey's arm as they got into the elevator. The elevator man would notice Dokey, but it didn't matter. Dokey wasn't going to be mixed up in this. That was the only thing Kip was sure about. Dokey wasn't to figure. Dokey hadn't hunted Don Redhair. He hadn't killed Jake Grimsley. He wasn't the murderer of Hyacinthe Fouré.

The night elevator man was not curious, however. Two men going to their rooms at three a.m. meant nothing in the Clark Street hotel. Kip ushered Dokey into the room, switched on the light and pointed to the bed.

Jude wasn't coming yet. First Kip would have to call Jude, and tell him. But he wanted to talk with Dokey first. Dokey sat down on the edge of the bed and pulled his hands out of his pockets. He didn't rest. He sat there stiffly, fiddling his hands.

Kip said, "Who stood you the drinks?"

"She did." Dokey slurred out words, not good words to hear spoken. He was himself again. He wasn't afraid or sorry. He was obsessed by hate.

"Why?"

"It was cold. She said she was cold. She didn't look cold. She told me I needed a drink." He looked sly. "Jude don't let me drink."

Kip saw something in Dokey's hand."

"Why did you get that?" he cried, and snatched it away before Dokey could protest.

Dokey said, "It was in her hair. It smelled nice. I took it to smell."

Kip thrust it into his pocket with the gun and the bloodstained handkerchief. Dokey dropped flat, with his face in the pillow.

Kip said, "I'd better call Jude."

Dokey was already asleep.

Kip looked through the classified directory, found the number he wanted and gave it to the operator. He heard the sirens screaming before he got the connection. Someone else had found Hyacinthe.

He said into the phone, "I want Jude."

"It's Jude, Kip."

"I found him." He kept his voice dull. "Come to my room in the hotel, number three hundred, at once. Don't talk to anyone."

Jude quivered, "What—"

"Get over here quick and be quiet."

Jude wouldn't give anything away. He'd been one of Ott's men. He knew what quiet meant. Kip put out the light and stood at the window. They'd found her. He could see far up Clark Street. The police car was pulling up to the curb. Both officials and the curious people were gathering there. Someone had stumbled across her and called the police. No alley derelict would have reported it. That would have solved the case quick enough—a bum and a girl.

She'd been found because someone wanted her found, because

someone had tipped the police off. Over the phone, anonymously? That
was the usual way. Now would they point to Dokey? Dokey would have
to be kept out of sight. No! That would be a give-away. That was what
the murderer was depending on and hoped Jude would try to hide
Dokey. No one would believe that Dokey was innocent unless he stood
his watch at night under the lamp post. But how could they keep him
quiet?

Kip heard a cautious knock. He strode over and asked without
opening the door, "Who is it?"

"Jude."

Kip opened up and let Jude slip inside. Even the grimy hotel
electric bulbs gave enough light to show how white Jude's face had
become. He spoke to Kip between stiff lips.

"Cops! On Clark!"

"That's why I put out the light." Kip went back to the window.
Jude followed him. "Dokey—he's here?"

"It was a gag," Kip said. "He thought she was a Jap. She said she
was a Jap. Someone told her to say that for a gag. Before that somebody
had got hold of his gun and loaded it. And she was a fool. She gave him
liquor." Kip let out his breath. "Somebody murdered her. Only Dokey
held the gun."

Jay's face was screwed up with worry.

Kip said, "I'm not a detective. But now I'm going to be one. I'm
going to find out who that someone is."

"I'll find out," Jude said. There wasn't much change in his voice
but it was the voice of a killer.

"I'll find out," Kip said savagely. "It's mixed up with Don
Redhair. There's three men and—" His lips came together in a hard
line. It couldn't be Mariel. But then again, maybe it was. "There are
two women left in it. One of them is guilty. The rest of them helped
her."

Jude didn't know what he was talking about but the words didn't
matter. The intonation was enough.

Jude said, "Maybe you don't know. There's a lot of folks who had
it in for Ott. Maybe it's gang stuff."

Kip looked at him and spoke wonderingly. "Diana Rudyar didn't
get killed. It was Hyacinthe Fouré."

He turned his back on Jude's animal grunt. He didn't know why it had been Hyacinthe, and not Diana. But it was always like that. The defenseless were out of luck. If life had it in for you, she didn't stop until she had you flattened. The Dianas never got hurt.

It took the police a long time to carry a battered girl out of an alley. More cars were there, more figures in the dark. Fingerprint men and photographers and newspaper reporters. They might find Dokey's fingerprints but they wouldn't match them to Dokey's fingers. He wasn't going to be a suspect.

From habit Kip moved his gaze to Grimsley's windows. They should have been dark now, but they were glowing, lemon-hued. As he watched, a shadowy shape crossed them. Kip scowled and swung around.

"I'm going out."

He passed Jude standing over Dokey, looking down at him with hopeless eyes.

"Don't let him leave. Stay here till I get back." Kip stepped into the hall, turned and opened the door again. "Lock the door."

He ran then. Without bothering to ring for the elevator, he clattered down the cement stairs to the lobby. Outside the biting air stabbed him, and he was glad he hadn't removed his coat and hat. He cut across the street, almost ghost-quiet at this hour. The building was locked. Of course, it would be locked. That must have been the night watchman's shadow he had seen. Kip angrily produced his keys. The night watchman really had no legitimate reason to be in Grimsley's at this hour. So it couldn't have been the night watchman, after all.

Kip let himself in and, walking softly, started up the stairs. He walked as quietly as a cat on the balls of his feet, toward the office, hoping the uninvited visitor was too absorbed to listen. Without a sound Kip unlocked the door to the private office, swung it wide and stood in the doorway.

The men inside didn't care about Kip. They'd heard him approach, all right, but hadn't bothered to hide. Peppo didn't take his hands out of the desk drawer. Cy Borg didn't close the files.

"Make yourself at home," Kip said.

Probably they had guns, too, both of them. They didn't need the weapons for this. Either of them could have taken care of Kip unaided by weapons other than their fists.

XIV

Kip sauntered on into the room.

"Find anything?"

He flung himself down in the client's chair, pretending an arrogance he didn't feel. He also lighted a cigarette he didn't want because their eyes were watching him.

"If you'd tell me what you're looking for, maybe I could help you," suggested Kip.

Peppo looked at him, poker-faced, "Hyacinthe Fouré was murdered tonight."

"I know." Kip squinted at the cigarette between his fingers. "I know. I just came from there."

Cy Borg lurched up to the desk. His ugly face was not nice to see. "Who bumped her off?"

Kip looked at him, level-eyed. "Do you want to hire me to find out?"

"Why was she bumped off?"

"I've been asking myself those same questions," Kip said. "I don't know. But I think it's tied up with Don Redhair."

Peppo said thinly, "Ghosts don't walk."

"No, ghosts don't walk." Kip stared at Peppo. "But the danger that threatened Don hasn't been exorcised. It walks, and Hyacinthe got in the road. That's the way I figure things out."

"I don't know what he's talking about," Borg complained.

Peppo said, "Maybe he'd better explain."

Kip asked insolently again, "Do you want me to find out who killed Hyacinthe? And why?"

Cy Borg figured with ten fingers and ten toes. He said, "Yeah, find out." His lower lip jutted out as he uttered the dare.

Kip said, "First there's a small retainer fee. Fifty dollars. Then it costs twenty-five dollars a day, and expenses."

Peppo asked, "What makes you think you can find the murderer?" There was insinuation in the way he said it. Borg was figuring again.

Kip pulled up in the chair. "Because I'm going to discover who did it, whether I'm hired or not. Maybe Hyacinthe knew Don Redhair too well."

Peppo's lips tightened. "I told you that Hyacinthe—"

Kip cut in, "Too well to feel safe. She knew too much. She was Don's"—he gave the word the inflection the girl had "—fiancée."

It was as if Kip had slashed Peppo across the eyes.

"She told me that herself," Kip added. He was sorry for the man.

Borg laid a thick palm on Peppo's shoulder and pushed him down. "Let it go." There were bills in Borg's other hand. "I'll hire him. Maybe he's smarter than he talks. If the girl said she was something to Don, she had a reason." He dropped the bills on the desk. "Go on. Find out."

Kip reached over and scooped them up. He smoothed them, new bills, a fifty against two tens and a five.

"How did you know she was murdered?" Borg watched as Kip put the money in his wallet.

Peppo said, "When I was closing the club—"

Borg said, "A guy who works in the club told us. He heard the sirens. He went to see what was beating. He came back and told us."

"So you drifted up here. Why?"

Peppo's laugh was not pleasant. "You were interested in Hyacinthe. She was killed." He lifted his padded shoulders.

Borg said, "Go on and tell him. We were looking for what you'd put down about her—what she told you."

"You found nothing," said Kip.

"Nothing." Borg said. "Nothing but Grim's old stuff. Where's Grim?"

Kip looked at the pushed-in face. He could read curiosity there, but that was all. Peppo's face was as blank as a mask. Kip leaned forward and squashed out his cigarette in the nicotined dish on the desk. When he straightened again, he let them have the truth.

"Grim is dead."

So they hadn't known! Neither of them could put on such an act otherwise—eyes rounded, mouths open, jaws slack. After the first shock had passed, they showed fear.

Borg's breath whistled from his mouth. "Grim's dead?"

"Yes, he's dead."

"Who killed him?" Borg, big Borg, almost had been afraid to ask, for his voice squeaked.

"I don't know who killed him," Kip answered. "Probably the same one who killed Hyacinthe Fouré."

"Aw, she didn't know Grim," Borg objected.

"She knew Don Redhair," Kip said.

Peppo asked, "How do you know Grim's dead?"

"I buried him." That was enough to make them afraid of Kip. Until now, they hadn't been. He didn't look tough as they were used to toughness. But they certainly were afraid of him now.

"Then I took over Grimsley's," went on Kip. "To find out about Don Redhair." He pushed back his hat. "Grim's dead because he knew too much about Don Redhair and was going to spill it to me." That increased their worry. "Somebody got Grim, just as somebody got Hyacinthe Fouré, before she could talk." He didn't know if he were right or wrong when he added, "Why don't you both open up before it's too late?"

Borg sneered, "What about?"

"Who tried to kill Don?"

"He died in battle," Peppo said.

"Sure he died in battle." No more beating around the bush, now. "Who tried to kill Don before that? Why are they saying he's come back? What's behind it? Who wants him to show up? What did Don have that made him worth killing? What happened to Ott's fortune?"

Peppo's eyes had masked again. And Borg's hands went into his pockets.

"Is that what you asked Grim?" Borg's eyes had narrowed.

"Maybe it was."

"Then you come into this even before anybody asked you to find Don?" The big man's eyes were mean and wise. "Who put you up to it?"

Kip knew then he'd told them too much. But he didn't care. He flung out a challenge they could not refuse.

"Don Redhair asked me to come here and browse around."

Fear returned to them—under their wariness, under their disbelief.

"But Don's dead," Borg insisted. But he was not sure now.

Peppo looked at the big man. "Of course, he's dead, Cy. You saw the War Deprtment notice yourself. Didn't you?" His voice rose sharply. "You did, didn't you?"

"I saw it. Sure I saw it."

Kip said, "The War Department can make mistakes. Sometimes men return from the dead." Let them think that. Let them quarrel among themselves. Let them fear. Kip alone knew where the cross stood, the cross that marked the spot in France. He twisted his head around.

"There's someone coming," he said. He had heard before they did, because his ears were attuned to the sounds of the old building. Whoever the person was, he was still on the staircase.

Borg's hand streaked to his armpit. "Put it away," Kip said. He had prescience. "It's probably the police."

"Why should they come here?" Peppo asked softly.

"I don't know the answer to that one," Kip said. "But you'd better let me do the talking." They'd never guess it was because of Dokey he wanted to handle matters here.

The feet stopped near the open door. Borg's big face showed panic. It must have been a long time since he had been trapped in a room with the police outside, but he remembered what had followed only too well. Peppo's features were expressionless. He controlled them skillfully.

There was no knock, no preliminaries. The man who walked in from the hall was in plainclothes. He had a small, wiry frame. His appearance was almost mild looking. Behind him clumped a thickset flatfoot.

The small man said, "Kip Scott?" His voice wasn't mild.

Kip said, "Yes."

"I'm Lieutenant Cagle."

He moved nearer, the flatfoot at his heels.

"Good evening, Lieutenant," Kip said. "Can I help you?" His words didn't sound like he intended them to be. They quavered.

Cagle halted at the edge of the desk. He blinked at the two other men and said, "Hello, Cy. Hello, Peppo. Hear what happened tonight?"

Kip answered for them. "We were just discussing it."

"You didn't read about it in no paper," the flatfoot growled.

"No." Kip controlled his temper. "I was on my way home when I saw the police cars. I was curious enough to investigate. It's my business to know about such things."

"A waiter in my club brought the news to Cy and me," Peppo said.

Cagle looked from Peppo to Kip, back again. "What time did the girl leave the club tonight?"

Peppo waved a careless hand. "I didn't see her leave. I was with Cy and his party at a table."

Cy put in, "Me and Monty Wentworth and Diana Rudyar. After they went I stayed on, talking business with Peppo. Pretty soon a waiter tells us about Hyacinthe and we come here. We was together all the time."

There was sweat rolling down his neck when he finished giving his alibi.

"Mr. Borg dropped over to ask me to find out who killed Hyacinthe Fouré," Kip added quietly.

Lieutenant Cagle stuck a cigarette in his mouth and scratched the match along the top of the desk. Kip didn't care. Another scratch didn't matter.

"What business you in now, Cy?"

"I'm a wholesale liquor dealer," Cy said. "Honest."

"Honest enough," Cagle admitted wryly. Suddenly he switched his eyes to Kip.

"You," he said. "What time did she leave you? When did you see her last?"

XV

Kip could hardly believe it. They suspected him of murder. His astonishment must have showed plainly upon his face. Cagle, however, seemed unimpressed. He was watching Kip as a hawk watches a chicken. Kip drew a long breath. He had been asked a question and it must be answered. He shook his head.

"I didn't see that girl tonight."

Cagle thought he was lying. His lips curled with contempt.

"That's the truth!" Kip shook with anger. "I saw her last night at Peppo's. I haven't laid eyes on her since. Anyone who says otherwise is a liar."

He was sweating as Borg had, and it occurred to him that maybe Borg had nothing to hide about Hyacinthe's death, after all. It was knowing he was right and knowing Cagle didn't believe a word of it that made him squirm. Then a new idea hit him. Perhaps Peppo and Borg had steered the police here, deliberately, to incriminate a nosey guy who had gotten in their way. Their faces showed they weren't at all displeased at the way Cagle had turned on him.

Kip fought for self-control. "Miss Fouré hired me professionally, Lieutenant Cagle." His anger had been a mistake. "She came here last night. Later I went to see her at the club where she was employed— Peppo's club." It didn't matter now who knew about Hyacinthe coming to him. "I haven't seen her since then. I was in the club earlier tonight but I didn't see her."

Cagle listened. His expression didn't change. His gaze remained on Kip while he fished in his watch pocket, brought out a fold of paper, and tossed it across the room to Kip.

Kip had to wrench his eyes away from those of the police lieutenant in order to inspect the paper. Inwardly Kip was afraid. It was a fear he'd never known before—the fear of the outlaw facing the law— similar to the fear that had turned Borg to jelly when he, unasked, had given his alibi. Kip felt his anger return. He wasn't an outlaw and there was no reason for him to experience these tremors. He read the slip with cold deliberation.

It was on Grimsley's faded letterhead. The battered machine over there in the corner had typed the message:

> Meet me in my office when you are free tonight. Use the
> service entrance. The front door is locked on Sunday. Be sure
> no one sees you come.
> Kip Scott.

The signature was typed. There were interlaced initials penciled over it.

"I didn't write this," said Kip. "I know nothing about it." Kip handed it back to Lieutenant Cagle. "I left the office this morning and didn't return." He turned cold eyes on Peppo, on Borg. There was no reason to help them now. "Until I"—he must not mention his hotel room—"noticed the lights on in the office. I came up to see who had broken in. I found these men here, paying my office an unannounced visit."

"We didn't bust in," Borg said. "The door was wide open."

That was a lie. It couldn't have been open. The door was self-locking, and Kip had shut it when he had gone out.

"And the front door downstairs?" Cagle queried.

"It was open, too," Borg said.

More lies. Was Borg protecting himself or deliberately trying to incriminate Kip? Kip didn't know. Any one of several persons could have typed the message and penciled the initials.

"The door fastens itself," Kip said. "The front door downstairs is always shut on Sunday nights. I didn't type that message and I didn't sign it. I don't know what can be proved."

"This much," Cagle said. He was deceptively casual. "The girl had this message but she told no one about it. She came to the back door, by way of the alley. The service door was locked. She stood outside, stood there quiet a little while. But no one came. Finally she left. It was when she was starting out of the alley that she got hers."

Kip said, "You think that is what happened?"

"We know," Cagle said. "We found the message in her coat pocket. She told the doorman when she left the club that she was meeting her sister. Various things have shown how much time she spent waiting to get in."

Kip repeated, "I know nothing about it."

He wasn't believed.

Cagle said, "I'm afraid we'll have to take you in for questioning, Scott."

Peppo and Borg were too silent. Kip gazed at them. If they'd talk—they could reveal more than he could. He hadn't enough proof to accuse them.

Borg spoke. "Guess we'd better be on our way, Peppo." The big man moved gingerly, as if he really didn't expect Cagle would allow him to leave.

Peppo lifted himself out of the chair. "You know where to find me, Lieutenant," he said.

Kip protested, knowing all the time how futile it was. "What about that? What about their breaking in here tonight?"

"They didn't break in," the flatfoot said. "The door was open."

"Then why didn't Hyacinthe walk in?" Kip ignored the flattie for Cagle.

"The service door was locked," Cagle said.

Kip watched as Peppo walked heavily to the door. He watched the elephantine Borg sidle after him.

Kip said, "Maybe she did walk in."

Borg looked back. His little eyes skittered to Kip alive with hate. His voice was tough. "Not when we was here."

"Come on, Cy," Peppo said. He waited by the door until Borg was there.

Kip spoke again, his face sardonic. "You still want me to find Hyacinthe's murderer?"

Peppo didn't wait for the machinery of Borg's mind to fashion an answer. Seizing the big man's coat sleeve, he pushed him through the door.

Peppo's mouth was twisted as he paused for a moment. "Ask him about Jake Grimsley's death." He went out. The flatfoot kicked the door shut after them.

Kip took out a cigarette and lighted it. He leaned back in the chair.

"Let's go, Scott," Cagle said.

Kip turned his eyes to meet the inscrutable ones of the police lieutenant.

"You don't actually believe I killed her?" he said.

Cagle shoved his hands into his pockets. "Maybe not. But there's too much against you right now. I'll have to take you in."

"Am I under arrest for murder?"

"Not yet. Questioning."

Kip shrugged and got out of his chair. It didn't matter. Perhaps by answering questions, he could get a few answers. Cagle knew Peppo and Cy Borg. Cagle must have known Ott Redhair. His hand closed on the phone as he stood by the desk.

"Want to call your lawyer?" Cagle asked.

"I haven't one—not in Chicago." He should call Jude, but not now, not in front of the cops. Too much risk of the call being traced, of Cagle's pale seeing eyes following the motions of the dial. If the police found his room, if they saw Dokey, they'd have a solution. They wouldn't care if it wasn't the whole picture. Dokey must be kept out of it until the picture was complete.

Kip said, "Let's go." He led the way to the door. Cagle and the flatfoot moved in on either side of him when they reached the hall outside.

The flattie said, "Aren't you going to lock the door?"

Kip said, "It locks itself when it's closed. I've told you that twice." He didn't say any more. That was enough.

Randolph Street was deserted, cold and dark and empty, stripped of its flashing red and green and blue signs, its incessant footsteps. Not even a derelict shuffled into a doorway—not with a police sedan at the curb in front of Grimsley's. Cagle got into the tonneau after Kip. The flatfoot took the wheel.

"Been in Chicago long?" Cagle asked.

"Not long."

The lurch of the car was matched by a sudden lurch inside of Kip. For, as he had thrust his hands down into his overcoat pockets for warmth, one of them had touched something that had entirely slipped his mind. Imbecile! He'd forgotten about that. In his anger at Borg and Peppo and his suspicion of them, he had failed to remember it, until his hand touched ice-cold steel.

The gun that had killed Hyacinthe Fouré was still in his pocket.

On it were Dokey's fingerprints and God knew how many others. But chief among them, superimposed over all the others, were his own. He had taken the gun away from Dokey. He had been the last to handle it. Beside the gun was a handkerchief, stained with Hyacinthe's blood. And underneath the handkerchief was that rose from her hair—the rose Dokey had thought smelled so sweet.

XVI

He was trapped. He couldn't get away now. A break from the car would mean a bullet pumped into him—more than one if the flattie was doing the shooting. If he killed a fugitive, he'd have his mug plastered all over the front pages of the newspapers, and maybe he'd even get a promotion. He would have killed the fiend who had murdered the beautiful girl in the alley, and the case would be closed. It wouldn't matter if the case hadn't been solved. The police wouldn't care about that.

Kip gave a start. Cagle was asking a question. It was the second time he had asked it. "What brought you here?"

Questioning? Perhaps they didn't search someone brought in for questioning. Kip didn't know about that. He'd had no experience with the police. If they searched him, he was hung. He'd never be able to make them believe the truth. Not without bringing Dokey into it and he couldn't do that. Dokey must not be hung for another's crime.

"Business," Kip answered.

If Cagle would only be reasonable. Cagle wasn't dumb. But behind Cagle was the wheel of politics.

The drive to the city hall didn't take long. Cagle's arm brushed his as they crossed the sidewalk. He could cut and run—and die. If he got away, they'd pick him up for he didn't know where to go. He was without experience, without wile. The flatfoot clumped along behind them as they went into the deserted building. Their tread echoed as they went along a bare corridor. Cagle opened a door and Kip followed him inside. The palms of his hands were sweating.

It wasn't a torture chamber. It was just an office, a plain, unvarnished one, not as moldy as Grimsley's, but nothing like the offices he knew before Chicago. The room was warm, steamy.

Cagle hung his coat on a clothes-tree, topped it with his hat. He went behind the desk, and sat down.

He said, "You wait outside, Mordik."

The flatfoot went out. He didn't like it. The door banged with his displeasure.

Cagle pulled out the lower drawer. He set a fifth on the litter of papers. "Drink?"

"No, thanks," Kip said. He wanted one but he wouldn't take it. Far more he needed his wits undrugged.

Cagle tipped the bottle in his mouth. "Wards off pneumonia." He wiped his lips with his thumb, put the bottle away. "Sit down, Scott."

There were two straight chairs. Kip sat in the one farthest from the desk.

Cagle said, "Take off your coat and hat. Smoke if you like. We'll take this slow and easy."

Kip didn't want to remove his overcoat. He didn't want it away from him, not as far away as the clothes-tree. But the room was warm, too warm, even if his spine and the pit of his stomach were cold. He took the coat off, folded it and laid it on his knees as if he were at a theatre. He left his hat on.

He asked again, "You don't think I killed that girl, do you?"

Cagle was moving a red pencil through his fingers. He said, "I stopped thinking a long time ago. All I know is what I find out. Let's start way back. Just when did you come to Chicago?"

Kip knew that, knew every day of it, but he pretended to tally. He said, "It's six weeks and four days."

"And you came—"

"On business."

Cagle asked, "What was the nature of the business?"

Kip hesitated before answering. "I came on business for Don Redhair."

"Don Redhair's dead."

"I know it." Kip curbed his anger, the anger that always rose in him when he thought of Don Redhair dead. He repeated, "I know he's dead. I was with him when he died."

"How did it happen?"

Kip glanced at the police lieutenant. Cagle had spoken as if he didn't know that Don had died in the war, as if some one man had been responsible.

"He died in battle," Kip answered.

Cagle nodded. He didn't speak.

Kip said, "At Cherbourg. On the beach."

"It actually happened that way." It wasn't a question but it required corroboration.

Kip said, "I was beside him."

Cagle's smile was mirthless. "A lot of folks would like to know what you've just told me."

"I know it." Kip didn't smile. "That's why I'm not telling."

Cagle leaned back in the chair. "I don't get it. You were with Redhair when he died. You know he's dead. So how can you be here on business for him?"

Kip said, "I came to carry out his last request."

"Which was?'

He could mention it here. Lieutenant Cagle couldn't possibly be on their side.

Kip said, "To keep them from getting his dog." Again he recalled the phrasing. "The spotted pup."

Cagle didn't get it. He was trying to, he was reaching back into memory, but nothing came up. He shook his head.

Kip said, not hiding his disappointment, "You don't know about it?"

"I don't," Cagle admitted. "It doesn't mean a thing. What about the dog?"

"That's it," Kip said. "I don't know. I want to find out without asking. I want them to give it away. They talk plenty but they don't mention the dog."

Cagle asked, "Was it valuable?"

"I don't know. It meant a lot to Don. Most men dying call for Mother or the girl back home. Don didn't. It was the dog—the spotted pup." Kip took a breath of the stale office air deep into his lungs. "I didn't know who Don was. I didn't know until this week. But after I was mustered out, I couldn't get Don out of my head. It didn't do any good to tell myself he was wandering there at the end. His mind didn't wander. He died too fast. And he was talking to me, not to anyone else. He was telling me not to let them get his pup. So I had to come to Chicago."

Cagle said, "You knew he was from Chicago?"

"Yes, I knew that. It was always Chicago when we were shooting the breeze. I went to the War Department to find out who to look up here. His next of kin." He'd talked too much; he was at Grimsley's name. Cagle hadn't picked it up on Peppo's warning but the police lieutenant wouldn't have forgotten. He wasn't a man who forgot. Kip couldn't keep the name out of his mouth now. He said it, "Jake Grimsley."

"What about Grimsley?" The voice was quiet enough, but the eyes were whittled to sharpness.

"He's dead," Kip said.

Cagle was easy, not ready to pounce yet. "You seem to know a lot about dead men, Scott. Men that no one else knows to be dead."

"You won't admit the long arm of fate?" Kip asked. "That's how it was."

Cagle said, "Randolph Street thinks Jake's away on a vacation."

"I told them that."

"Did you see him die, too?"

"No," Kip said. "He died in a hospital. Under the name of Jacob Grey. He lived under that name a good many years away from Grimsley's."

Cagle was tracing Jacob Grey's name on a piece of paper.

He said, "You might as well tell me the rest of it."

"Maybe you won't believe me." He didn't expect to be believed. "I came to Grimsley's. I told him what I was looking for, Don's dog. He was excited about it—" Kip broke off. "Did you know Grimsley?"

"Known him for years," Cagle said. "One of Ott Redhair's gang."

"Yes." Kip nodded, and then his anger returned again as he remembered the man. "He was a dirty little scoundrel. His excitement was—repulsive is as good a word as any. I'd told him something he wanted to know. I'm still not sure what it was. He died before he talked."

XVII

Cagle was watching Kip with open curiosity, now.

"He gave me an address and the name of a man I was to see that night—a man named Jacob Grey," Kip resumed. "I went to the apartment. I found Grimsley. He'd been shot. He was conscious and he wasn't scared. He almost seemed to relish the idea of being shot. You see, whoever had plugged him hadn't killed him, and that gave him a hold over the killer. He didn't know he was going to die."

Kip looked at Cagle. "Don't get the idea I killed him. I didn't want him to die. I wanted him to talk. That was why Grimsley had been shot—to prevent him from talking."

Cagle made a gesture which showed he understood.

"He didn't want a doctor but he was afraid to go to the hospital and have the wound dressed. I took him there. He was admitted as Jacob Grey. I went back to my room at the hotel. I wasn't there more than an hour when the hospital called. They'd removed the bullet but the operation hadn't been a success. Grey was sinking. He insisted on seeing me. He told them it was a big business deal and he had to close it that night. By the time I got there, he was dead."

"The hospital wasn't suspicious of you?"

"No. Grey—Grimsley—had taken care of that. He used the old cleaning-the-gun gag when he went in. He told them if I hadn't arrived when I did, he'd have bled to death in his office. Grimsley, even while posing as Grey, wasn't particularly prepossessing. I didn't look like a suspicious character."

"No, you don't," Cagle said softly.

Kip wondered if that could be true. He had been living so long in a Clark Street hole-in-the-wall he felt as if he must be contaminated.

He said, "That's what happened to Grimsley. Believe it or not. I moved into his office. I didn't say he was dead. Even his murderer can't know that. He was buried as Jacob Grey. I'm looking for the one who tried to murder Don Redhair before he enlisted, though he didn't have a dime. I'm sure it's the same mob who got Grimsley, who murdered Hyacinthe Fouré tonight." He lifted his eyes to Cagle's. "I must be close or they wouldn't have tried to frame me."

Cagle said, "What were Peppo and Cy Borg doing in your office?"

Kip answered carefully. "I think they were looking for a report on Hyacinthe Fouré—what she'd told me. There wasn't any report. It's here." He tapped his forehead.

"You said they'd hired you."

"Borg did." His smile was sardonic. "I forced that on him. If he refused, it was as good as admitting he killed her." He lost the smile. "Ordered her killed."

"Hyacinthe Fouré told you what?"

"Nothing." Kip's lips twisted. "Nothing but that she was Don's fiancée. Diana Redhair hired me but told me nothing. Not even that Don had a sister. I found that out myself." He was silent on Mariel Smith. He knew he should add her to the list but he didn't. "They both hired me to find Don. Why? Because they'd found out Don had something worth money. It must be the dog."

Cagle said, "I never heard of a two-million-dollar dog."

Kip's eyebrows raised.

"That's the amount of dough missing from Ott's estate. It never turned up. Some say he left it for Don."

"But Don was broke, he didn't have a dime," Kip objected. "Grimsley was paying his room rent."

"Don found out."

That was clear enough. Don had found out after they did, found out when they started hunting him. He hadn't stayed around to flush the hunters. There was the war. In those days a young fellow left his business, however important, for a bigger thing—to clean up the world.

After Don was dead, why hadn't anyone claimed the two million? There was only one reason why Grimsley, next of kin, wouldn't, or why Diana, the actual next of kin, hadn't. Perhaps Hyacinthe had been hiding something. Was she more than a fiancée? Could there have been a secret war-time marriage—a marriage she was afraid to admit? Because if she admitted it, she would stand in the same danger that Don had?

Kip was thinking carefully, now, trying to clear things up in his mind. There could be only one reason why the fortune hadn't been claimed. They didn't know how to get hold of it. And the key to that was the dog. Whoever had the dog, had the key. That was what Kip had to find out—who had it. It could have been Hyacinthe. That could be the reason she was trapped in the blind alley and shot down. And that meant someone else would get the dog.

He'd forgotten where he was, had forgotten Cagle across the room. Cagle's eyes hadn't left his face. Kip met them now. He laughed a little.

"Sorry. I was trying to figure out who might have the dog."

"I want to show you something." Cagle beckoned him to the file in back of the desk.

Kip didn't want to move for he didn't trust the man with the quiet voice and gimlet eyes, but there was nothing else he could do. If he carried the coat with him, he couldn't hold it and examine the bulky manila folders Cagle was pulling out. He could lug it to the lieutenant's desk and lay it there, but Cagle might pick it up. By accident or design. He should have kept the coat on, despite the stifling steam heat. Finally he got up from the chair, and left it on the chair, still folded, neatly, as if in a theatre.

Cagle was laying the files on the desk. There were three of them— Ott Redhair's, the bulkiest; Jacob Grimsley's; and Don Redhair's, a slight one.

Kip opened the first package. "You had a lot on the old man."

Cagle tapped it with his pencil. "I have three drawers devoted to Ott. This one is just loose ends for my own curiosity."

Kip was feeling the Ott reports. "You think the answer to the dog is here?"

"Could be." Cagle was looking past him to the door.

"Come in, Nelson."

A young fellow in uniform, with horn-rimmed glasses on his curved nose, was bringing in a fresh sheaf of papers. He carried them to the desk.

Cagle said, "Kip Scott. Charles Nelson. This is the Fouré file."

Nelson said, "I'll have some more a little later."

It wasn't accident, it was design. Cagle had signaled. Nelson stopped at the chair, took up the overcoat.

He said, "I'll hang up your—" He held the coat upside down. It was no accident. The gun was heavy. It thudded to the floor.

Nelson put down the coat. "I'm sorry." He managed to look sorry, not smug.

Cagle's eyebrows were on Kip. "Yours?"

Kip could have lied but it wouldn't have helped. The gun would be checked before he left here. "It's the gun that killed Hyacinthe Fouré," Kip said. "My fingerprints are all over it."

Nelson picked up the gun.

Cagle said, "Check it." He didn't say any more until Nelson closed the door.

Kip went back to the chair. He took up the coat, carried it to the desk. "The gun isn't mine," he said. "You won't believe me but I might as well tell you. I picked it up by Hyacinthe's body. I got there before the police. But I didn't kill her." Savagely he pulled the handkerchief from the overcoat pocket. "This is her blood. I wiped it off my hands after I'd lifted the body to see who the girl was. And this—"

Kip dug out the rose and flung it on top of the handkerchief. Her blood was old now; the artificial flower was stiff. The perfume was gone, too.

Cagle said harshly, "You didn't call the police."

"I went to my office to do just that. I heard the sirens when I was walking upstairs. Borg and Peppo told me she was dead. Maybe they called the cops."

"They didn't call. It was a sandwich girl at Walgreen's. She was starting home." Maybe it had been a sandwich girl. They could have checked on that. Cagle shrugged. "It probably doesn't make a hell of a lot of difference who called."

Kip said, "You're going to book me. You're making a mistake. I had nothing to do with any killing. I'm not that kind."

Cagle said, "You don't look that kind. You said so yourself." His voice became harsh. "I don't go by looks. I don't go by hunches. I'm a policeman. I go by facts."

"Facts can be erroneous."

"I grant that, Scott. They can be manufactured." Cagle rubbed his hand down his cheek. "If I could think, maybe I'd think you didn't do it. It isn't my job to think. If I didn't book you, I'd be pounding pavements tomorrow or answering the phone like Nelson. I'm not the boss. I'm a hireling.''

"I can't locate the dog from jail," Kip said.

It wasn't haggling. Cagle wasn't a man you could influence. He was a cog in a political machine and couldn't move unless the whole machine was set in motion.

Cagle smiled. "You might locate the dog from jail. You might do just that. I've seen queerer things happen since I joined the force."

Kip followed him to the door. Bitterness was like acid in his veins. Because you tried to help a guy who couldn't know, who couldn't care now, you landed behind bars. That was where you belonged. If you knew the score, you'd know that Don Quixote was dead. And that anyone who followed his example deserved this fate.

XVIII

Kip hadn't expected to sleep. The wheels had whirred in his head until gray dawn seeped through the small barred window. Cagle had been decent, and had given him privacy. He'd had a chance to think. As Cagle said, he might have been able to find the dog, here behind bars. He hadn't. Only one thing was clear. With a two-million-dollar dog at stake, murder had been the outgrowth. . . .

He heard the chant of the turnkey through sleep. "Wake up in there. Come on. Wake up!"

He opened his eyes, but not to sunlight. The window was still as dank and gray as if he'd slept at Grimsley's. His watch said nine-twenty. Another special privilege granted by Cagle. He sat up, combed his fingers through his hair.

"Come on," the turnkey growled. "Your lawyer's waiting to see you."

Kip's eyes widened. "I have no lawyer."

"That so?" The man's rheumy mouth chewed the words. "Wait'll you see what he brought you for breakfast."

Kip followed the jailer.

"In there." The jailer kicked open the door.

Kip entered, still dubious. His jaw dropped.

The lawyer was Monty Wentworth. His dark Chesterfield was knife-pressed. He might have been attending a society soiree rather than visiting a jail. What he'd brought for breakfast was Diana. Her hair, her brown furs were warm in the room. She seemed friendly now. Her lips were moist red.

She cried, "I don't know how they had the nerve to lock you up! I told Lieutenant Cagle—"

Wentworth's smile was amiable, too. "With what Di told Cagle, I'm surprised I didn't have to bail her out, too."

Kip asked, "Do you mean I'm out?"

Wentworth's shrug was apologetic. "On bail. I couldn't quite carry off getting the charge squashed. It's been changed from suspicion of murder to material witness."

"You went my bail?" Kip asked.

"Cy did," Diana said. "The minute he told me what that stupid Cagle had done, I rushed to Monty's office."

Wentworth took up the conversation again. "Borg insisted on going bail. He has some influence. He talked to the D.A. personally."

Kip was wary. "I don't like charity from strangers."

"Don't be difficult." Diana tossed back her hair. "You're working for Cy, aren't you? He said you were. And he said you couldn't very well work for him when you were locked up. That's just what he told Cagle."

"Let's get out of this place. We'll go have some breakfast at my club. You can clean up there, Scott." Wentworth fingered his small moustache. "I can't understand why I couldn't squash the charge. Cagle must have something against you."

Kip smiled sardonically. "He has." He watched them. "The gun that killed Hyacinthe Fouré."

Wentworth's mouth was hidden behind his hand. Diana's eyes darkened with wonder. It was she who whispered, "Where did you get it?"

"In the alley. Before the police got there."

Fear caused her throat to twitch.

"No, I didn't kill her," Kip said. "But Cagle finds that hard to believe, and I can't prove I didn't—not yet."

Wentworth's hand left his moustache. He glanced warningly at Kip.

"If you did, you'd better be careful. Peppo feels badly about her death."

"I'm always careful." Kip slurred the words. "You might warn Peppo to be as careful as I will be." He added, "If he and Hyacinthe were such good friends the murderer might just possibly believe Peppo shared her knowledge—death knowledge."

Wentworth didn't answer. He put his arm on Diana's. "Let's go. This place depresses me. Okay, Scott?"

It was right with him. But once outside he said, "I'm skipping the breakfast."

"You can't!" Diana cried.

She didn't like to have her plans changed. It wasn't Wentworth who'd engineered this jail deliverance; the man wouldn't soil his hands in a criminal case. It wasn't Borg; he didn't like Kip Scott. It had to be Diana. But again he was sure she didn't like him any better than Borg did and he didn't trust her interest in him. She was just pretending to be friendly. And there were Dokey and Jude waiting. At least, he hoped they were waiting.

"I've got to get back on the job," Kip said. His smile was wry. "I haven't found Don Redhair yet."

"You know he's dead."

He answered her as quickly, as heatedly. "If he's dead, why did you hire me to find him?"

She was quiet again. "I couldn't take the chance. If he—if he is in Chicago—I have to know."

"My job is to find out."

He went away quickly after saying that, but not far. Only far enough to step into a doorway out of sight, and look back. He could see them getting into her car. He waited where he was until the car U-turned and started off. He let it get out of sight, to prevent them from following him to his hotel. He made certain this didn't happen. When he reached his room, he inserted and turned his key before he realized it shouldn't turn, that he was supposed to rap the signal. His room was empty.

The bedspread was crumpled where Dokey had lain. There was cigar ash in the tray. Jude didn't smoke cigars. Neither did Dokey. Plenty of men did. One man who did was Cy Borg.

Kip stood in the middle of the room, feeling as if someone had ground a heel in his stomach. Someone big and bulky who reeked of cigars had been here. There had been a reason for Borg to go Kip's bail—if Borg had the man who fired the gun. If Borg knew.

Kip stripped himself savagely, showered and dressed in quick time. He didn't stop for coffee. He left the hotel, cut across Randolph into the sluggish cold to the white front. Jude wasn't there. Jude didn't come on before noon.

The day manager didn't want to give the phone number, but Kip made him tell. The phone didn't help, for there was no answer from the other end of the wire. He pocketed the returned nickel, crossed the street in mid-traffic to the Elegante. There wasn't anyone around. Night-clubs are dead places by day.

He returned to the white front, took a cup of coffee and carried it with him to the heavy telephone stand. Borg wasn't listed. Nor was Peppo. Not under their right names. Or perhaps they lived in hotels, with no private wires. He looked up Wentworth's office address. It was on North Michigan, not far away. He swallowed the coffee, slammed the cup down on a table and went out. There was no cab so he decided to walk it. Soon he was pushing through the weight of the wind, biting on the cold as if it were anodyne, as if it would ice his rage.

The building on Michigan rose tall and proud over the lake. Wentworth wasn't a Grimsley. He had position, money. The elevator carried Kip to the fourteenth floor—to the rugs and blanched wood and supple leather of a Wentworth anteroom. It was like coming home. But he hadn't headed for this place to hug nostalgia. He had an icy purpose. He took one step toward the switchboard and stopped.

The girl at the board was Mariel Smith. Then she, too, was a part of this. She was looking at him as if she'd never seen him before.

"Yes?" she said.

Kip didn't smile at her. He acted as if he hadn't seen her before. "Mr. Wentworth."

Things were happening too fast. He couldn't fit things in yet. And he had to make the last piece fit. She was ringing the inner office.

"Your name?"

The corners of his lip curled. "Mr. Smith," he said.

She didn't hesitate. Only her eyes flickered. He heard her say, "Mr. Wentworth, a Mr. Smith to see you." She asked, "Have you an appointment, Mr. Smith?" She was cool as a spatter of ice.

He said, "No. But I think Mr. Wentworth will see me. I'm from Mr. Borg."

She repeated into the mouthpiece, "Mr. Smith was sent by Mr. Borg." She broke the connection. "If you'll wait a moment, Mr. Wentworth will see you."

XIX

Scott didn't go over and sit down, but stood where he was, looking down at her, waiting for his mockery to fray her nerves. She took it. But she had to speak, to break the silence.

"If you'll sit down, Mr. Smith, it won't be long," she said.

He barely moved his lips. "I was arrested last night."

She didn't answer, not even with her eyes.

"For the murder of Hyacinthe Fouré."

She spoke under her breath. "Borg bailed you out." There was hostility in the set of her chin but in her eyes the glint of fear. "What are you doing here?"

"I didn't expect to find you," Kip said. "It never entered my head." He was bitter without knowing why. "I didn't think you were part of the gang." Chiefly he was resentful because she was clean, because she had been too good an actress. She'd fooled him.

She hadn't time to answer him. A door opened and a girl was there, a sleek, sloe-eyed girl with reddened lips and nails—a girl that belonged on display at Peppo's, not in a tailored suit in a law office.

"Mr. Smith?" Her voice was cultured. "Mr. Wentworth will see you now."

He followed her into the corridor, up to the office at the front, the best office, Wentworth's. Behind the other doors were junior partners, readers, assistants. Wentworth was alone. He was no anachronism in the elegance of his office.

He said, "I wasn't expecting you." But he wasn't hostile, only hesitant.

Kip smiled. "I didn't want to telegraph my approach." He didn't explain. Wentworth was in this too deeply to make explanations necessary. Not only did he know about Diana, but the girl outside, too. Kip didn't try to figure it now. "I don't make a habit of being in debt," he said. "I want to pay off Borg."

Wentworth wasn't easy to read. His worn face, his trimmed moustache was cautious. "You're not planning to skip out?"

"I have no plans," Kip said. "All I want is Borg's address."

Wentworth's smile was superficial—no deeper than that. "Mr. Borg isn't worried about the money, Mr. Scott. There's no hurry. Any time."

"I'm not accustomed to owing." Kip's jaw was unyielding. "I have the money for him."

"Very well. If that is how you wish it." The smile again. "I'll send it to him at once."

Kip smiled now. His was more real. "I want to thank him in person. If you'll give me his address?"

Wentworth was dubious. He could have orders. It could be unprecedented that anyone cared to brave Borg's sanctum. Kip waited. Wentworth fingered his moustache. He fingered the telephone.

"I could run you over."

"I want to see him alone," Kip stressed the word, added, "To thank him."

Wentworth gave the information reluctantly. "He lives at the Palmer House."

He'd probably phone as soon as Kip left the room. But Kip could get there first. He said, "Thanks."

Wentworth stood on his feet. He extended his hand across the desk. "You're not much like the little man who was your predecessor. Grimsley never paid a debt." His handclasp was firm. "Cy says he's dead." The lawyer's pale eyes were curious.

"Yes, he's dead."

"How did it happen?"

"He was cleaning a gun."

"Accident?" Wentworth was skeptical.

"The hospital authorities had it that way," Kip said. "I was called to the hospital before he died. He sent for me on a matter of business."

Wentworth persisted. "You were fortunate to have the opportunity to conclude your business."

Kip's lips twisted. They wanted to know what he'd found out. It wasn't Grimsley's death that fretted them, it was what Grimsley might have told. The truth would sound a lie. He spoke it.

"I was unfortunate that he died before I reached the hospital." He started to the door, turned to face the lawyer. "I didn't know Mariel Smith worked for you."

"Mariel Smith?" Wentworth showed only bewilderment. "Mariel Smith?"

"Switchboard."

"Oh. Miss Smith." He did it well—the realization. If it wasn't for the tieup, he wouldn't necessarily know her name, not her first name. Wentworth's eyebrows lifted. "She is a friend of yours?"

"You might call it that."

He ignored Wentworth's curiosity, and left, finding his own way back to the anteroom. The girl at the switchboard had cotton-colored hair and a receding chin.

"Where's Miss Smith?" Kip demanded.

Her voice was a chirp. "She hadda go home. She was sick all of a sudden."

All of a sudden she was sick! Kip couldn't delay now—not if he wanted to get to Borg before the others or before the big man could hide out. "Too bad." The girl looked at him as if he had fangs.

His luck was good. There was a cab letting out a passenger at the street door. It wasn't five minutes to the Palmer House. He called on the house phone. Borg himself answered.

Kip gave his right name. He said, "I want to see you. I have something you want." He expected argument but there was none. Borg told him the suite number.

It could be the elevator was lifting Kip into danger, great danger. It could be he wouldn't come down again. It wasn't something he could think about. He had to move by instinct now, without thought. He hoped his reflexes were functioning and in the right direction.

Borg opened the door, the gold and green stripes of his massive bathrobe glistening. Diana's taste showed in that. His suite was also to Diana's taste, not that of the Palmer House. Palmetto wood, a green tufted rug, gold and green hangings. It didn't go with its owner.

"I thought you was in jail," Borg said.

Kip closed the door after him carefully.

"You bailed me out." He sat down without being invited.

"You the one? Monty said—that's right, that's the name, Scott." Borg was too big for the tasseled love seat. "What you got to show me? Did you find Don?"

Kip took a check book from his pocket. "Ten thousand," he said. He filled out the check with his pen. "That's what it was?"

Borg's face screwed up. "What's this for?"

"That's my bail. I'm paying you back."

"You going to skip?"

It was the same question. This time the question could have masked eagerness. Was that what the pachyderm wanted?

XX

Kip laid his hat on the circular green glass table.

"No, I'm not planning to run," he said. "Not yet. I just don't like to be beholden to any man." He looked into Borg's little eyes. "It was Monty who wanted me out?" he asked.

"I don't know. I never know what Monty wants. He's my lawyer." Borg rubbed the back of his head. "Diana wanted you loose. She said you couldn't find"—his hesitation was infinitesimal, the pause for substitution "—Don when you was in jail. She's right."

Kip spoke coldly. "It isn't Don you're looking for. It's the pup."

Borg's head jerked up. He wasn't slow when he was on the defensive. Anger, fear—and he was dangerous.

"You got it?"

"I haven't."

"You know who has got it?"

"I don't." Kip didn't care if he were believed. He said slowly, "Grimsley knew, but someone bumped off Grimsley."

"He didn't know. He was trying to find out."

"He knew something. That's why he was silenced. So he couldn't tell me."

Borg's mouth was a slit. "Grimsley didn't know. He was looking for it. Because if he found it, it was his. Because Don was dead, and Grimsley was his heir. Like he signed the paper."

Kip's spine straightened. It took this hulk to make him see things—this slob who couldn't think straight. But if Borg's thinking were crooked, he could think fast.

"And Grimsley was killed so he couldn't inherit. And Hyacinthe." Don's fiancée. Here it was again. A secret bride? Diana would inherit. Diana! Was Borg or was Monty Wentworth the man waiting for Diana to inherit?

Kip was soft-tongued. "Why did you kill Hyacinthe?"

Borg's forehead became beaded. "I didn't kill the little girl. I was with Peppo."

"You and Peppo."

Borg's fear was gone quickly. He wiped a thumb down his flat nose. His voice was lugubrious.

"You gotta find who killed her for Peppo. She was Peppo's little girl."

"Don's girl."

Borg shook his ponderous head. "I don't mean like that. Peppo's little girl. His kid."

"His daughter?" Kip didn't believe it.

"Yeah. For business he don't say so. But she was his kid."

That left one person in the clear. Peppo hadn't killed his daughter. Not that way. In anger perhaps, by accident, but not with a gag. It wasn't Peppo who was guilty and Peppo didn't know who it was. If he did, he would kill. Kip could talk to Peppo.

"Peppo didn't know she was engaged to Don Redhair. Why not?"

Borg sweated some more. "Maybe she wasn't. Maybe she just made that up so you'd listen to her, so you'd help her find the pup."

"She didn't ask me to find the pup. It was Don."

Borg walked to the window. "That's right. To find Don."

Kip knew there was more—a lot more. But Borg wouldn't admit anything easily. And there wasn't time. Kip must get to Jude and warn Jude to watch Dokey.

He stood up, said, "That's that. You're paid. There's nothing out of your pocket if I decide to skip."

Borg turned his flat nose away from the window. His voice was almost plaintive. "I wouldn't skip if I were you." He followed Kip to the door. "Ten grand's a lot of dough these days."

It might be the money. Ten grand was a lot of it. It might be a hint that it wouldn't be too healthy to leave town, that Kip Scott knew too much. . . .

He called Jude's number from a lobby booth but got no answer. Jude wasn't hiding Dokey out at home. If he'd taken the kid out of town, there could be trouble. Yet there shouldn't be any more trouble, for anyone except a murderer. A dirty back alley murderer.

He was leaving the booth when he thought of Mariel Smith. He was suddenly sure, cold sure, that she knew all the answers. Monty

Wentworth had got her out of the office quick enough on Kip's arrival. Too quick. He looked up Wentworth's office, dialed. Miss Smith wasn't there. The cotton-headed girl on the switchboard didn't know Miss Smith's home address or phone number. Reluctantly she agreed to look them up.

He hung on, despite altercations with the operator, until the girl returned. She nasaled, "Sorry, but we aren't allowed to give out our staff's phone numbers."

Kip repressed his irritation. "I'm her Uncle Oswald. I'm only in town for a few hours. I've lost Muriel's address!"

"Sorry." She might have been an automaton.

He hadn't time to intercept her after work, and throttle the information out of her. He needed it now, before the police found Dokey. With the amount of evidence against Kip, Kip wouldn't be out on bond unless someone had offered a substitute.

He barged out of the phone booth. Since he couldn't reach Jude or Mariel, he could go back to Grimsley's and wait—wait for someone to come looking for him, wait for Peppo to open the club. He was fed to the teeth with the impotence of waiting.

A cold wind bit at his face as he left the hotel. Hoping he could think better while walking the few blocks to Grimsley's, he refused a cab. The way from State to Randolph was as crowded as if the sun were a bright awning overhead, as if it weren't swaddled in the dirty gray flannel of Chicago afternoon.

He saw the person he wanted to see above all others while he was waiting for the light to change on the corner in front of Field's. Mariel Smith was directly across the street and she saw him. She dived across Randolph with the last second of the east-west light. As he cut across State she, too, crossed it on the west side in the opposite direction. The lights changed again and he watched her reach the corner where he formerly stood, watched angrily as she slid deftly into the protective coloring of the crowd.

He moved then, the way in which she was moving, east on State, watching the navy coat, the small navy hat across the street. It wasn't difficult, both were halted by the same light and she didn't seem to know he was following from afar.

She didn't know? She'd vanished. He stopped savagely halfway down a block. She'd lulled him into security and she'd vanished into dirty gray flannel air. Then he noticed the hooded subway entrance across the way.

He ignored traffic lights, cut directly across the street and half ran to the entrance.

He didn't know when she'd disappeared. He didn't know just when he'd relaxed vigilance. She could have slipped into any one of the shops in these blocks. But he ran down the subway stairs, fumbling in his trousers for the fare as he ran, expecting at each step to hear the rush of a coming train that would frustrate him utterly.

His luck held good. He wasn't too late. She was there. She was caught. Fear whitened her face as he came through to the platform. At least a dozen other persons were waiting for the train. She could scream; she could beg for help. But she didn't. She stood there as he came up to her—silent, the pulse in her throat throbbing with terror.

He had to quiet her before she could drop. He hoped his words were for her alone.

"I didn't kill Hyacinthe Fouré."

XXI

The train whirred into the station as he spoke. He couldn't hear her answer. He only knew what her eyes expressed. Grimly he ignored her warning and followed her into the car. It wasn't filled but she didn't enter the lighted interior. She stood in the vestibule.

"I didn't kill her," he repeated.

"You are a fool," she said.

She wasn't afraid of him now but she was still nervous. Her eyes were watching faces in the car while she spoke.

"Don't you know you shouldn't be seen with me? Not now."

"I don't know anything," he said. He had thought that he did but he was wrong. On second thought he didn't know the reason why she was involved. "I know you were afraid to be seen with me."

"Because you were mixed up with them. It would have been dangerous for me. Now you've given it away."

He didn't know what she was talking about. He followed her as she left the car, climbed the steps.

"Don't you know they have to get to me first?" she said under her breath.

Again he said, "I don't know anything. What did I give away? When?"

Wherever they had emerged, it was still Chicago, gray turning to dark. He was beside her crossing the street, walking in some direction past old apartment houses.

"Knowing me at the office. Telling Monty Wentworth."

"I didn't tell him anything."

"Whatever you told him was enough. He asked Cecile to send me in when I returned. I didn't go back." She looked over her shoulder. No one was following and she stopped at a darkened brick facade. "If you're wise, you'll go on your way. You won't know where I am or anything about me," she said.

Kip said, "I don't scare." He smiled at her in the dusk. "I want to know about you. And if I've put you in danger, the least I can do is stick around. Maybe I'm not as big a fool as I look."

He heard the catch of her breath. He followed again. She turned into the building but she didn't stop before any apartment. She went through the lower hall, out the service entrance, across the back alley to another building on another street. He followed her through the rear of the building, up the back stairs. Her apartment was on the third floor, facing the street. He didn't say anything while she put her key in the lock. She hadn't been pretending. The hand holding the key wavered.

"You can come in," she invited.

She locked the door behind her, put the chain in its bolt. Her face was milky in the dusky room. She didn't say anything, not until she'd steadied herself. Then she studied him for a long, oddly intense moment.

"I'm Don's wife!" said Mariel Smith.

He hadn't expected it. He didn't have anything to say. He stood like a dolt, as if she hadn't spoken, until the yellow of the lamp pooled on the ash-pale carpet. He saw then, not the room but what was in the room. He was shame-faced.

"I thought it was a real dog."

There were a dozen and more, Dalmatians, terriers, Springers, half-breeds, of clay, of plastic, of pipe cleaners, of fur—spotted pups.

He recovered quickly. "It can't be safe."

"It was," she said. "No one knew about me." She had thrown off her hat, was unbuttoning her coat slowly. "No one knew I'd ever laid eyes on Don."

"But Wentworth?"

She sat down on the arm of the flowered couch. "I got the job in his office after Don left Chicago. I thought maybe I'd hear something about Don, working there. It was secret—our marriage. He didn't tell me why. Only that it had to be, and that he'd be in trouble—bad trouble—if anyone knew. I solemnly promised him I'd never tell. I haven't until tonight."

"Your family?"

"I don't have a family." Her face was without expression. "I think that's why he picked me. It was a business arrangement. I was at Field's—in advertising. I scarcely knew Don."

"You didn't love him?"

She cried, "What if I did?" and was quiet again. "Maybe I would have if there'd been time. Maybe he would have, too." Even her hands were quiet. "Maybe not. There was a girl in the East."

A girl. Who wouldn't want to know Don Redhair. But Mariel Smith was proud even now in her humiliation. She was fine and honest and lovely.

He was puzzled. "Why the marriage?" When she didn't answer, he repeated, "Why did you marry him?"

A trace of red came into her cheeks. "I've wondered. Every girl wants to marry. He was—he was fun and nice looking. I didn't know who he really was." She explained. "I'm from Pennsylvania. I didn't know about the Redhairs. He kept asking me to marry him after he'd enlisted." She turned her eyes on Kip. "I refused. I told him to wait. Then he told me the truth."

Kip sat down at the far end of the couch. He heard her voice but he didn't look at her.

"He told me it would be strictly a business arrangement. He wanted a safe place to leave his personal effects."

The words hurt her. "Personal effects" to Don. Nothing else.

Kip asked quickly, "Did Don know?"

"He must have. He warned me never to tell anyone. To hold on to the spotted pup. I found the key myself."

"Safe deposit?"

"I suppose so. It was wadded in paper inside the pup."

He looked at the collection. "Which one?"

"None of these." Sensing his curiosity, she smiled. "They're red herrings. I collected spotted pups." She went into an inner room, returned with a piece of dull iron, sculpted into an incredibly ugly dog with liver-white spots. She put it in Kip's hands. "His father used it for a paperweight. It opens."

He turned it in his hands. "The key isn't in it."

"No."

He set the pup on the couch between them. "Did Don mention what you were to do with his things if he didn't return?"

"They were to be mine," she said simply. "Because I was his wife."

"But after his death?"

She lifted her shoulders. "I didn't know what to do." She turned to him swiftly. "Don't you see? If I did anything—if I tried to do anything—they'd kill me."

He asked it pointblank. "Who are 'they'?"

"I don't know." She whispered as fearfully as if "They" were outside the walls. "He wouldn't say. Before his father died they tried to kill him because he was to inherit. He wasn't hurt. Poison in a drink. He knew in time. Once he was shot at from a car. The bullet only grazed his shoulder. He was lucky."

Lucky. Yes, lucky. It had taken mass murder, war, to kill a man and his luck.

"There's Wentworth," said Kip. "He'd have known about the will. Diana—he could have told her, and Borg and Peppo." He thought about it. "Then there was Grimsley. Why did Don pick Grimsley as next of kin?" He couldn't have trusted the dirty little man.

"To keep me out of it," she answered.

"He couldn't have trusted Grimsley." This part of it still puzzled Kip. It didn't make sense. Grimsley had been such an obvious crook and Don Redhair had been anything but a fool.

"He didn't." Her eyes were sad. "He didn't trust anyone."

"You."

"No." She shook her head slightly. "Only a very little. He didn't tell me about the key. I don't know now why it's important."

He looked at her and he spoke slowly. "It's important because two million dollars were missing from Ott Redhair's estate."

She hadn't known. She hadn't even surmised. The color went from her face, leaving it ivory white.

"That's what Don Redhair left you," Kip said.

She began to cry, soundlessly, piteously.

He kept his voice hard. "Don't cry."

"You don't know how poor he was," she said. "He didn't have enough to eat. His shoes—"

He stood up then. "Quit thinking about it," he said. He didn't want her to think about the boy who couldn't mention her name, because he wanted her to be safe. She mustn't remember a boy on the beachhead, with his blood sinking into the sand.

"He loved you," Kip said gently. "I know he did." He put his hand out but he didn't touch her. "You mustn't. I need you tonight. I know what to do now. I'll have to tell you, instruct you. Will you listen?"

She raised her face to him. She couldn't see him through the blur of her eyes. She said, "I'll do anything you say."

XXII

Kip was calling number after number, from a telephone booth in a cigar store, ignoring the fat and impatient blonde outside. To each person he gave the same message, "I have the pup. Grimsley's at nine."

One more call—to Cagle. Kip gave Cagle the message, hoping that his surmise was correct.

Next came Randolph Street, after dark, with its fret of noise, its jiggle of lights, its scrawl of faces and endless sanding of feet. The bitter dark wind was sucking into doorways, and hoar frost was falling from the faraway sky. Kip moved past the white front. No Jude stood behind the steam table. Across at the Elegante, brawling jungle music sounded, a strange wake for a singer forever mute. Clark and Randolph. The lamp post jutted up, alone and lonely.

Kip didn't know just what would happen. The murderer might come early, and be waiting now in the scabrous corridor, in the shadows of Grimsley's. He opened the vestibule door and went inside. He pressed the buzzer for Adams, pressed his finger against the button until he heard the scrape of the cage below. His watchful eyes scanned the staircase.

Adam was grumbling. "What's the rush?" His old eyes peered at Kip. "It's you, Mr. Scott. Where you been? Now you're in a big hurry."

"Did you take anyone up for Grimsley's? I've been in jail. Wasn't it in the headlines?"

The old man stopped the cage on Third. "You didn't kill that little girl. Nobody thinks you done that. Nobody came tonight."

Kip was afraid, afraid to move out of the open-work cage into the uncharted corridor. Their conversation echoed cavernously in the hollow gloom.

"Nobody comes to Grimsley's," Adam said. "You expecting somebody?" His eyes were sharp.

"Yeah," Kip said. "I'm expecting a murderer. I don't know his name. I've got to find out his name." He had to learn it to keep Mariel safe. He laughed harshly. "I'm expecting a lot of clients. Watch out for them."

Kip walked away slowly, fearing to move into the no-man's land, forcing each step. He turned the bend and took a few more steps to the locked door. When he reached it, his hands were wet, his mouth dry as dust.

The sound of danger came to his ears. He swung about. Jude's face was a blur of white, his eyes were lamp black. His hands in his pockets could be pushing forward a gun, pointing it at the belly of a man who'd sold out his brother.

"They took Dokey." Jude's voice rasped. "The police came for Dokey tonight."

"It's all right, Jude," Kip said. He was surprised the way his voice sounded, comforting, unafraid. "Don't worry."

He grasped Jude's arm and he led him to the office door. He kept saying words while he put in the key, turned it.

"They'll know he didn't do it. I'm going to find out tonight who did it. You're going to help out."

They were in the office, the office that was never dark, that couldn't be dark because the lights of Clark and Randolph spilled across the rotting floor. There was no one else in the room. Kip turned on the green shaded lamp above the desk and opened the top drawer. His gun was still there. He broke it and it was loaded. He put his overcoat over the back of the chair, still saying words in that empty comforting voice.

Jude said, "I took Dokey away. I saw Borg coming. I didn't

answer the phone. I sent Mamma and the kids to her brother's in Cicero. I stayed with him all day. He slept a lot. He felt awful bad, Kip.''

Kip said, "We need four or five more chairs, Jude. Give me a hand with them, will you?"

Cautiously he opened the connecting door to the waiting room. No one was in there. He made certain the outer door was locked. Mariel had the key. If she followed orders, exact orders, she wouldn't be hurt, not if she waited in the dark doorway across Randolph until she was certain they were all inside, until he signaled.

The chairs were snag-toothed. He lined them up in the office in front of the desk. Not too straight a line, just casual. One in the corner, the corner of Clark and Randolph.

"You sit there. Don't talk. Listen, and watch. Watch their faces, Jude. Don't say anything. Watch."

The waiting part was difficult. Kip paced up and down the scarred floor.

Jude didn't say anything.

''I thought a lot of Don,'' Kip explained. "I was beside him when he died. I saw many men die, men I thought a lot of. But I couldn't forget Don—what he asked me to do. That's why I came to Chicago.''

"I knew." Jude was becoming quiet. "First time you happened into the joint for coffee, I knew you didn't belong."

''I'm from New York. I'm a lawyer. I thought I was too busy to come out here but I had to come.''

He heard someone moving down the corridor and sat down on the creaking swivel chair. He lighted a cigarette, and the door was opened, just shoved open. There was no knock.

It was Cy Borg. Behind him came Peppo.

Kip said, "Come in. Have a chair."

Peppo's face was like granite.

Borg said, "Where is it? How did you find it? Did Grim—" His little eyes licked the files. He saw the man in the shadows. His voice quivered. "Who's that?"

"You know Jude."

"Didn't recognize him."

Borg slumped into the client's chair.

Peppo said, "Hello, Jude. You, too?"

Kip broke in, "Grimsley didn't know where to find it."

"Where is it?" Borg demanded again.

"Let's wait for the others," Kip said gently. "They want to know, too." He looked at his watch. "I don't think they'll keep us waiting long."

Peppo's voice was edged. "How did you know where to find it?"

"I'm smarter than Grim." Kip's eyes held Peppo's. "I'm smarter than all five of you put together." He heard the staccato sound of heels outside. "That includes the beautiful Diana and her lawyer."

Scott opened the door. Diana's fiery hair was frosted from the night. Wentworth was impeccable but the tip of his nose was red.

"Good evening," Kip said. "Won't you join us?"

He closed the door, and stood against it watching her settle the flame and gold of her dinner dress, arrange the golden pouch of her evening bag, smooth off her white gloves.

He moved then, walked to the window, opened the center one an inch, and spoke with his eyes on the doorway across the street, seeing the slight figure taut there.

"If it gets too cold, let me know."

He came back to the chair, sat down in it.

Diana smiled. "You found the pup?"

"Yes."

She was eager. "Incredible. How did you do it?"

He cut into her words. "Grim couldn't. I'm smarter than Grim. I'm alive."

They were solid against him at once, an ugly solid line.

Peppo asked, "Who killed Grim?"

"I don't know who killed him," Kip said. "But I know why he was killed. Someone was afraid he'd spill it to me. Someone had found out he was cutting himself a big slice of personal effects. Grimsley was trying to find the pup for too many of you."

Peppo said, "He didn't have to cut anyone in. He was Don's heir."

"That wouldn't stand up in court." Diana was heated. She flung her head towards Wentworth.

"It would never have stood up," Monty said unctuously. "Diana was the real heir. Grimsley knew it wouldn't stand up. He was glad enough to be paid to hunt for the spotted pup."

Kip began, "If Hyacinthe Fouré was more than a fiancée—"

Peppo grew rigid.

Kip spoke to Borg. "If Hyacinthe was so close to him, why did you send her to me?"

"I didn't do that."

Kip began laying out ten-dollar bills on the desk. "These are from you and these are from Hyacinthe. Read the serial numbers."

Borg murmured shakily to Peppo, "I didn't know she'd be hurt."

Kip said, "She was probably glad to do a little favor for her father's friend—just ask a few questions about Don Redhair and pretend to be his—fiancée. She didn't know the pup was mixed up in it—the deadly pup. When she saw me doodling on the scratch pad she was terrified. She knew her father and Borg wanted that pup badly enough to kill."

"You can't frame me, Monty!" Borg said.

Monty unfolded his white muffler.

Kip went on inexorably. "They had remembered by then that something might have been hidden—possibly in old Ott's paper weight. Yes, they'd remembered it was hollow. Whoever found it—well, the heirs could whistle for their share."

Diana's eyes smouldered at the two men.

"I know why Hyacinthe was killed. But her murderer made a mistake." Kip heard then the soft movement of someone in the other office. He relaxed and raised his voice to cover the sound. "I have the spotted pup." He put his hand in his pocket, slowly brought out the toy Dalmatian, and set it on the desk.

XXIII

All their eyes were on it. Jude crept from his corner and stood behind Kip. Wentworth spoke.

"That isn't it!" he complained.

Diana's mouth dropped. "That isn't the one," she said.

Kip smiled. "No. That isn't the one. I brought the wrong one. But I've sent for the other. It should be here at any moment."

"Who has it?" Diana cried.

Kip Scott let the words drop, like two cold pebbles, in the silence. "Don's wife."

That silence now was more impressive than sound.

Diana whispered, "Don's wife!"

"Yes. She's bringing the real pup."

These words were a prearranged cue. There came a tap on the door.

"Come in," Kip called. But he didn't watch her as she entered— he kept his eyes on the hands of the four and his own hand clenched on the gun in his pocket.

"Come in, Mariel," he said.

Mariel Smith advanced to the desk and laid the ugly iron pup on it.

"That's it," Borg said. He gave a deep sigh.

Diana's hand moved toward the pup.

"The key isn't in it now," Kip said pleasantly.

He was on his feet, pressing Mariel into his chair. "May I present to all of you Mrs. Don Redhair?"

Diana's eyebrows straightened. "She's your office girl, Monty!" she cried.

Wentworth's hands tightened on the arms of the chair. "Yes."

"She was in charge of the phones," Peppo cried, and his face had grown cruel.

Borg spoke in a plaintive voice. "You mean she listened?"

"That's what he means," Diana said.

Kip spoke harshly. "It won't do you any good to kill her. Diana can't inherit now. It would go to Mrs. Redhair's next of kin." He kept near Mariel in the chair. "It was a mistake to kill Hyacinthe. She wasn't married secretly to Don. She played her part well that night—at Borg's direction."

Not one of them spoke.

"Murder is always a mistake," Kip went on softly. "Someone thought she had the pup, because I'd sketched it while she was there. Someone found that sketch. It was a mistake to kill Grim, too. Certainly he had threatened to sell out to me unless the ante was raised. Fifty per cent of the findings, wasn't it? He was a greedy little man."

Diana smiled across at Mariel. "I don't know how you came to be mixed up with this man. I don't know what he's promised you for your part. Maybe you don't know he's a murderer."

Wentworth looked at Kip. "The police are coming for you again tonight." He was almost apologetic. "They have sufficient evidence for an indictment, Scott."

Kip's fingers tightened on the gun in his pocket. But his lips could still fake an easy smile. "I don't doubt that."

Cy Borg bellowed, "If he's a killer, why did you ask me to go bail? Do you want him to bump off the rest of us like he did Grim and Hyacinthe?" He moved his big rump uneasily on the decrepit chair.

Cagle should have been here by now. He was long past due.

Wentworth smoothed his moustache. "How, may I ask, could we lay hands on the pup if he were in jail?"

"How'd you know he had the pup?" Borg's pig eyes were mean.

Diana caressed the clasp of her golden handbag. "He was in Don's company. Don gave the pup to him." She shrugged. "Or told him where it was." Her lips curled at the sight of Borg's stupid face. "Monty can add two and two, Cy."

Kip's ears ached from straining for some sound, such as a car stopping below, or a step in the hall. Why did Borg talk so loud?

Borg was shouting now. "What was all that hocus pocus about Don being in Chicago? Who started that?"

"Dokey spread that," Kip said. "I told him to. I wanted to get you moving fast."

"No one pays any attention to Dokey." Diana's tone was scornful.

Under cover of his pocket, Kip loosed the safety catch of the gun in his pocket. He'd heard something. It could be Cagle. His eyes taunted Diana. "That depends on what Dokey has to say."

He could hear sounds plainly now. There was no mistake. He pulled out the gun and warned them. "That'll be our friend, Cagle. Keep your hands quiet—all of you." He stepped back from Mariel's chair. "Get back in the corner, Jude." The gun covered the four, and protected Mariel's back. He raised his voice. "Come in!"

Sweat trickled greasily down Borg's face. Peppo's hands were knotted on his knees. Kip couldn't see Mariel's face, but Diana's eyes were trembling like lake water. Monty Wentworth's mouth had become pinched.

"Come in," Kip called again, and again warned, "Don't move."

The door swung open, Cagle stood there undisturbed, holding Dokey by the arm.

"Having trouble?" he asked Kip.

"Quiet," said Kip. He held the gun steady. He asked coaxingly. "What'd she say, Dokey? Tell me again. What did she say?"

Dokey's black eyes were on Kip. "She said she was a Jap," he whispered. "She wasn't a Jap. I killed her." He gulped.

"Steady," Kip said. "Take a good look. Somebody gave you a lot to drink. Jude won't let you drink. You fooled Jude, you and she. Look at them, Dokey."

Kip had stepped out where he could watch them all. He could see the horror on the faces of Mariel and Jude.

"She said she was a Jap." Dokey again husked. There was a terrible smile on his thin lips. Cagle released his arm as he moved forward, soft as a cat. "She said she was a Jap."

Diana screamed, "No, no! I'm not a Jap! I'm not a Jap! I'm Diana Redhair."

She couldn't get out of the chair. Dokey was in front of her, with that smile on his lips, with that soft accusing whisper.

"She said she was a Jap."

Kip had been sure he'd fixed it so nothing could happen, at least he thought he had. But he was a bungler, a fool amateur. Even with the gun in his hand, he couldn't fire quickly enough. Diana could—and did. She must have had it in the sleeve of her coat. She kept screaming even as she fired.

"No—no!"

Then Peppo grabbed her hand and smashed it.

Dokey didn't totter. He stood there smiling that terrible smile down at her and rasped out a few words.

"Diana—said—Hyacinthe—was—a—Jap." He fell then, like a tree, upon Diana who was still screaming.

Cagle got to Dokey first, eased him off the floor.

Jude was shaking the desk.

"He told me, but I didn't understand," said Jude. "You didn't have to do this to him."

Cagle said, "He isn't dead." He was working as he spoke. "I carry sulfa—as we did in the big fight."

Kip put his arm around Jude's shoulders. "He'll pull through. Maybe the shock will clear his mind. There are new treatments, Jude. You are going to be all right."

Mariel got the hospital on the phone. "Emergency." Through the confusion that one word sounded like a bell in Kip's ears.

The flattie waddled importantly in through the open door. "Shall I take him in now?" He glared at Kip as if he'd like to take him apart.

Cagle stood up. He wiped the blood from his hands on his handkerchief and stuffed it back into his right hip pocket.

"Take her," he said, nodding at Diana. "She's a killer."

"You can't do this!" Furiously she tossed her scarlet head. "You never got my father. You can't get me on this. You haven't any proof."

"Get her out of here," Cagle snarled.

Borg's voice was like wet putty. His voice shook with fear. "Diana—Diana."

The flattie had to use handcuffs.

Wentworth spoke as the door closed. "I was afraid she was—that she might be the one. Only she seemed so sure it was Scott. She insisted she had proof."

"Because she knew," Kip said.

"She tried to kill the old man once," Wentworth murmured.

Peppo spoke quietly. "Maybe she did kill him."

Wentworth opened his eyes. "That's why he wrote the will as he did. It was to safeguard Don."

Cagle took the deposit key from his pocket. It fell metallically on the desk. "We found the box. There's nothing in it."

A whisper of surprise ran through the circle like a breaking wave on the beach.

"Nothing!" Cagle repeated.

Borg's heavy nostrils distended. "Grim!" he cried.

Kip had mastered his amazement. "What did he do with two million? He was in debt." Strangely enough, he felt relieved. Then he realized why and his face grew warm.

"The dirty skunk," Borg said. "He must have stolen the key from Don, pretending to be his friend. After he got the dough, he was afraid to use it. Afraid Don might come back. Afraid Diana would figure it out and get to him."

Wentworth said, "She would. She had Grim watching all of us."

Kip looked at Mariel now. She was serene. She too seemed relieved.

He bent down, spoke to her alone, his lips close to her ear.

"I need a secretary. I think you'd like New York."

Her eyes met his solemnly. Then a smile curved her lips.

Peppo's voice was heavy. "We'll find where Grimsley hid it."

Kip spoke from the window, looking down at Clark and Randolph, not seeing the lonely lamp post and the misty lights, not smelling the cheap perfume and the bite of a gray lake wind, not hearing the loudspeaker's blare and the shuffle of feet, or even the wail of an ambulance cutting through the traffic. He spoke from a light heart.

"If you ever find it," he said, "let us know. We'd be very interested."

ABOUT THE AUTHORS

Robert Bloch

This mild-mannered master of the macabre is best known for his novel *Psycho* (1959), made into the shuddersome film of that name by Alfred Hitchcock. Born in Chicago in 1917, Bloch made his first professional sale (to *Weird Tales*) two weeks after his high school graduation. His early fiction, much of the best of which appears in his first collection, *The Opener of the Way* (1945), was strongly influenced by H. P. Lovecraft, but Bloch soon developed his own distinctive style in suspenseful tales of modern, neon-lit horror that climaxed with his best known short story, the much anthologized "Yours Truly, Jack the Ripper," in which the immortal Red Jack stalks his victims in the fog-shrouded streets of today's Chicago. Many of Bloch's works are set in Chicago, such as his novels *Terror* (1962) and *American Gothic* (1974), the latter based on the career of mass murderer H. H. Holmes during the Columbian Exhibition of 1893, when the female lodgers at his hotel mysteriously disappeared. In 1959 Bloch moved to Hollywood, aided by the success of *Psycho*, to concentrate on films (many based on his stories, such as "Asylum") and TV plays for such series as *Star Trek* and Rod Serling's *Night Gallery*. His twenty-some novels and nearly four hundred shorter works are about evenly divided into supernatural and mystery fields. A former president of the Mystery Writers of America (1970–71), he has won the Science Fiction Writers of

America's prestigious Hugo for the best short story of 1959 ("That Hell-Bound Train") and the World Fantasy Convention's Lifetime Achievement Award (1975). His lastest novels bring back his two most famous characters—*Psycho II* (1982) and *Night of the Ripper* (1984).

Jon L. Breen

A multi-talented man, Breen is known in the mystery field for scholarly reference works such as *What About Murder?* (1981) for which he won the MWA Edgar, best non-fiction category, an annotated bibliography of critical works about crime fiction; *Novel Verdicts* (1985), an annotated listing of courtroom fiction; but also for his own suspenseful mystery novels such as *Listen for the Click* (1983) and *The Gathering Place* (1984) and detective story parodies collected in *Hair of the Sleuthhound* (1982). Born in Montgomery, Alabama, in 1943, Breen was educated in California's Pepperdine University (B.A., 1965) and University of Southern California at Los Angeles (M.S. in Library Science, 1966). After Army service he worked as a librarian at several colleges and is currently at Rio Hondo College, Whittier, California. A longtime and frequent contributor to such leading journals of mystery criticism as *The Armchair Detective*, his best-known series character is Ed Gorgon, mystery fiction's only umpire detective.

Richard Connell

Born in New York in 1893, Connell claimed to have been the world's youngest professional writer. He covered baseball games at the age of six for his father, who was the editor of New York's *News-Press*, receiving a dime a game as wages. Connell attended Georgetown College for one year, but graduated from Harvard in 1915, after which he worked as a reporter for the *New York American*. He served in France with the Twenty-seventh Division during World War I. From 1919 on he was a freelance writer of more than three hundred short stories (some collected in *Variety*, 1925), novels (*Murder at Sea*, 1929) and screenwriting (most notably an original story with Robert Presnell, "Meet John Doe"). Connell died in 1949, best remembered for his classic adventure story, "The Most Dangerous Game," filmed three times and much imitated, and "Brother Orchid," filmed in 1940 starring Humphrey Bogart and Edward G. Robinson, and included in this volume.

Dorothy B. Hughes

The author of *The Fallen Sparrow* (1942), made into a suspenseful film starring John Garfield and Maureen O'Hara, Ms. Hughes has had double careers in the mystery field, first for fiction in the forties, next for non-fiction in the fifties and beyond. Born in Kansas City, Missouri, in 1904, she received a B.J. degree in 1924 from the University of Missouri at Columbia, with further studies at the University of New Mexico and New York's Columbia University. A reporter in the twenties, she began reviewing mysteries in the thirties for newspapers including the New York *Herald-Tribune*, the Los Angeles *News* and the Los Angeles *Times*. Her first book, *The So Blue Marble* (1940), was a notable debut, featuring series detective Inspector Tobin, murder, and hidden treasure. Most of her fourteen novels feature rich heroines suddenly thrust into danger. *In a Lonely Place* (1947) and *Ride the Pink Horse* (1946) were both made into A-budget movies, the former starring Humphrey Bogart and the latter Robert Montgomery. After the forties she concentrated on non-fiction, doing reviews and the authorized biography *Erle Stanley Gardner: The Case of the Real Perry Mason* (1978). In 1950 the Mystery Writers of America awarded Ms. Hughes an Edgar for Best Criticism; in 1978 she won the coveted Grandmaster Award. Ms. Hughes was something of a pioneer in the use of accurate, detailed city backgrounds to intensify realism; see, for example, "The Spotted Pup," her never-before-reprinted short novel included in this volume.

Fredric Brown

Chicago itself is one of the major characters in Fredric Brown's first book, *The Fabulous Clipjoint* (1948), which won the Mystery Writers of America's Edgar award for Best First Novel. It also began the career of his only series characters, the nephew-and-uncle team of Chicago-based private eyes Ed and Am Hunter. An entertaining writer whose stories sparkle with the unexpected, Brown has risen rapidly in critical estimation in recent years; even his earliest works are now being reprinted in expensive limited editions. Born in Cincinnati, Ohio, in 1906, Brown was educated at the University of Cincinnati (night school) and Indiana's Hanover College (one year), working as a proofreader for the Milwaukee Journal from 1936 to 1947 when he set out as a full-time writer. His work first appeared in the pulp magazines and was about evenly divided between science fiction and mystery fields. His most notable books are probably *What Mad Universe* (1949) and *Nightmares and Geezenstacks* (1961), science fiction; and such novels of murder as *Madball* (1953), *The Screaming Mimi* (1949), made into a film starring Anita Ekberg, and *Night of the Jabberwock* (1950). Much of his work had a characteristic macabre touch, such as "I'll Cut Your Throat Again, Kathleen," the chilling and suspenseful short story included in this volume.

Edward D. Hoch

A popular and ingenious writer, Edward D. Hoch is a legend in his own time for his more than seven hundred short stories, most of them in the demanding field of the classical fair-play detective story and many using the difficult theme of the impossible crime. Born in Rochester, New York, in 1930, Hoch turned to writing after two years each in the University of Rochester (1947–49) and the U. S. Army (1950–52) and became a fulltime author after advertising and editorial work (1952–68). His first published story, "Village of the Dead" (1957), was a remarkable foreshadowing of the mass suicide at Jonestown years before it happened. In 1968 Hoch received the Mystery Writers of America's award for the best short story, "The Oblong Room," and was elected president of the organization in 1982. Hoch has created more series characters than any other author, including Dr. Sam Hawthorn, specialist in the impossible; the unusual Simon Ark, who may (or may not) be two thousand years old, hunting the world to find and battle Satan Himself in human form (*The Quests of Simon Ark*, 1984); Nick Velvet, the professional thief, who, for a high price, offers to steal only worthless objects—and gets a surprising amount of business (*The Thefts of Nick Velvet*, 1978); and hard-working Homicide Captain Leopold, whose exploits appear in the recent collection, *Leopold's Way* (1987).

Craig Rice (Georgiana Ann Randolph)

It's not every detective story writer who's ghostwritten a mystery for a stripteaser, but Craig Rice—real name Georgiana Ann Randolph—has. *The G-String Murders* (1941), published as by "Gypsy Rose Lee" and written while Ms. Rice was publicity agent for the stripteaser, remains her best-known book. Ms. Rice was born in Chicago, the setting for many of her stories, in 1908. Privately educated, she worked as a reporter through the twenties and the heyday of Al Capone, often covering murder trials, from 1925 to 30; as a radio writer and producer of a half-hour, thrice-weekly mystery show from 1931 to 38; and as a freelancer from 1938 onwards. Her first book, *8 Faces at 3* (1939), featured her most famous series detective, the hard-drinking Chicago lawyer John J. Malone, often aided by the husband-and-wife team of press agents Jake and Helene Justus. Her novels, filled with imaginative concepts and screwball humor, have often been filmed, and include *Trial by Fury* (1941), *Having Wonderful Crime* (1943) and *Home Sweet Homicide* (1944). Her own screenplays during the forties included two mysteries in the Falcon series. Also notable are *People vs. Withers and Malone* (with Stuart Palmer, 1963), in which Malone co-stars with old-maid schoolteacher Hildegarde Withers to solve murder cases; and (in a grimmer mood) a group of true crime cases, *45 Murderers* (1952).

Howard Browne

The first time he saw Chicago, at seventeen, Browne said, "I fell in love with that town the way you fall in love with a woman . . . Chicago was one hell of a city . . . every corner you'd turn you'd either get rich or get shot." Born (1908) and reared in Nebraska, Browne moved to Chicago in his teens and turned to writing to escape his hated job as department store credit manager (1929–41). He was soon selling a large amount of fiction to Chicago publisher Ziff-Davis's pulps, which led to an offer of an editor's post and eventually management of the firm's entire pulp line, including *Amazing Stories, Fantastic Adventures, Mammoth Detective*, and *South Sea Stories* (1941–56). His first novel, *Warrior of the Dawn*, published in Chicago in 1943, was a prehistoric adventure modeled after the Tarzan stories and admired by Edgar Rice Burroughs fans; Browne himself would like to forget it. The discovery of Raymond Chandler's hard-boiled novels featuring Philip Marlowe changed Browne's life and led to four books in the Chandler manner with Chicago private eye Paul Pine, whom critics rank with Marlowe: *Halo in Blood* (1946), *Halo for Satan* (1948), *Halo in Brass* (1949), all as by "John Evans"; and in 1957 his finest book, *A Taste of Ashes*. His most profitable and best known book, however, is *Thin Air* (1954), televised four times including the CBS Movie of the Week and an episode of "The Rockford Files." In 1957 Browne moved to Hollywood to work as story editor for Twentieth-Century Fox, writing a total of 127 TV episodes for such series as *Cheyenne* and *Mission Impossible*, and several films, including two set in Chicago: *The St. Valentine's Day Massacre* (1967) and *Capone* (1975). Gangster Mickey Cohen liked them so much he asked Browne to ghost-write his autobiography, an offer Browne quickly refused. "So Dark for April," included in this volume, is the only Pine short story.

Ray Russell

One of the men who made *Playboy* one of the greatest successes of magazine publishing history, Ray Russell refers to his work as its executive editor (1954–60) as "a delightful detour from the main highway of my life, writing." Born in Chicago in 1924, Russell was educated at its Conservatory of Music and Goodman Memorial Theatre. After Air Force service (1943–46), Russell set the tone for *Playboy's* fiction—hip, fresh, sophisticated and literate—and wrote a fair amount of it himself, largely surprise ending short-short stories. The most memorable of his more than seventy stories and articles, however, are such longer works as *Sagitarius* (1971), a macabre novella of Jack the Ripper, and the title tale of *Sardonicus and Other Stories* (1961).

Sara Paretsky

With only three novels and four short stories, Sara Paretsky has created one of most memorable female detectives of modern times—V. (for Victoria) I. Warshawski, a Chicago private eye who can walk the dark and dangerous streets of today without ever losing her charm and femininity. One of the new generation of skilled mystery writers who have created independent women who thwart crime, such as Linda Barnes's Carlotta Carlyle, Sue Grafton's Kinsey Millhone, Marcia Muller's Sharon McCone and Lillian O'Donnell's Sgt. Norah Mulcahany, Ms. Paretsky was born and raised in Kansas. Currently an executive of a large insurance company, she lives in Chicago with her husband, physicist Courtney Wright of the University of Chicago. The first V. I. Warshawski novel was *Indemnity Only* (1982), followed by *Deadlock* (1984) and the recent *Killing Orders* (1985). Her latest exploit, "Skindeep," was inspired by Chicago locations, including its most expensive and glamorous beauty salon, and appeared—appropriately—in *New Black Mask Quarterly* No. 8. A vividly detailed picture of Chicago as well as some of V. I.'s early life—glows in the background of "The Old Swimming Hole," included in this volume.

James M. Ullman

Born in the late twenties, Chicago newspaperman James M. Ullman won a prize in Ellery Queen's 1953 Contest with his first story, "Anything New on the Strangler?" Ullman was educated at Chicago's Wright Junior College and De Paul University, receiving a Master's Degree in Journalism from Northwestern University in 1954, shortly before his first story appeared. His eleven years of study were interrupted by service in WWII and the U. S. Navy—two and a half years—and one year as an Air Force civilian employee on Guam. He's been a newspaperman ever since, a police reporter on the La Porte, Indiana, *Herald-Argus*; editor of the Skokie, Illinois, *News*; and lately head of the United Press Bureau's Chicago desk. His first book, *The Neon Haystack*, won First Prize in Simon & Shuster's Inner Sanctum Mystery contest in 1963 and a Mystery Writers of America Scroll. *Good Night, Irene*, (1965) presents a believable picture of a big city newspaperman's investigation of a murder. In his series detectives, Michael James Dane and Ted Bennett, Ullman created a new kind of detective and police procedural, securities investigation, in "The Stock Market Detective," *Ellery Queen's Mystery Magazine*, December 1962.